Using Literacy World in the Classroom

Planning

Literacy World provides complete units of work for both fiction and non-fiction in a flexible way that reflects the genre requirements and teaching objectives of the term. Across the fiction and non-fiction strands, *Literacy World* provides 14 weeks of work for Term 1, 11 for Term 2 and 11 for Term 3. These are broken down in the following way:

STAGE/TERM	FICTION	NON-FICTION
Stage 1 Term 1	5 units over 9 weeks	2 units over 5 weeks
Stage 1 Term 2	3 units over 7 weeks	2 units over 4 weeks
Stage 1 Term 3	5 units over 8 weeks	2 units over 3 weeks

The units of work vary in length, from 1 week to 3 weeks. Some of the sessions are optional, putting the teacher in control of how much time he or she wants to spend on a particular focus. For example, in Stage 1, Unit 4 on poetry is a flexible one- or two-week unit. The second week provides consolidation and reinforcement of the key teaching points covered in Week 1.

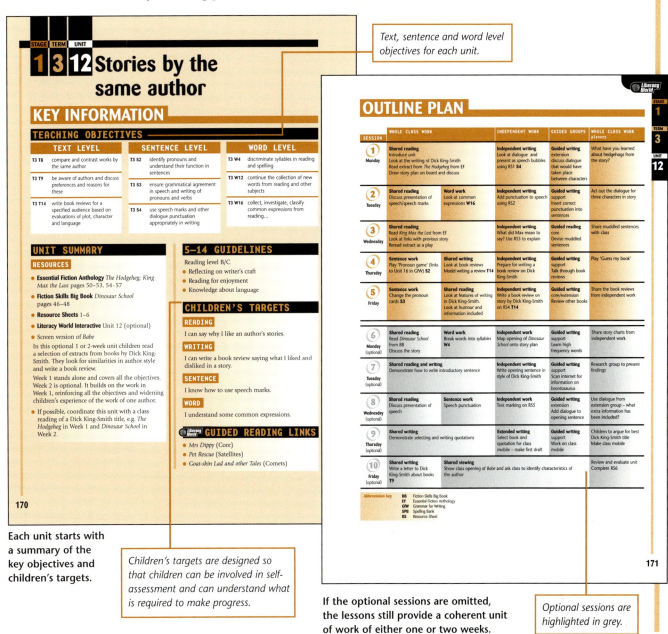

Each unit starts with a summary of the key objectives and children's targets.

Text, sentence and word level objectives for each unit.

Children's targets are designed so that children can be involved in self-assessment and can understand what is required to make progress.

If the optional sessions are omitted, the lessons still provide a coherent unit of work of either one or two weeks.

Optional sessions are highlighted in grey.

TEACHING NOTES

SESSION 1

FOCUS
- What is a story setting?

RESOURCES
- *The Twelfth Floor Kids* Essential Fiction pages 4–5

WORD WORK
Select some high frequency words from the text and discuss strategies to help the children with their spelling, e.g. 'sometimes' (compound word), 'when', 'what', (revision of 'wh' words), 'bought' (link with others with the same letter pattern: fought, sought, thought, brought). Remind the children about using Look Say Cover Write Check when memorising words.

SHARED READING
? Limbering Up Give me the settings of three different soap operas. Think of three settings within each soap opera.

In this unit the children will explore how authors use settings. Tell the children they are going to write a setting for a story of their choice.

Discuss the targets for the unit and then read *The Twelfth Floor Kids*.

◁) **Listening focus** What do you learn about the setting in this story opening? Why do you think the author set the story on the twelfth floor of a block of flats? How can you work out what this vocabulary means? ('balcony', 'glitters', 'since')

Look for vocabulary in the text that describes the setting, e.g. 'high up', 'far down below'.

Discuss what it would be like to live in a high-rise flat.

INDEPENDENT WORK
Ask the children to think about life in a tower block. Ask them to note what they can see, hear and do.

⊙ **Extension** Children can write two sentences to describe the tower block, using some of the vocabulary they have collected.

GUIDED WRITING — SUPPORT
Help the group to generate descriptive phrases to describe life in the tower block. Encourage them to attempt spellings on a whiteboard.

PLENARY
Write the reading target on the board and discuss with the class how this will be met, e.g. by reading different story openings and comparing them. Share suggested vocabulary from the independent work. Demonstrate orally how to expand their descriptions into complex sentences, e.g. *old lift/hundreds of stairs: The battered old lift is often out of order so you have to climb hundreds of steep steps up to the twelfth floor.*

14

SESSION 2

FOCUS
- What effect does a setting have on a story?

RESOURCES
- *The Twelfth Floor Kids* Essential Fiction pages 4–5
- Resource Sheet 1 'Story planner'

SHARED READING
💭 **Time out for thinking** With partners, ask the children to think of two things they would like about living on the twelfth floor of a block of flats.

Look again at *The Twelfth Floor Kids*. Focus on one character, e.g. Amy. *What information can you find about Amy?* (part of a big family) Draw a grid with the following headings: Characters, Setting, Problems, Solutions. *How might a story about Amy develop? What problem might she have?*

SENTENCE WORK
Write the following simple sentence on the board and show the children how the sentence can be expanded, e.g. *The boy ate lunch. The ___ boy ate his ___ lunch. The ___ boy with no money ate his ___ lunch.* Discuss with the class the effect of expanding the sentence. Use more examples to work through with the class (Links to Unit 6 of *Grammar for Writing*).

INDEPENDENT READING
Working in pairs, children choose another character from *The Twelfth Floor Kids* and complete the story planner on RS1 for that character. They select one of the problems and then develop a solution, taking into account the setting. *How might a story about their character develop?*

GUIDED READING — CORE
Choose short stories with settings that are familiar to the children and focus on drawing out how the setting influences the characters' actions.

PLENARY
Ask the children to reflect on the way the setting for their character affected their story ideas, e.g. Dan's Mum worries when he goes down to play football because she can't see where he is playing.

Speaking and listening

*Planned opportunities for developing speaking and listening skills are provided. There are specific activities under the headings **Time out for discussion**, **Time out for thinking** and **Listening focus**.*

Guided reading

*Suggestions are given for reinforcing the the focus of the shared and independent work in guided reading sessions, using any suitable book. Links to **Literacy World** Guided Readers are given in the 'Key Information'.*

Shared reading and writing

Reading and writing are covered equally. Where the focus is on demonstration writing, exemplar texts are provided for support.

Essential Fiction
Teaching & Planning Guide

Contents

| Introduction | 2 |

Unit 1 Narrative: Setting
Key information	12
Teaching notes	14
Resource sheets	19

Unit 2 Narrative: Dialogue
Key information	25
Teaching notes	27
Resource sheets	32

Unit 3 Shape poems
Key information	38
Teaching notes	40
Resource sheets	43

Unit 4 Poetry: Observation
Key information	47
Teaching notes	49
Resource sheets	54

Unit 5 Plays
Key information	60
Teaching notes	62
Resource sheets	67

Unit 6 Oral and performance poetry
Key information	79
Teaching notes	81
Resource sheets	86

Unit 7 Narrative: Traditional tales
Key information	92
Teaching notes	94
Resource sheets	100

Unit 8 Myths, fables and parables
Key information	108
Teaching notes	111
Resource sheets	119

Unit 9 Narrative: Plot
Key information	129
Teaching notes	131
Resource sheets	136

Unit 10 Point of view
Key information	142
Teaching notes	144
Resource sheets	149

Unit 11 Humorous poetry
Key information	157
Teaching notes	159
Resource sheets	164

Unit 12 Stories by the same author
Key information	170
Teaching notes	172
Resource sheets	177

Welcome to Literacy World!

Literacy World is a complete fiction and non-fiction literacy programme for juniors. It offers resources for shared and independent work for both reading and writing. The fiction and non-fiction strands both work in the same way, and can be used alongside each other.

In this updated edition, we have brought *Literacy World* into line with the latest advice on whole-class teaching, flexible planning and child-friendly target setting. The one-, two- and three-week units of work reflect the National Literacy Strategy's Medium Term Plans. As ever, the starting point for the programme has been to maintain a selection of superb quality texts for both fiction and non-fiction.

Shared Reading and Writing Components

FICTION for each of Years 3–6 (Primary 4–Primary 7)

FICTION TEACHING & PLANNING GUIDE | ESSENTIAL FICTION ANTHOLOGY | FICTION SKILLS BIG BOOK | WHOLE CLASS INTERACTIVE SOFTWARE

NON-FICTION for each of Years 3–6 (Primary 4–Primary 7)

NON-FICTION TEACHING & PLANNING GUIDE | ESSENTIAL NON-FICTION ANTHOLOGY | NON-FICTION SKILLS BIG BOOK | WHOLE CLASS INTERACTIVE SOFTWARE

Literacy World also provides an extensive range of guided reading books and teaching support for both fiction and non-fiction, for children of all reading ability. For further information on the Literacy World Guided Reading components, please see the inside back cover.

SESSION 3

FOCUS
- How can you introduce a character and setting?

RESOURCES
- *The Twelfth Floor Kids* Essential Fiction pages 4–5
- Resource Sheets 2 'New character' and 3 'Introducing a new character'

SHARED WRITING
? Limbering Up *Work with a partner and introduce yourself and tell her/him four facts about yourself, e.g. Hi! My name is … I am … years old. I live with … My favourite book is …*

Explain to the children that they will be writing their own introductory paragraphs about a new character from Beechtree Flats. Demonstrate how to introduce a first person introduction showing how to present the facts about the character and introduce the problem of the story. You may wish to use RS2 as a prompt.

WORD WRITING
Collect spelling errors that the children have made. Ask the children to help you to categorise the words in ways that will help with the spelling, e.g. list together the words with silent letters; the words with a modified 'e'; those words which have a smaller word inside them etc. Remind children about using Look Say Cover Write Check to help with learning spellings.

INDEPENDENT WORK
Using RS3, ask the children to write an introductory paragraph about a new character who lives on the twelfth floor. Remind them about sentence punctuation.

GUIDED WRITING — SUPPORT
Using RS3 discuss with the group how to use the structure that they have read in the shared text and demonstrated by you: start with the basic introductory facts; add details about the setting; introduce the problem of the story.

PLENARY
Share some of the introductory paragraphs. Discuss with the class what makes a good story opening. Start a class checklist of 'Good ideas for story openings'. (set the scene, introduce the characters, powerful adjectives to describe the character, suitable name to sum up the character, clues to tempt the reader to read further)

SESSION 4

FOCUS
- How can writers help the reader to picture the setting?

RESOURCES
- *The Littlest Dragon* Fiction Skills Big Book page 2
- Resource Sheet 4 'Sentence punctuation'
- Screen version of *The Secret Garden*

SHARED READING
Read the opening of *The Littlest Dragon*. Check against the class checklist of 'Good ideas for story openings' created in Session 3.

Discuss the concept of long, medium and close-up shots as a means of introducing a setting and characters. The long shot starts from a distance, outside the cave, then the camera moves closer inside the cave and finally the camera focuses on the main character of the story. Using the acetate, mark on the text the long, medium and close-up shots.

Demonstrate how this opening effect is achieved using details of the school you attended as a child. Roughly sketch three views – the school from a distance, a closer view of the buildings and playground and into the classroom where you are sitting at a desk. Add labels with descriptions, e.g. long shot: set on a hill just outside the village, next door to the church; medium shot: playing fields all around, small playground, surrounded by stone wall; close-up: cluster of children around the teacher's desk, one child sitting alone in the book corner. Explore this further looking at film footage from *The Secret Garden* or by reading the opening of *The Worst Witch*.

INDEPENDENT READING
Give the children RS4 and ask them to read through the text and spot what is missing. Ask them to decide where the punctuation should go and add it, and then reread the text to make sure it makes sense.

GUIDED READING — CORE
Invite the children, one by one, from the group to practise reading aloud from a book at a suitable reading level, paying particular attention to the punctuation.

PLENARY
Expand some of the labels (from the shared reading work on long, medium and close-up shots) with further descriptions to make complete sentences. Involve the children in suggesting the punctuation for these sentences. Check their understanding, e.g. *Why do we need a full stop here?*

15

Independent work
Suggestions follow on from the shared reading and writing. Where appropriate, these are differentiated for lower ability groups (support) and higher ability groups (extension). The activities take a range of forms, including group discussions, IT and research, sometimes making use of photocopiable resource sheets.

Guided writing
Support for guided writing sessions follows on from the shared work. These are often differentiated for ability groups.

Grammar for Writing/ Spelling Bank
*Where appropriate, references are given to units in **Grammar for Writing** and **Spelling Bank** activities. However, access to these documents is not obligatory in order to run the **Literacy World** sessions. The references are there if further work on the focus is required.*

Recurring activities

There are a number of activities that occur regularly throughout the programme, which provide opportunities for active participation.

?	✏️	📜	💬	☁️	🔊
Limbering up Warm-up oral games, puzzles and questions, linked to the focus of the unit.	**Ready, steady, write** Children write on individual whiteboards.	**Living sentences** Physically constructing and deconstructing sentences.	**Time out for discussion** Giving children, in pairs, brief discussion time during whole class work.	**Time out for thinking** Giving children brief thinking time during whole class work.	**Listening focus** Giving children a specific question or focus while the teacher reads. Feedback is generally required.

How to use Literacy World Interactive

Literacy World Interactive CD-ROMs add a new dimension to whole-class sessions, providing resources to help the teacher integrate ICT into literacy in a meaningful way as they are linked directly to the units of work in the *Teaching and Planning Guide*. For each stage of *Literacy World* there is one CD for fiction and one CD for non-fiction.

On each of the CDs there are:

- electronic versions of the Big Book pages
- additional stimulus material, in the form of audio recordings, short video clips and photographs
- a range of interactive word and sentence activities
- some additional reading extracts
- the Resource Sheets contained in this guide to edit and customise
- notes to help the teacher make the most of the resources

The activities in *Literacy World Interactive* can be used alongside the activities suggested in the units of work in this *Teaching and Planning Guide*. They are intended as an optional way of extending literacy teaching in a fun and motivating environment, and can be used to reinforce and consolidate learning.

Details of the resources for each of the *Literacy World* units of work are given at the end of teaching notes for that unit. Notes on how to use the interactive resources are on the CD itself.

Literacy World and the NLS Objectives

Literacy World covers the full range of NLS Objectives, as described in the NLS Framework for Teaching, and mirrors the approach set out in the Medium Term Plans. These charts show how the objectives have been linked together to form units of work.

STAGE 1 TERM 1

	UNIT TITLE/FOCUS	WEEKS	LITERACY WORLD RESOURCES	TEXT	SENTENCE	WORD	SPEAKING & LISTENING	OUTCOME
1	Narrative: Setting	2	Essential Fiction anthology: *The Twelfth Floor Kids; It's Not Fair…that I'm little*; Fiction Skills Big Book: *The Littlest Dragon; The Grumpy Princess; At the Park*	T1 compare story settings T9 generate ideas related to topics T11 develop the use of settings in own stories T12 investigate and collect sentences for openings and endings T16 organise stories into paragraphs	S1 use grammar to decipher words S6 secure knowledge of question marks S10 identify the boundaries between sentences S11 write in complete sentences S12 demarcate sentences correctly	W1 spell words containing long vowel phonemes W5 identify misspelled words in own writing W6 use independent spelling strategies W7 use 'look, say, cover, check' W14 infer the meaning of words from context	Take part in discussions about settings in stories and their experience	Story opening, focusing on setting
2	Narrative: Dialogue	2	Essential Fiction anthology: *The Tasting Game*; Fiction Skills Big Book: *The Punctuation Game; Quackers; Who Said What?; Penalty*	T2 how dialogue is presented T3 different voices in stories T9 generate ideas related to topics T10 use reading as a model for own writing T12 investigate and collect sentences for openings and endings T16 organise stories into paragraphs	S1 use grammar to decipher words S2 take account of grammar and punctuation S6 secure knowledge of question marks S7 understand speech punctuation conventions S8 use the term speech marks S9 investigate devices for presenting speech	W8 spelling of verbs with 'ing' W16 use a thesaurus W17 generate synonyms for high frequency words W18 use the term 'synonym' W19 identify common vocabulary for dialogue	Listen to dialogue in stories, and act out events and dialogue between characters	Story, focusing on dialogue and ending
3	Poetry: Shape poems	1	Essential Fiction anthology: *Ten Ways to Travel; The River*; Fiction Skills Big Book: *Cats Can; Spider*	T6 read aloud and recite poems T7 comment on the impact of a layout T9 generate ideas related to topics T13 collect words and phrases for poems T14 invent a range of shape poems	S4 use verb tenses with accuracy S5 use the term 'verb'	W9 investigate spelling pattern 'le' W16 use a thesaurus	Recite and listen to poems Discuss the choice of words in poems, and generate ideas for poems Express personal preferences clearly	Class poetry book
4	Poetry: Observation	1 or 2	Essential Fiction anthology: *Listen; Bed in Summer*; Fiction Skills Big Book: *Wings; The Lake*	T6 read aloud and recite poems T7 comment on the impact of a layout T8 express views about poems T9 generate ideas related to topics T13 collect words and phrases for poems	S3 explore the function of verbs S5 use the term 'verb'	W2 identify phonemes in speech and writing W9 investigate spelling pattern 'le' W16 use a thesaurus	Recite and listen to poems Discuss the choice of words in poems, and generate ideas for poems Express personal preferences clearly	Observation poem
5	Plays	2	Essential Fiction anthology: *Rumpelstiltskin*; Fiction Skills Big Book: *Rumpelstiltskin playscript; Dick Whittington*	T3 different voices in stories T4 read, prepare and present playscripts T5 recognise the difference between prose and playscripts T15 write simple playscripts	S6 secure knowledge of question marks S9 investigate devices for presenting speech S10 identify the boundaries between sentences	W3 read and spell KS1 high frequency words W10 recognise and spell common prefixes W11 generate new words from root words W12 use the term 'prefix'	Rehearse and present a play Act out dialogue between characters	Pantomime for class to perform

7

STAGE 1 TERM 2

UNIT TITLE/FOCUS	WEEKS	LITERACY WORLD RESOURCES	TEXT		SENTENCE		WORD		SPEAKING & LISTENING	OUTCOME
Oral and performance poetry	6 2	Essential Fiction anthology: *If You Want To See An Alligator; Fisherman Chant; Gran, Can You Rap?; The Travellin' Britain Rap* Fiction Skills Big Book: *With My Hands; The School Kids' Rap*	T4 T5 T11	choose and prepare poems for performance rehearse and improve performance, write new/extended verses	S8	understand uses of capitalization	W2 W3 W4 W6 W13 W14 W16	identify phonemes in speech read and spell high frequency words discriminate syllables in reading spell by analogy recognise and spell common suffixes use knowledge of suffixes to generate words use the term 'suffix'	Rehearse and perform poems Comment on dramatic features of performances	Poetry performance; new verses for a poem
Narrative: Traditional tales	6 2	Essential Fiction anthology: *The Gifts at the Bottom of the Well* Fiction Skills Big Book: *Traditional Tales*	T1 T2 T6 T8 T9	investigate styles and voice of traditional story language identify story themes plan main story points write character portraits write a story plan	S4 S5	extend knowledge of pluralisation use the terms 'singular' and 'plural'	W6 W7 W8 W9 W11 W24	use independent selling strategies use 'look, say, cover, check' how words change when 'er', 'est', 'y' spelling rules for plurals with 's' use the terms 'singular' and 'plural' explore opposites	Prepare a story for telling out loud Use expression in reading aloud	Oral storytelling; traditional story
Narrative: Myths, fables and parables	8 3	Essential Fiction anthology: *Birth of the Stars; Baira and the Vultures Who Owned Fire; The Crowded House; The Dog and the Bone; The Stag and His Spindly Legs* Fiction Skills Big Book: *Why The Moon Shines At Night; The Sly Builder; The Bear and the Travellers*	T2 T3 T6 T7 T9 T10	identify story themes identify main and recurring characters plan main story points describe and sequence incidents write a story plan write alternative sequels	S1 S2 S3 S6 S7 S10 S11	use grammar to decipher unfamiliar words understand the function of adjectives use the term 'adjective' understand the function of commas use the term 'comma' understand verbs in the 1st, 2nd and 3rd person understand the need for grammatical agreement in speech and writing	W12 W15 W24	recognise and generate compound words use the apostrophe to spell shortened word forms explore opposites	Use talk for writing to discuss themes and characters	Sequel to a well-known story

STAGE 1 TERM 3

	UNIT TITLE/FOCUS	WEEKS	LITERACY WORLD RESOURCES	TEXT	SENTENCE	WORD	SPEAKING & LISTENING	OUTCOME
9	Narrative: Plot	2	Essential Fiction anthology: *Stranded!* Fiction Skills Big Book: *Quackers; Trapped!*	T1 retell main points of a story T2 refer to significant aspects of the text T10 plot a sequence of episodes T11 write openings for stories	S4 use speech marks and dialogue punctuation S6 investigate how words and phrases signal time sequences	W1 spell words containing the long vowel phonemes W5 identify misspelled words W9 recognise and spell prefixes: mis, non, ex, co, anti W10 use prefixes to generate new words	Explain views about stories, giving reasons Use drama to explore stories	Adventure story, using language for effect
10	Narrative: Point of view	2	Essential Fiction anthology: *The Toad Tunnel* Fiction Skills Big Book: *The Pied Piper*	T1 retell main points of a story T3 distinguish between 1st and 3rd person accounts T4 consider credibility of events T5 discuss characters' feelings, behaviour and relationships T12 write a 1st person account T13 write extended stories S1 use grammar to decipher unfamiliar words	S4 use speech marks and dialogue punctuation S5 understand sentences can be joined, using conjunctions	W2 identify phonemes in speech and writing W5 identify misspelled words W6 use independent spelling strategies W12 collect and use new words	Investigate characters' feelings and behaviour through talk and role-play	First person account
11	Humorous poetry	2	Essential Fiction anthology: *How Can I?; My Dad's Amazing; Recipe for a Disastrous Family Picnic; Through the Staffroom Door; At the End of School Assembly* Fiction Skills Big Book: *Sunday in the Yarm Fard; The Grumpy Princess; Baira and the Vultures; Teacher Said...; All The Things You Can Say*	T6 compare forms or types of humour T7 select and recite poetry that plays with language T15 write poetry that uses sound for effect T21 use IT for publication	S1 use grammar to decipher unfamiliar words S7 use commas in marking grammatical boundaries	W4 discriminate syllables in reading and spelling W8 identify short words within longer words W11 use the apostrophe to spell contracted words W13 collect synonyms for dialogue W14 explore homonyms	Perform poems with expression	Poetry performance; humorous poem
12	Stories by the same author	1 or 2	Essential Fiction anthology: *The Hodgeheg; King Max the Last* Fiction Skills Big Book: *Dinosaur School*	T8 compare and contrast works by the same author T9 be aware of authors and discuss preferences T14 write book reviews	S2 identify pronouns and understand their function S3 ensure grammatical agreement in speech and writing S4 use speech marks and dialogue punctuation	W4 discriminate syllables in reading and spelling W12 collect new words from reading W16 collect, investigate and classify common expressions	Express and justify preferences for authors	Book review

Literacy World and the Scottish 5-14 Guidelines

Literacy World has been developed with many aspects of the 5-14 Guidelines in mind, and teachers will find it works well in the Scottish classroom.

- Stage 1 is suitable for Primary 4
- Stage 2 is suitable for Primary 5
- Stage 3 is suitable for Primary 6
- Stage 4 is suitable for Primary 7

5-14 Reading and Writing Strands

In general, *Literacy World* Stages 1 and 2 are suitable for children working at Levels B and C of the Attainment Targets. Stages 3 and 4 are suitable for children working approximately at Levels C and D. At the start of the teaching notes for each unit, you will find detailed reading levels for that unit, along with a summary of how the resources and teaching suggestions match the Programme of Study for reading.

Opportunities to develop writing skills are interwoven throughout the units, and *Literacy World* recognises the importance of writing by dedicating approximately half of the sessions to different forms of writing. Children are led through the supportive structure of talking and planning for writing in response to their reading, teacher demonstration and scribing, and supported composition before moving on to writing independently.

Literacy World offers opportunities for functional writing, personal writing and imaginative writing in a number of ways. The unit notes provide ideas for shared writing, independent writing using response journals and writing frames. Punctuation and structure, and knowledge about language are introduced in the shared reading and taught explicitly during shared writing. Many of the Resource Sheets give practice in the use of these skills.

Listening and Talking

Throughout *Literacy World*, there are planned opportunities for children to develop their communication skills, through discussing ideas and opinions in pairs and groups, giving feedback to the class, role-play and drama. These activities are highlighted in the notes under the headings **time out for discussion**, **time out for thinking** and **listening focus**, as well as being built into the plenary sessions.

Literacy World and the Northern Ireland Curriculum

Literacy World supports reading, writing and talking and listening strands within the Programme of Study for English at Key Stage 2. *Literacy World* Stages 1 and 2 are suitable for children working at approximately Levels 2 and 3 of the Attainment Targets. Stages 3 and 4 are suitable for children working at approximately Levels 3 to 5.

Reading

Literacy World provides a full range of genres and text types, including narrative, poetry, playscripts and non-fiction. For a detailed description of these, please see the charts on pages 7–9. The programme's approach encourages silent reading, reading for enjoyment and reading aloud for different audiences.

Children are given a range of reading activities including: listening to and understanding a range of texts; participating in shared reading; exploring stories and texts through discussion; expressing opinion and justifying responses; considering aspects of stories and the writer's craft.

Writing

Opportunities to develop writing skills are interwoven throughout the units, and *Literacy World* recognises the importance of writing by dedicating approximately half of the sessions to different forms of writing. Work on grammar and punctuation is built into writing. Children are led through the supportive structure of talking and planning for writing in response to their reading, teacher demonstration and scribing, and supported composition before moving on to writing independently.

The *Literacy World* fiction strand offers opportunities to write stories, diaries, poems, notes, dialogue and playscripts. The non-fiction strand gives support in writing reports, instructions, notes, explanations and discussions.

Talking and Listening

Throughout *Literacy World*, there are planned opportunities for children to develop their communication skills, through discussing ideas and opinions in pairs and groups, giving feedback to the class, role-play and drama. These activities are highlighted in the notes under the headings **time out for discussion**, **time out for thinking** and **listening focus**, as well as being built into the plenary sessions.

1 1 1 Narrative: Setting

KEY INFORMATION

TEACHING OBJECTIVES

TEXT LEVEL

T1 T1	compare a range of story settings and select words and phrases that describe scenes
T1 T9	generate ideas related to a topic by brainstorming, word association etc.
T1 T11	develop the use of settings in own stories by: writing short descriptions of known places; writing a description in the style of a familiar story
T1 T12	investigate and collect sentences/phrases for story openings and endings – use some of these formal elements in retelling and story writing
T1 T16	begin to organise stories into paragraphs

SENTENCE LEVEL

T1 S1	use awareness of grammar to decipher new or unfamiliar words ...
T1 S6	secure knowledge of question marks and exclamation marks in reading, understand their purpose and use appropriately in own writing
T1 S10	identify the boundaries between separate sentences in reading and in own writing
T1 S11	write in complete sentences
T1 S12	demarcate the end of a sentence with a full stop and the start of a new one with a capital letter

WORD LEVEL

T1 W1	spell words containing each of the long vowel phonemes ...
T1 W5	identify misspelled words in own writing
T1 W6	use independent strategies
T1 W7	practise new spellings regularly by Look Say Cover Write Check strategy
T1 W14	infer the meaning of unknown words from context

UNIT SUMMARY

RESOURCES

- **Essential Fiction Anthology** *The Twelfth Floor Kids; It's Not Fair... that I'm little* pages 4–9
- **Fiction Skills Big Book** *The Littlest Dragon; The Grumpy Princess; At the Park* pages 2–5
- **Resource Sheets** 1–6
- **Literacy World Interactive** Unit 1 (optional)
- Screen version of *The Secret Garden*

In this 2-week unit children study a variety of story settings. They contribute to a class checklist of features of good story settings. They plan in pairs and write the first paragraph of a story introducing the characters in a setting.

5–14 GUIDELINES

Reading level A/B
- Reflecting on writer's craft
- Reading for enjoyment
- Knowledge about language

CHILDREN'S TARGETS

READING
I know the purpose of settings in stories.

WRITING
I can write a setting which draws the reader into the story. I can organise my story into paragraphs.

SENTENCE
I understand when to use a question mark.

WORD
I can recognise long vowel phonemes.

SPEAKING AND LISTENING
I can present information clearly and take part in discussions.

Literacy World GUIDED READING LINKS

- *Twelfth Floor Kids* (Core)
- *Fair's Fair* (Satellites)
- *Quackers* (Comets)

OUTLINE PLAN

STAGE 1 · TERM 1 · UNIT 1

SESSION	WHOLE CLASS WORK		INDEPENDENT WORK	GUIDED GROUPS	WHOLE CLASS WORK plenary
1 Monday	**Word work** High frequency words **W6**	**Shared reading** Read and discuss *The Twelfth Floor Kids*. Discuss pros and cons of living in a high-rise flat **T1 T9 S1 W14**	**Independent work** Suggest vocabulary to describe the flats **W7**	**Guided writing** support Generate descriptive phrases	*What will we need to do in this unit?* Share suggestions for vocabulary. Compose sentences
2 Tuesday	**Shared reading** Read EF pages 4–5. Develop story about Amy using story grid **T9**	**Sentence work** Demonstrate expansion (Links to Unit 6 of GfW) **S10 S11 S12**	**Independent reading** Complete the story grid for another character **RS1**	**Guided reading** core Review influence of setting on characters	*How did the story setting affect the ideas for your story?*
3 Wednesday	**Shared writing** Create a new character for Twelfth Floor flats **T11**	**Word work** Identify misspelt words in own writing **W5 W6 W7**	**Independent writing** Write opening setting and introduce a new character **RS3**	**Guided writing** support Identify structure for own story	*What makes a good story opening?*
4 Thursday	**Shared reading** Read *The Littlest Dragon* in the BB and check against criteria. Introduce long, medium, close-up approach **T1 S6**		**Independent reading** Sentence punctuation **RS4**	**Guided reading** core Discuss features of punctuation and its effect on how we read	Share examples from independent work. Add punctuation
5 Friday	**Sentence work** Play the 'Construct' game (links to Unit 6 of GfW) **S10 S11 S12**	**Shared reading** Talk about the three shot approach to setting in BB **T11**	**Independent writing** Draw and label three shot approach to own school	**Guided writing** support Help group to draw and label three shot approach to their own school	Create sentences for opening settings
6 Monday	**Word work** Identify long vowel phoneme 'O' and sort under the different vowel combinations	**Shared reading** Read and discuss *It's Not Fair* from EF **T11**	**Independent writing** Complete the story grid for *It's Not Fair*. Problem and Solution	**Guided writing** support Revise story grid	Review sample of completed story grids
7 Tuesday	**Plan for writing** Groups to role play scenes from the park **W1**	**Talk for writing** Brainstorm what you can see, hear, smell and taste in *At the Park* in BB **T9**	**Independent writing** Map chosen scene onto story grid	**Guided writing** support Work through planning process	Selected groups perform their scene from the park
8 Wednesday	**Shared writing** Demonstrate how to write a three paragraph story using a nursery rhyme (links to Unit 8 of GfW)		**Independent writing** Map chosen nursery rhyme into paragraph boxes **T16**	**Guided writing** support Deconstruct nursery rhymes	Refer to class checklist. Decide on paragraphs for nursery rhyme
9 Thursday	**Shared writing** Write the opening scene from the BB park scene using three shot description	**Extended writing** Write opening paragraphs using story plan and three shot description		**Guided writing** support Write opening paragraph of own story	Children work in pairs to discuss writing and comment
10 Friday	**Sentence work** Play 'Complete' sentences game or use suggested sentences (links to Unit 6 of GfW)	**Shared reading** Children evaluate story openings	**Independent writing** Work in pairs to check spelling and punctuation **W5**	**Guided writing** support Edit opening paragraph of own story	*Have you reached your targets?* Complete self-assessment sheets

Abbreviation key
- **BB** Fiction Skills Big Book
- **EF** Essential Fiction Anthology
- **GfW** Grammar for Writing
- **SPB** Spelling Bank
- **RS** Resource Sheet

TEACHING NOTES

SESSION 1

FOCUS
- What is a story setting?

RESOURCES
- *The Twelfth Floor Kids* Essential Fiction pages 4–5

WORD WORK
Select some high frequency words from the text and discuss strategies to help the children with their spelling, e.g. 'sometimes' (compound word), 'when', 'what', (revision of 'wh' words), 'bought' (link with others with the same letter pattern: fought, sought, thought, brought). Remind the children about using Look Say Cover Write Check when memorising words.

SHARED READING
Limbering Up Give me the settings of three different soap operas. Think of three settings within each soap opera.

In this unit the children will explore how authors use settings. Tell the children they are going to write a setting for a story of their choice.

Discuss the targets for the unit and then read *The Twelfth Floor Kids*.

Listening focus What do you learn about the setting in this story opening? Why do you think the author set the story on the twelfth floor of a block of flats? How can you work out what this vocabulary means? ('balcony', 'glitters', 'since')

Look for vocabulary in the text that describes the setting, e.g. 'high up', 'far down below'.

Discuss what it would be like to live in a high-rise flat.

INDEPENDENT WORK
Ask the children to think about life in a tower block. Ask them to note what they can see, hear and do.

Extension Children can write two sentences to describe the tower block, using some of the vocabulary they have collected.

GUIDED WRITING — SUPPORT
Help the group to generate descriptive phrases to describe life in the tower block. Encourage them to attempt spellings on a whiteboard.

PLENARY
Write the reading target on the board and discuss with the class how this will be met, e.g. by reading different story openings and comparing them. Share suggested vocabulary from the independent work. Demonstrate orally how to expand their descriptions into complex sentences, e.g. *old lift/hundreds of stairs: The battered old lift is often out of order so you have to climb hundreds of steep steps up to the twelfth floor.*

SESSION 2

FOCUS
- What effect does a setting have on a story?

RESOURCES
- *The Twelfth Floor Kids* Essential Fiction pages 4–5
- Resource Sheet 1 'Story planner'

SHARED READING
Time out for thinking With partners, ask the children to think of two things they would like about living on the twelfth floor of a block of flats.

Look again at *The Twelfth Floor Kids*. Focus on one character, e.g. Amy. *What information can you find about Amy?* (part of a big family) Draw a grid with the following headings: Characters, Setting, Problems, Solutions. *How might a story about Amy develop? What problem might she have?*

SENTENCE WORK
Write the following simple sentence on the board and show the children how the sentence can be expanded, e.g. *The boy ate lunch. The ___ boy ate his ___ lunch. The ___ boy with no money ate his ___ lunch.* Discuss with the class the effect of expanding the sentence. Use more examples to work through with the class (Links to Unit 6 of *Grammar for Writing*).

INDEPENDENT READING
Working in pairs, children choose another character from *The Twelfth Floor Kids* and complete the story planner on RS1 for that character. They select one of the problems and then develop a solution, taking into account the setting. *How might a story about their character develop?*

GUIDED READING — CORE
Choose short stories with settings that are familiar to the children and focus on drawing out how the setting influences the characters' actions.

PLENARY
Ask the children to reflect on the way the setting for their character affected their story ideas, e.g. Dan's Mum worries when he goes down to play football because she can't see where he is playing.

SESSION 3

FOCUS
- How can you introduce a character and setting?

RESOURCES
- *The Twelfth Floor Kids* Essential Fiction pages 4–5
- Resource Sheets 2 'New character' and 3 'Introducing a new character'

SHARED WRITING
Limbering Up Work with a partner and introduce yourself and tell her/him four facts about yourself, e.g. Hi! My name is … I am … years old. I live with … My favourite book is …

Explain to the children that they will be writing their own introductory paragraphs about a new character from Beechtree Flats. Demonstrate how to introduce a first person introduction showing how to present the facts about the character and introduce the problem of the story. You may wish to use RS2 as a prompt.

WORD WRITING
Collect spelling errors that the children have made. Ask the children to help you to categorise the words in ways that will help with the spelling, e.g. list together the words with silent letters; the words with a modified 'e'; those words which have a smaller word inside them etc. Remind children about using Look Say Cover Write Check to help with learning spellings.

INDEPENDENT WRITING
Using RS3, ask the children to write an introductory paragraph about a new character who lives on the twelfth floor. Remind them about sentence punctuation.

GUIDED WRITING — SUPPORT
Using RS3 discuss with the group how to use the structure that they have read in the shared text and demonstrated by you: start with the basic introductory facts; add details about the setting; introduce the problem of the story.

PLENARY
Share some of the introductory paragraphs. Discuss with the class what makes a good story opening. Start a class checklist of 'Good ideas for story openings'. (set the scene, introduce the characters, powerful adjectives to describe the character, suitable name to sum up the character, clues to tempt the reader to read further)

SESSION 4

FOCUS
- How can writers help the reader to picture the setting?

RESOURCES
- *The Littlest Dragon* Fiction Skills Big Book page 2
- Resource Sheet 4 'Sentence punctuation'
- Screen version of *The Secret Garden*

SHARED READING
Read the opening of *The Littlest Dragon*. Check against the class checklist of 'Good ideas for story openings' created in Session 3.

Discuss the concept of long, medium and close-up shots as a means of introducing a setting and characters. The long shot starts from a distance, outside the cave, then the camera moves closer inside the cave and finally the camera focuses on the main character of the story. Using the acetate, mark on the text the long, medium and close-up shots.

Demonstrate how this opening effect is achieved using details of the school you attended as a child. Roughly sketch three views – the school from a distance, a closer view of the buildings and playground and into the classroom where you are sitting at a desk. Add labels with descriptions, e.g. long shot: set on a hill just outside the village, next door to the church; medium shot: playing fields all around, small playground, surrounded by stone wall; close-up: cluster of children around the teacher's desk, one child sitting alone in the book corner. Explore this further looking at film footage from *The Secret Garden* or by reading the opening of *The Worst Witch*.

INDEPENDENT READING
Give the children RS4 and ask them to read through the text and spot what is missing. Ask them to decide where the punctuation should go and add it, and then reread the text to make sure it makes sense.

GUIDED READING — CORE
Invite the children, one by one, from the group to practise reading aloud from a book at a suitable reading level, paying particular attention to the punctuation.

PLENARY
Expand some of the labels (from the shared reading work on long, medium and close-up shots) with further descriptions to make complete sentences. Involve the children in suggesting the punctuation for these sentences. Check their understanding, e.g. *Why do we need a full stop here?*

SESSION 5

FOCUS
- How can you use film techniques to create a setting?

RESOURCES
- *The Grumpy Princess* Fiction Skills Big Book page 3

SENTENCE WORK
Ask the children to work in pairs to play a 'Construct' game. Each pair will need a piece of paper. Child 1 writes a sentence starter made up of a determiner, an adjective and a noun, e.g. 'The old teacher', folds the paper and slides it across to her/his partner. Child 2 (without looking at the sentence starter) completes the sentence, starting with a verb and adding an ending, e.g. 'sank wearily into her chair.' The pair should then read their completed sentence and check the punctuation. Share the resulting sentences. (Links to Unit 6 of *Grammar for Writing*.)

SHARED READING
Read *The Grumpy Princess* extract. Check against the criteria for 'a good story opening' on the class checklist. Make comparisons with the other story settings that the children have looked at. Discuss how the 'three level' description introduces the story. Using the acetate, mark on the Big Book the long, medium and close-up shots.

INDEPENDENT WRITING
Based on the teacher example from the previous session ask the children to sketch three views of their school showing long, medium and close-up shots. They should label each view, e.g. fields/streets in long shot; building in medium shot; pupils in close-up.

GUIDED WRITING — SUPPORT
Support this group as they draw and label their school. Remind them that labels only need to have words or short phrases. Encourage them to use their phonic knowledge to attempt to spell words.

PLENARY
Ask the children to imagine they are creating the first three sentences of a story set in their school. Tell them to orally create one sentence based on their labels for each of their sketches. Share these sentences.

🔊 **Listening focus** *Is each description a complete sentence?*

Ask the class to sum up what they have learned about successful story settings.

SESSION 6

FOCUS
- How does dialogue tell you about the characters?

RESOURCES
- *It's Not Fair! … that I'm little* Essential Fiction pages 6–9

WORD WORK
Ask the children to think of words that rhyme with 'hole', e.g. foal, bowl, soul. Jot down their suggestions. Separate each word into phonemes (h-o-l). Ask the children to decide how the words could be sorted (e.g. 'oa' 'o-e' 'ow' 'ou'). Study the longest list (o-e): dole, hole, mole, pole, role, stole, whole. Test their spellings on their whiteboards.

SHARED READING
? Limbering up Tell the children to turn to a partner and to think of a time recently when they have said: "It's not fair!" Discuss the children's experiences.

Read *It's Not Fair!* to the class and ask the following questions:
- Who are the characters in the story?
- Where is the story set?
- What was Kitty's problem?
- How did Kitty solve her problem?
- What does the dialogue reveal about the characters?

Draw a story grid (Characters/Setting/Problem/Solution) on the board and ask the class to help you complete the 'Characters' and 'Setting' sections.

INDEPENDENT WRITING
Complete the story grid for *It's Not Fair!* under the headings 'Problem' and 'Solution'.

GUIDED WRITING — SUPPORT
Revise the purpose of a story grid to include all the story elements. Discuss Kitty's problem and enter it on the story grid. Support the group as they complete the 'Solution' section of the grid.

PLENARY
Review a sample of completed story grids. Demonstrate how to enter information briefly in note form, e.g. bullet points.

SESSION 7

FOCUS
- How can you make a scene come alive?

RESOURCES
- *At the Park* Fiction Skills Big Book pages 4–5

SHARED WRITING

Look at the picture of the park scene.

Select a character from the scene. Talk to the class about what is happening to the character and why, what has happened before this moment and what will happen next.

Explain that you can use your observation and imagination to make up a short story about them, e.g. *My character is going to be called Jaydon and he's in the park and I can see he's talking on his mobile. I need to explain why he has come to the park so I could imagine he's calling his mate to ask him why he hasn't turned up to play football, so I put on my story grid:*

Characters: Jaydon and Mark;	Setting: in the park
Problem: Where is Mark? What has happened to him? Has he had an accident?	Solution: Use mobile – Mark is fine. He lost track of time playing on his computer. Invites Jaydon to come and play.

Plan for writing Divide the children into groups of two or three and distribute the different scenes depicted in the Big Book. Remind them that in order to bring their stories alive they should discuss what those characters could see, hear, smell, feel and taste. They could make this into a mini drama to be presented in the plenary.

INDEPENDENT WRITING

Ask the children to map their dramatised scene onto a story grid: Characters/Setting/Problem/Solution. Remind them to give their characters names and to write in note form, e.g. using bullet points.

GUIDED WRITING — SUPPORT

Focus on support for the planning process. Work with the group on their selected scenarios and discuss it in terms of Characters/Setting/Problem/Solution. Support the children as they make brief notes based on the discussion.

PLENARY

Select one or two groups to perform their two-minute drama re-enacting their allocated scene. They should concentrate on the dialogue of the characters using it to reveal information and insight about the character, e.g. what they say, how they say it.

SESSION 8

FOCUS
- How can paragraphs help you to structure our stories?

RESOURCES
- Resource Sheet 5 'The story of Humpty Dumpty'

SHARED WRITING

Recall the nursery rhyme *Humpty Dumpty*. Draw three boxes on the board. Explain that the boxes represent the main stages of the story of *Humpty Dumpty*. Box 1 introduces the setting and the characters (Humpty sits on wall). Box 2 outlines the problem facing the character (Humpty has a fall). Box 3 provides a solution to that problem (Humpty cannot be repaired).

Show the children how to expand the basic action with a description. You may wish to use RS5 as a prompt. (Links with Unit 8 of *Grammar for Writing*).

INDEPENDENT WRITING

In pairs children select one of the following nursery rhymes and divide it into paragraph boxes: *Hickory Dickory Dock*, *Jack and Jill* or *Incy Wincy Spider*.

GUIDED WRITING — SUPPORT

Check children are familiar with one of the nursery rhymes. Discuss with the group how to divide up the action into three or four paragraph boxes.

PLENARY

Ask the children to help you to map *Little Miss Muffet* into paragraph boxes. Summarise what you have found out about paragraphs and how you decide when to start a new paragraph in a story.

SESSION 9

FOCUS
- What do you need to include in a good story opening?

RESOURCES
- *At the Park* Fiction Skills Big Book pages 4–5
- Resource Sheet 6 'At the Park'

SHARED WRITING
Demonstration writing Demonstrate how to write an effective story opening for a story about one of the characters in the park scene from the Big Book. Use all the elements that you have worked on in the previous sessions: the story grid, the paragraph boxes, the three-level description for the setting, and the dialogue from the oral activity. (You may wish to use RS6 as a prompt.)

Time out for discussion Ask the children to work in pairs and make suggestions for the end of the story.

EXTENDED WRITING
Invite pupils to write the opening of their story based on their notes in Box 1 of their story grid completed in Session 7. Remind them to use the three-level description to introduce the setting.

GUIDED WRITING — SUPPORT
Support the group as they write the opening of their story based on their notes in Box 1 of their story grid. Encourage them to compose their sentences orally before writing them down and to continually reread what they have written to check that it makes sense.

PLENARY
Ask the children to read their story openings to a partner. The listener needs to look out for the elements of a good story opening from the checklist. Ask children to nominate good examples of, e.g. use of descriptive language, the three-level description of setting, drawing the reader in and making them want to read more.

SESSION 10

FOCUS
- What makes a good story opening?

RESOURCES
- Some examples of children's extended writing from Session 9
- Resource Sheet 12 Unit 5 'My evaluation sheet'

SENTENCE WORK
Play the 'Complete' game with the children. Give them sentence starters made up of sentence, conjunction and pronoun:

The dog picked up the stick and he …
The skater fell over but she …
The footballer missed the goal because he …

Then ask them to complete each sentence starter.

SHARED READING
Evaluate the children's writing from the previous session with the whole class. Divide the class into groups, and give each group an example of the children's writing. Tell the children to read the story opening and find examples of:
- the three levels of description using the long shot medium shot and close-up
- description of the senses to bring the scene alive
- powerful adjectives to sum up the character
- clues that tempt the reader to read on.

INDEPENDENT WRITING
Ask the children to work with a partner and check for spelling mistakes in their own writing.

GUIDED WRITING — SUPPORT
Support the children as they edit and amend their opening paragraphs. Draw attention to ways that they can use the good examples that they found earlier to improve their own work.

PLENARY
Look again at the children's targets for the unit. Discuss what has been learned and which aspects of the targets have been met. What do they need to work on? Ask the children to complete their self-assessment sheets on 12 (Unit 5), reflecting on what they have learned in this unit and what they still need to work on.

On the Literacy World Interactive CD for Stage 1 Fiction, you will find the following resources for this unit:
- Copies of all the Fiction Skills Big Book pages for interactive work (*The Littlest Dragon* page 2, *The Grumpy Princess* page 3, *At the Park* pages 4–5)
- Interactive word and sentence work for Sessions 3, 6 and 10
- Extra reading (*The Owl who was Afraid of the Dark* and *Julian, Secret Agent*)
- All the Resource Sheets for independent work for you to customise
- Comprehensive Teaching and Planning Guides for the unit are also available on the CD.

Name   Date

Story planner

Choose a character and a problem in the setting shown. Put a circle around each choice. Write a solution.

Characters	Setting

Problems	Solutions
Out of order / KEEP OFF THE GRASS / No ball games	_____ _____ _____ _____ _____ _____

STAGE 1 | TERM 1 | For use with Unit 1 Session 2 as independent work.
© Harcourt Education Ltd. 2004. Copying permitted for purchasing school only. The material is not copyright free.

PROMPT: Writing exemplar

New character

> I'm going to introduce an older character who lives on the twelfth floor, so I won't start with "Hi"! An older person might say "Hello"

Hello, my name is Joan. I will be sixty next birthday. I have lived on the twelfth floor for five years.

> Then I need to say who she lives with. I'll have her living on her own … no, I'll give her a parrot as a pet …

I live on my own but my parrot, Polly, keeps me company.

> I want to write about things she likes about living on the twelfth floor and things that are not so good …

I like living high up above the noise of the traffic. The worst thing that happened here was when the lift broke down and I had to climb all the way up 120 steps with two heavy bags of shopping!

> To round off my introductory paragraph I'll make a joke …

I was certainly ready for a cup of tea when I finally got to my flat!

> … and put an exclamation mark after that sentence to show that it is meant to be funny.

Name _____ Date _____

Introducing a new character

Sketch a new character from Beechtree Flats. Then write a paragraph to introduce them. Don't forget to write in the first person.

New character	Setting

_____
_____
_____
_____
_____
_____
_____
_____
_____

STAGE 1 | TERM 1 | For use with Unit 1 Session 3 as independent work.

Name _____ Date _____

Sentence punctuation

Write the following with the correct punctuation.

hello I am a full stop I come at the end of a sentence after me you will always see my friend the capital letter when you are writing dialogue you must remember to start each speaker on a new line

do you know what a question mark looks like you must put one at the end of a sentence that is a question exclamation marks are fun they go at the end of a sentence to show surprise such as Tim said he was the best reader in the world

! . " , " ? " . , " !

PROMPT: **Writing exemplar**

The story of Humpty Dumpty

1 Humpty sits on wall

I'm going to set the scene and introduce the character.

It was a lovely sunny day and Humpty Dumpty thought he would sit on the wall and enjoy the sunshine. He looked down to the street below. He could see children playing, mothers shopping and, in the distance, some soldiers marching near the castle.

I'll give hints about later events.

2 Humpty has a fall

Then I'll start a new paragraph for the main action/problem.

At that moment, Humpty leaned forward to get a better view of the soldiers. He began to lose his balance. He wobbled and wobbled and then he fell from the wall on to the street below.

Repeating verbs will create tension and drama.

3 Humpty cannot be repaired

Lastly, I'll present my solution to the problem.

Poor Humpty was smashed into a thousand pieces. The soldiers hurried over to help Humpty but there was nothing they could do.

PROMPT: Writing exemplar

At the Park

I'm going to introduce the characters and establish the setting with a three-level description in the first paragraph ...

It was a beautiful sunny Saturday afternoon. The park was full of people. Some children were waiting impatiently for their turn on the merry-go-round. There was a queue for the hot dog stall and one boy was chatting away on his mobile phone.

... then add colour by describing things that can be seen, heard and smelled.

A close-up shot focuses on one character.

Mrs Daniels loved to come to the park on sunny days. She wheeled her wheelchair past the hot dog stall and the ice cream van. She could hear the happy cries of the children on the merry-go-round. She decided to buy a bunch of flowers.

Dialogue moves the action on.

"It will be like having the park in my living room," she said sniffing the flowers. But when Mrs Daniels looked in her handbag her heart nearly stopped beating. Her purse wasn't there! She must have left it at home.

The third paragraph introduces the problem ... and hooks the reader in.

Let's pause for a moment ... *How could the story end?*

"Never mind, dear," said the lady on the stall. "Take the flowers today and pay me next time."
"What a lovely day this has turned out to be," said Mrs Daniels.

STAGE 1 | TERM 1 | For use with Unit 1 Session 9 as a prompt for shared writing.
© Harcourt Education Ltd. 2004. Copying permitted for purchasing school only. The material is not copyright free.

1 1 2 Narrative: Dialogue

KEY INFORMATION

TEACHING OBJECTIVES

TEXT LEVEL

T1 T2	how dialogue is presented in stories
T1 T3	be aware of the different voices in stories using dramatised readings
T1 T9	generate ideas relevant to a topic by brainstorming
T1 T10	use reading as a model to write own passage of dialogue
T1 T12	investigate sentences/phrases for story openings and endings
T1 T16	begin to organise stories into paragraphs; begin to use paragraphing in presentation of dialogue in stories

SENTENCE LEVEL

T1 S1	use awareness of grammar to decipher new or unfamiliar words
T1 S2	take account of the grammar and punctuation e.g. sentences, speech marks, exclamation marks and commas to mark pauses when reading aloud
T1 S6	secure knowledge of question marks and exclamation marks
T1 S7	understand the basic conventions of speech punctuation
T1 S8	use the term speech marks
T1 S9	notice and investigate a range of other devices for presenting text, e.g. speech bubbles

WORD LEVEL

T1 W8	notice how the spelling of verbs alter when 'ing' is added
T1 W16	use a thesaurus
T1 W17	generate synonyms for high frequency words
T1 W18	use the word 'synonym'
T1 W19	identify common vocabulary for introducing and concluding dialogue

UNIT SUMMARY

RESOURCES

- **Essential Fiction Anthology** *The Tasting Game* pages 18–21
- **Fiction Skills Big Book** *The Punctuation Game; Quackers; Who Said What?; Penalty!* pages 6–11
- **Resource Sheets** 1–6
- **Literacy World Interactive** Unit 2 (optional)
- Screen version of *Pingu*

In this 2-week unit the children look at dialogue in stories, consider how the characters might speak, the words they might use and see how authors draw stories to a conclusion. They plan and write their own stories using what they have learnt about dialogue and story endings.

5–14 GUIDELINES

Reading level B/C
- Knowledge about language
- Reflecting on writer's craft
- Reading aloud

CHILDREN'S TARGETS

READING
I can make a story more interesting by the way I read aloud.

WRITING
I can include dialogue in my story and use it to move the action forward.

SENTENCE
I know the basic conventions for speech punctuation.

WORD
I know many ways of introducing and concluding dialogue.

DRAMA
I can act out events and dialogue between characters.

GUIDED READING LINKS

- *Twelfth Floor Kids* (Core)
- *Fair's Fair* (Satellites)
- *Quackers* (Comets)

STAGE 1 TERM 1 UNIT 2

25

OUTLINE PLAN

SESSION	WHOLE CLASS WORK		INDEPENDENT WORK	GUIDED GROUPS	WHOLE CLASS WORK plenary
1 Monday	**Spelling** How the spelling of verbs alter when adding 'ing' **W8**	**Shared reading** Introduce focus for the unit – dialogue in stories. Read *The Tasting Game* in EF **S1**	**Independent reading** Reread *The Tasting Game* and use the dialogue as a play **T3**	**Guided reading** support Practise reading dialogue	Present dramatised readings Discuss targets
2 Tuesday	**Shared reading.** Look at ending *The Tasting Game* from BB Talk about good story endings **T2 T12**	**Sentence work** Talk through the principles of speech punctuation. Create a class list of 'what we know about punctuation (links to Unit 4 in GfW) **S2 S7 S8**	**Independent writing** Write the conversation that took place in *The Tasting Game* using RS1 **S6**	**Guided writing** core Prepare dialogue prior to writing **T2**	Invite children to give dramatised reading of their independent work Link to checklist for punctuation
3 Wednesday	**Word work** How spellings alter when 'ing' is added **W8**	**Shared reading** Read *Quackers* in BB Discuss how the character of Polly is portrayed through the dialogue **T10**	**Independent work** Select fiction book from library and find 10 alternative verbs for 'said' for dialogue presentation **S6 W17 W18 W19**	**Guided reading** extension Find phrases from *The Tasting Game* that portray characters	Collect in speech verbs **W19**
4 Thursday	**Oral language and word work** Collect in ideas about how the character speaks Discuss the effect of different verbs to show emotion and aspects of character from *Who Said What?* in BB **Role play** Children present sentences with intonation and expression. Point out powerful verbs **T3 S7 W18 W19**		**Independent work** Complete speech using RS2 **S9**	**Guided reading** support Find speech marks and speech verbs	Share work from RS2 Add speech into speech bubbles in *Who Said What?* in BB
5 Friday	**Word work** How spellings alter when 'ing' is added **W8**	**Shared writing** Demonstrate how to turn speech bubbles into written dialogue Check conventions using class list of speech punctuation **T2**	**Independent writing** Add correct punctuation and speech verbs using RS3 **S7**	**Guided writing** core Punctuate sentences	What do we know about the conventions of writing a dialogue?
6 Monday	**Shared reading and writing** Remind the class about story openings Brainstorm ideas about opening of *Penalty!* in BB Model opening paragraph **T9 T16**		**Independent writing** Use planning notes and write opening paragraph to own story **T16**	**Guided writing** support Revise planning notes	Share checklist of good story opening features
7 Tuesday	**Oral language and shared writing** Children role play their conversation between Mr Brown and head teacher, Miss Sharp Demonstrate writing of next part of story		**Independent writing** Use story plans and write dialogue between Mr Brown and headteacher	**Guided writing** core Compare dialogue	What are the common pitfalls when writing dialogue?
8 Wednesday	**Shared reading and writing** Show class paragraph plan. Scribe possible options for conclusion and talk about paragraph connectives **T12**		**Independent writing** Plan final episode of their stories	**Guided writing** extension Devise alternative endings	Swap and evaluate story endings
9 Thursday	**Shared writing** Demonstrate ways to edit and refine writing of *Penalty!* story	**Extended writing** Children to write own conclusion based on their plans Check for writing making sense, correct punctuation and choice of vocabulary **T12**		**Guided writing** support Edit own work	Share resolution of story and how they edited their stories
10 Friday	**Word work** Ways of introducing and concluding dialogue	**Review and evaluation** Talk through the self-evaluation on RS12 (Unit 5)	**Independent work** Use self-evaluation to assess progress towards targets in this unit	**Guided writing** support Revise each stage of own story	Discuss features of a good story Create class checklist on good advice for writers

Abbreviation key
BB Fiction Skills Big Book
EF Essential Fiction Anthology
GfW Grammar for Writing
SPB Spelling Bank
RS Resource Sheet

TEACHING NOTES

SESSION 1

FOCUS
- How can you make a story more interesting when you read aloud?

RESOURCES
- *The Tasting Game* Essential Fiction pages 18–21

WORD WORK
How does the spelling of verbs alter when you add 'ing'?

Write on the board the following verbs: *talking; running; coming; having; eating; sitting; asking; making; shopping.*

💬 **Time out for discussion** *What do you notice about the verbs?* (All end in 'ing', some drop final 'e' from root, some double final consonant after short vowel)

Group the words according to how they add 'ing'.

SHARED READING
❓ **Limbering up** *How would you speak if you were Great Big Billy Goat Gruff? Baby Bear? The wolf in Red Riding Hood? The Gingerbread Man?*

Introduce the unit by explaining to the children that they are going to look at dialogue in stories, consider how the characters might speak their words and see how authors draw stories to a conclusion. In the second week they will write their own stories.

Read *The Tasting Game* to the class. Ask the children the following questions:
- Why do you think Steve says "I hate being the oldest"?
- What were Steve's reasons for breaking the rules?
- Why do you think the parents were not cross?

💬 **Time out for discussion** Ask the children to discuss in pairs who they think behaved the best/worst: Steve? Ben? Or their parents? Discuss the children's thoughts.

INDEPENDENT READING
Remind the children that in a play only the dialogue is heard. Tell them they are going to read *The Tasting Game* up to line 60 as a play. Demonstrate with the first few lines of text. Children work in pairs, and just read the words that are spoken.

GUIDED READING — SUPPORT
Reread *The Tasting Game* up to line 60. Discuss how the children can identify when a character is speaking. Let them practise reading the dialogue only.

PLENARY
Invite the children to share their dramatised readings. Discuss how the reading brings the text alive. Look together at the targets for this unit and talk briefly about what they will be doing to help them to achieve the targets.

SESSION 2

FOCUS
- How does a writer show when a character is speaking?

RESOURCES
- *The Punctuation Game* Fiction Skills Big Book page 6
- *The Tasting Game* Essential Fiction pages 18–21
- Resource Sheet 1 'Speech punctuation'

SHARED READING
Recap the plot of *The Tasting Game* up to line 83 with the whole class. Ask the children to recall what happens in the end. What did they like/dislike about the ending? Talk about the importance of a good story ending.

SENTENCE WORK
Show the children the pages from the Big Book.

💬 **Time out for discussion** Ask the children to discuss in pairs what is missing from the text.

Using the acetate demonstrate how to punctuate the dialogue correctly. Talk through all the reasons why the speech marks, commas, question marks and exclamation marks are needed.

Do a 'Collect and Classify' activity to investigate conventions for punctuating direct speech. First, mark all the speech marks in a piece of text. Look at the words outside the speech marks. Classify their function. Create a class checklist of 'What we know about speech punctuation'. (Links with Unit 4 of *Grammar for Writing*.)

INDEPENDENT WRITING
In pairs ask the children to write the conversation that must have taken place in *The Tasting Game* between Steve and Ben in lines 27–29. Remind them to refer to the class checklist about speech punctuation.

👉 **Support** Children can use RS1 to help with speech punctuation.

GUIDED WRITING — CORE
Help the children to orally prepare the conversation between Steve and Ben before writing it down.

PLENARY
Invite the pairs of children to give a dramatised reading of the dialogue they created in the independent work. Ask them to check that they have used the correct punctuation for the conversation. *Why is it necessary to use punctuation here?* (to make it clear who is speaking etc.)

SESSION 3

FOCUS
- What can you find out about a character from the dialogue in a story?

RESOURCES
- *Quackers* Fiction Skills Big Book page 7
- *The Tasting Game* Essential Fiction pages 18–21

WORD WORK
Ask the children what can happen to a base word when 'ing' is added. (e.g. drop the final 'e', double the final consonant, just add 'ing'.) Write the following on the board: *write + ing, like + ing, take + ing, ride + ing, bake + ing, hope + ing*. Tell them to work with a partner and to write the correct spelling of each word with its 'ing' ending. They should come up with a rule to remind themselves about adding 'ing' to words ending in 'e', e.g. drop the 'e' before 'ing'. (Links to Spelling Bank page 4.)

SHARED READING
Read the extract from *Quackers* to the whole class.

◁) **Listening focus** What do you learn about Polly?

Collect in comments about Polly's character and link this to textual evidence, e.g. she is anxious about the party invitations because she pretends that she has forgotten them. Draw attention to the speech verbs which give clues to Polly's mood, e.g. 'sighed'.

💬 **Time out for discussion** Ask the children to discuss, in pairs, the range of punctuation. Compare this with the class checklist.

Invite individual children to come out and to identify specific features of punctuation.

In a good story there is a solution in the end. Ask the children to suggest possible solutions for the end of the story.

INDEPENDENT WORK
Give each child a fiction book. Tell them to find ten different speech verbs for 'said' and to write these on their whiteboards or in their writing journals.

GUIDED READING — EXTENSION
Select examples of dialogue from *The Tasting Game*. Ask the children what each utterance tells them about the character, e.g. line 25 "It always is.": an example of an older child's feeling of jealousy that the younger child gets away with things.

PLENARY
Collect in the speech verbs from the independent work. Invite the children to say sentences according to the speech verbs.

SESSION 4

FOCUS
- How do speech verbs affect the meaning of dialogue?

RESOURCES
- *Who Said What?* Fiction Skills Big Book pages 8–9
- Resource Sheet 2 'What do they say? How do they say it?'
- Screen versions of *Pingu*

ORAL LANGUAGE WORK
Look at the pictures in the Big Book. Using the acetate complete the speech bubbles for each character, e.g. *Can you help me?*, *Let me come in*. Ask the children how each character might have spoken their lines, using one of the speech verbs from the border.

WORD WORK
Point out the difference between using the verb 'said' and other more powerful verbs. Talk about the way that emotion and aspects of character can be expressed through the careful choice of the speech verb. Put three headings on the board and ask the children to suggest appropriate speech verbs, e.g. *speaking in a frightened way – whispered; speaking in a fierce way – roared; speaking in a happy way – laughed, chuckled*.

💭 **Time out for thinking** Tell the children to select a speech verb and a character from the Big Book and decide how to read the sentence in the speech bubble.

Invite individual children to say their chosen sentence with the appropriate intonation and expression. The rest of the class should guess which speech verb has been chosen. Discuss the effect of the different speech verbs.

INDEPENDENT WORK
Ask the children to complete the speech in RS2 with sentences of their own choice.

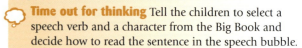 **Extension** Children can write a conversation between Pingu and his parents after viewing a screen version.

GUIDED READING — SUPPORT
Find examples of speech marks and speech verbs in the guided text. Discuss appropriate expression and practise reading aloud.

PLENARY
Invite children to write their dialogue from the independent work into the empty speech bubbles on the Big Book, using the acetate. Discuss which parts of the sentence are included and explain why the speech verb is not included.

SESSION 5

FOCUS
- How can you turn speech bubbles into dialogue?

RESOURCES
- *Who Said What?* Fiction Skills Big Book pages 8–9
- Resource Sheet 3 'Speech marks and verbs'

WORD WORK
Write the words *hop* and *hope* on the board. Ask the children to read each word and to decide which phoneme is different. Explain that after a short vowel the consonant is doubled before 'ing'; after a magic 'e' ending the 'e' is dropped before the 'ing' is added.
Demonstration writing Demonstrate adding 'ing' to the following: stop, chat, hate, drive, run, win. (Links to *Spelling Bank* page 4.)

SHARED WRITING
Using the speech bubble text in the Big Book, created in Session 4, ask the children to tell you how to turn the speech bubbles into written dialogue. *What speech punctuation is needed? What speech verbs are suitable?*
Refer to the class checklist of speech punctuation created in Session 2. Demonstrate how to correctly punctuate one speaker in each of the pictures.
Ready steady write Tell the children to write the reply for each of the pictures.

INDEPENDENT WRITING
Ask the children to use RS3 and add the speech marks and a suitable speech verb for the dialogue between the characters from *Little Red Riding Hood*.

GUIDED WRITING — CORE
Tell the group you want to write some sentences with dialogue on a whiteboard and that they are going to advise you on how to punctuate them. For example, you want to write: *Is it nearly lunch time moaned the pupil*. What must you think of first? (start a new line for the speaker, open speech marks, start first word with capital letter etc.)

PLENARY
Refer to the class checklist and recap on the rules for presenting dialogue in text and speech bubbles.

SESSION 6

FOCUS
- What makes a good story opening?

RESOURCES
- *Penalty!* Fiction Skills Big Book pages 10–11
- Resource Sheet 4 'Penalty! (story opening)'

SHARED READING AND WRITING
Limbering Up What would the headteacher of this school do if somebody kicked a football through her/his window?
Talk for writing Show the children the Big Book. Talk about the narrative the picture suggests. Encourage them to think about what led up to this moment and what will happen next. Explain that you will be using this picture to plan a story together and they will each have a chance to write their own version of *Penalty!*.
Plan for writing Draw out the planning grid used in Unit 1 (Characters, Setting, Problem, Solution) and demonstrate how to note ideas for names and character traits, details of the setting, a summary of the problems and the solutions. Give children time to note their own ideas on individual whiteboards. Explain that you will be writing the story in three parts: the opening where the story is introduced, a middle part where the story builds up and a final part where the problem is solved.
Demonstration writing Remind the children of the work on story openings in Unit 1 and ask them to recall the features of a good opening. Explain that you are going to use the same structure for the story opening as they were working on before.
Demonstrate writing the opening paragraph. You may wish to use RS4 as a prompt.

INDEPENDENT WRITING
Ask the children to use the planning notes that they made earlier and begin writing their own story opening. Encourage them to use the long, medium and close-up view of the school, to introduce the characters and to build up to the problem in the story.

GUIDED WRITING — SUPPORT
Help the children to review their planning notes. Encourage them to compose sentences orally before they write, refining and improving so they are sure that what they write makes sense.

PLENARY
Display the checklist of features of a good story opening from Unit 1. Ask the children to read through their writing so far. Can they find examples of any of these things? Ask one or two children to read out examples of particular features, e.g. the three shot description of the setting.

SESSION 7

FOCUS
- How can dialogue move the action on?

RESOURCES
- *Penalty!* Fiction Skills Big Book pages 10–11
- Resource Sheet 5 'Penalty! (middle)'

ORAL LANGUAGE AND SHARED WRITING

Remind the children of the story plan and the story opening written in the previous session. Today you will be writing the middle part where the story builds up. This part of the story will involve a confrontation between the headteacher and the person who kicked the ball.

Time out for discussion In pairs, the children discuss possible dialogue between Mr Brown and Miss Sharp, the headteacher.

Invite pairs to role play the dialogue they prepared.

Demonstration writing Demonstrate how to write the next part of the story. Emphasise how to compose dialogue which moves the action forward. An example of this can be found on RS5. Reinforce the children's understanding of speech punctuation and dialogue by involving them in decisions about where to put the speech marks, the choice of speech verb etc.

INDEPENDENT WRITING

Ask the children to read through their story plans and their story openings. Ask them to write the next part of the story, using dialogue between the headteacher and teacher to move the action on. Remind them to include ideas from their role play and to remember how to use punctuation correctly.

Support Children could present this part of the story in the form of speech bubbles to support them when writing dialogue.

GUIDED WRITING — CORE

Support the group in composing sentences and dialogue orally before writing. Challenge them to move the action on through the dialogue in the same way as was demonstrated in the whole class session.

PLENARY

Ask the children to reflect on their own writing. *What do you have to remember when writing dialogue?* Take the children's suggestions and draw out the idea that there are common mistakes, e.g. putting the speech verb inside the speech marks, forgetting to close the speech marks when somebody has finished speaking, repeating the word 'said' too often. Ask them to read through their work and circle anything they need to change or add.

SESSION 8

FOCUS
- How can you write a good story ending?

RESOURCES
- *Penalty!* Fiction Skills Big Book pages 10–11
- Resource Sheet 6 'Penalty! (end)'

SHARED READING AND WRITING

Limbering up Think of a penalty for a teacher who breaks a window!

Read through the story so far and explain that you will be working on the final part where the problems are solved. Remind the children of the work in previous sessions on good story endings. Read the text from RS6. *Do you think that this is a good ending? Does it solve the problems of the story?* Draw out the idea that a good ending needs to resolve the problems of the story and let you know what happens to the main characters.

Talk for writing Ask the children to discuss ways to round off the story. Organise the children in threes, with each child taking a different role: Mr Brown, Mrs Sharp, Kevin Kelly. Role play the rest of the conversation between them.

Draw together suggestions from the children and discuss how the solution needs to link to the problem. Talk about paragraph connectives to move the action forward. You may wish to use RS6 for ideas.

Discuss with the class how to round off their story with an author comment, e.g. It would be a long time before Mr Brown kicked a football again.

INDEPENDENT WRITING

Ask the children to review what they have written so far and to plan the final part of their stories. Remind them to think carefully about how to link the solutions to the problems introduced already and to tell the reader what happens to the main characters.

GUIDED WRITING — EXTENSION

Challenge the children to devise original and interesting ways to conclude the story. Ensure that they look back at their own stories and plans and make clear links between the problems and the solutions.

PLENARY

Ask the children to work in pairs. They should swap story endings and read them through. What do they like about their partner's story ending? Are there any questions that remain unanswered? Share some suggestions for more satisfactory endings.

SESSION 9

FOCUS
- How can you revise your writing?

RESOURCES
- *Penalty!* Fiction Skills Big Book pages 10–11
- Resource Sheets 4–6 'Penalty!'

SHARED WRITING

Read the complete *Penalty!* story (RS4–6). Explain that the next stage of the writing process is to make it as good as possible so that somebody else will enjoy reading it.

Start by checking the punctuation, drawing attention to the use of full stops, exclamation marks and question marks. Use the checklist produced earlier in the unit to check the speech punctuation.

Reread the story to check that it makes sense. Draw attention to the links between the three parts of the story, e.g. connecting words and phrases. Consider the choice of vocabulary and show how to clarify meaning or express emotion by choosing different words.

INDEPENDENT WRITING

Ask the children to complete their own stories based on their plans made in Session 8 and then read them through carefully. They need to check spelling, punctuation and the sense of the story and make changes as necessary.

GUIDED WRITING — SUPPORT

Support the group in reading through their own writing and checking it for sense and accuracy. Break the process down into three stages: checking it makes sense, checking spelling, and checking punctuation. Help them to identify specific errors and make changes where necessary.

PLENARY

Ask all the children to share examples of things that they have changed or improved in their work. Encourage them to think about the process of identifying errors, e.g. How did you know that a particular word was misspelt? How did you know where to put the speech marks?

SESSION 10

FOCUS
- What have you learned about story writing?

RESOURCES
- Resource Sheet 12 (Unit 5) 'My evaluation sheet'

WORD WORK

Display the word target: 'I know many ways of introducing and concluding dialogue.' Read out a sentence in different ways. Ask the children to write the missing words on their whiteboards. Write the verbs on the board, and tell them to select an appropriate verb, e.g.

'Get me out of here!' he _____
(shouted/whispered/sobbed/begged/muttered).

REVIEW AND EVALUATION

Present the self-assessment on RS12 (Unit 5) to the children and explain that this is for them to use as they think about what they have learnt. Go through each part with them, giving examples of the type of evidence they might find in their own work, e.g. *Look at the dialogue in your story. How does it move the action on?*

INDEPENDENT WORK

Ask the children to think about their own progress towards the targets by working through the self-evaluation sheet.

GUIDED WRITING — SUPPORT

Support the group as they go through each stage. Talk about the evidence that they are looking for and help them to consider what they still need to work on.

PLENARY

Draw together all the learning in Units 1 and 2. Discuss the features of a good story based on what they have learnt about openings, endings and use of dialogue. Write a checklist of 'Good advice for story writers.'

On the Literacy World Interactive CD for Stage 1 Fiction, you will find the following resources for this unit:

- Copies of all the Fiction Skills Big Book pages for interactive work (*Quackers* page 7, *Who Said What?* page 8 and *Penalty!* pages 10–11)
- An audio recording of *Quackers*
- Video clips of *Pingu*
- Interactive word and sentence work for Sessions 1, 2, 3, 4 and 10
- All the Resource Sheets for independent work for you to customise
- Comprehensive Teaching and Planning Guide for the unit are also available on the CD

Speech punctuation

Add the speech punctuation to this dialogue.

I cleaned everything up as best I could, and the game went on

See what you make of this said Steve

I know what that is said Ben it's cranberry jelly

Now you try me with something Steve said

I think you'll like this said Ben

Mmmm that's peanut butter said Steve Now I've found something different for you to try

Easy said Ben that's raisins

This is very sticky said Ben and it's really sweet

It must be syrup said Steve

STAGE 1 | TERM 1 | For use with Unit 2 Session 2 as independent work.

© Harcourt Education Ltd. 2004. Copying permitted for purchasing school only. This resource is not copyright free.

Name _____ Date _____

What do they say? How do they say it?

Choose some words for each character and describe how they say them.

_____ _____

_____ _____

_____ _____

_____ _____

Name _____ Date _____

Speech marks and verbs

Add the speech marks and a speech verb for each sentence.

Oh, Grandma! What big teeth you've got _____ Little Red Riding Hood.

All the better to eat you with _____ the wolf.

Help! Help! _____ Little Red Riding Hood.

A woodcutter heard her cries and he rushed into the cottage.

Stand back _____ the woodcutter.

The woodcutter cut open the wolf and out popped Grandma, safe and sound.

Thank you _____ Grandma you saved my life!

PROMPT: Writing exemplar

Penalty! (story opening)

> I'm going to write the opening paragraph for our story. I'll use a technique we used before – the camera shots from a long, medium and close-up view …

It was lunchtime at Westwood Primary School and the playground was packed with children rushing about and having fun. — *that's my long shot. Now I'll move in a bit closer …*

As usual, Kevin and his gang were playing a wild game of football.

> I think I should add an adjective there to describe the game of football. I know, I'll use the word 'wild'.

Mr Brown was hurrying across the playground on his way to the staffroom. — *now I need my close-up shot.*

> Now I need to link Mr Brown and the game of football.

Just at that moment Kevin kicked the ball to Jason but the ball bounced over Jason's head and landed at Mr Brown's feet. Mr Brown always thought he could have been a footballer if he hadn't become a teacher and, with all the boys watching him, he thought he would show them how it was done.

> I want my story to be slightly funny so I'll add in some detail about Mr Brown. Perhaps he always fancied himself as a footballer so …

> now I need some specific vocabulary to show his knowledge of football …

He steadied the ball with his right foot and booted it as hard as he could in the direction of the goal. The ball ~~went up in the air~~ … soared into the air. It went nowhere near the goal. It went straight through a window.

> no, I can think of a better verb, I'll write 'soared into the air'.

STAGE 1 | TERM 1 | For use with Unit 2 Session 6 as a prompt for shared writing.
© Harcourt Education Ltd. 2004. Copying permitted for purchasing school only. The material is not copyright free.

PROMPT: Writing exemplar

Penalty! (middle)

Next I need a reaction to Mr Brown's action in the story opening. I must remember to punctuate the speech and start the dialogue on a new line.

"Who did that?" demanded Miss Sharp as she leant out of the window. "Was it you Kevin Kelly, because if it was, I shall be speaking to your father tonight. I don't think he's going to be very happy about paying for a new window, do you?"

I need a question mark after that.

Now Mr Brown will reply so I'll write that on a new line ...

"Excuse me, Miss Sharp," said Mr Brown sheepishly, but before he could go on Miss Sharp spoke again.

and perhaps I'll use the word 'sheepishly' for the way Mr Brown spoke ...

"Just one moment please, Mr Brown, I need to find out who is the culprit."

"But ..." said Mr Brown but Miss Sharp silenced him with one look.

"It wasn't me!" said Kevin angrily.

we can see how dialogue moves the action forward.

PROMPT: Writing exemplar

Penalty! (end)

[Now I am ready to begin to finish my story I could write ...]

"It was me!" ~~said~~ blurted out Mr Brown. "It was an accident. I was trying to show the boys how to score a goal and I must have kicked a bit too hard."

[that's a bit weak, so I'll change the speech verb into something more powerful ...]

Miss Sharp stared open-mouthed. She could hardly ask Mr Brown's father to pay for a new window. "It seems to me, Mr Brown," said Miss Sharp, "that you're a better teacher than a football player!"

"I think you're right," said Mr Brown quietly.

"Well," said Miss Sharp smiling. "I think you need lessons in scoring goals."

She turned to Kevin. "What do you think, Kevin? Could you help Mr Brown improve his football skills?"

[I must remember to make sure the solution links to the problem ...]

[then I'll try and think of a humorous ending that makes light of the accident.]

Kevin looked at Mr Brown. "Yes," he said slowly, "I think so, but I don't think he stands much chance of getting into the school team."

[When the problems are solved I'll finish my story with the final paragraph ...]

It would be a long time before Mr Brown kicked a football again.

[in this case, an author comment to round off the story.]

1 1 3 Shape poems

KEY INFORMATION

TEACHING OBJECTIVES

TEXT LEVEL

T1 T6 read aloud and recite poems, ... discuss choice of words and phrases that describe and create impact

T1 T7 ... comment on the impact of layout

T1 T9 generate ideas relevant to a topic by brainstorming

T1 T13 collect suitable words and phrases, in order to create poems and short descriptions; design simple patterns with words, use repetitive phrases, write imaginative comparisons

T1 T14 invent calligrams and a range of shape poems selecting appropriate words and careful presentation. Build up class collections

SENTENCE LEVEL

T1 S4 use verb tenses with increasing accuracy in speaking and writing

T1 S5 use the term 'verb' appropriately

WORD LEVEL

T1 W9 investigate and learn to use the spelling pattern 'le'

T1 W16 understand the purpose and organisation of the thesaurus and then make use of it to find synonyms

UNIT SUMMARY

RESOURCES

- **Essential Fiction Anthology** *Ten Ways to Travel; The River* pages 22–23
- **Fiction Skills Big Book** *Cats Can; Spider* pages 12–13
- **Resource Sheets** 1–3
- **Literacy World Interactive** Unit 3 (optional)

This is a 1-week unit. The children read, discuss and present several shape poems. They use these as models for writing their own poems and then collect these together to make a class poetry book.

5–14 GUIDELINES

Reading level B
- Awareness of genre
- Reflecting on writer's craft
- Reading aloud

CHILDREN'S TARGETS

READING
I can understand why a poet chooses a particular shape for a poem.

WRITING
I can choose a shape for a poem which fits the subject.

SENTENCE
I understand when we use verbs in the past tense.

WORD
I can use a thesaurus to help me find new words and synonyms.

SPEAKING AND LISTENING
I can work with others to generate ideas for poems.

OUTLINE PLAN

STAGE 1 • TERM 1 • UNIT 3

SESSION	WHOLE CLASS WORK		INDEPENDENT WORK	GUIDED GROUPS	WHOLE CLASS WORK plenary
1 Monday	**Shared reading** Introduce focus for the unit. Discuss *Ten Ways to Travel* **T6**	**word work** Investigate and learn the spelling pattern 'le' **W9**	**Independent work** Discuss possible ways to read *Ten Ways to Travel* and practise presentation **T6**	**Guided reading** core Identify and make list of action words	Introduce and discuss targets Share oral reading of *Ten Ways to Travel*
2 Tuesday	**Sentence work** Discuss principles and explanations of verb tenses Brainstorm verbs which end in 'ed' and those which do not (links to Unit 2 of GfW) **S4 S5**	**Shared reading and writing** Read poem *Cat's Can* from BB Demonstrate writing a shape poem	**Independent writing** Write a shape poem selecting one of the animals discussed **W16**	**Guided reading** support Discuss ways to write shape poem	Share shape poems and mime actions
3 Wednesday	**Shared reading and writing** Choral reading of *The River* Brainstorm ways to present a class poem on a thunderstorm Demonstrate writing of poem		**Independent writing** Write own shape poem on a thunderstorm Use a thesaurus **W16**	**Guided writing** support Look at ways of presenting words in poem	Share completed storm shape poems
4 Thursday	**Sentence work** Use the correct form of the past tense for irregular verbs (links to Unit 2 of GfW) **S4 S5**	**Shared reading and writing** Read and discuss poem *Spider* in BB Demonstrate how to write a kenning shape poem on a bee	**Independent writing** Write a kenning poem using hyphenated nouns to describe the creature	**Guided writing** support Write a kenning poem on an earthworm Write own kenning shape poem with hyphenated nouns using RS3	Read kennings – class to guess insect
5 Friday	**Shared work** Present poem in best hand-writing for class poetry book	**Independent work** Present poem in best handwriting for class poetry book		**Guided writing** core Discuss presentation of own poem and final features of class poetry book	Share completed poems Discuss targets

Abbreviation key
- **BB** Fiction Skills Big Book
- **EF** Essential Fiction Anthology
- **GfW** Grammar for Writing
- **SPB** Spelling Bank
- **RS** Resource Sheet

TEACHING NOTES

SESSION 1

FOCUS
- What is a shape poem?

RESOURCES
- *Ten Ways to Travel* Essential Fiction page 22

SHARED READING

Limbering up Use the word 'rectangle' to make the shape of a rectangle. Ask the children why you have done this.

Ready, Steady, Write Ask the children to write another shape on their whiteboards using the word to make the outline of the shape.

Introduce the unit by explaining that the children are going to look at shape poems and then write their own.

Look at the poem *Ten Ways to Travel*. Discuss why each word is written in the way it is. Talk about the effect of arranging the words in this way, e.g. the poem is about movement and the words seem to be moving. Discuss ways of performing the poem, e.g. having a narrator whilst somebody acts out the movements.

Ask individual children to suggest ways to write the following words: climb, skate, march, wander.

WORD WORK

Write the words *rectangle* and *circle* on the board. Ask the children what they notice about the ending 'le'. Tell the children they are going to think of other words ending in 'le'. Draw attention to the word 'wriggle' in the poem. Ask the children for a word which rhymes with 'wriggle' (e.g. *giggle, jiggle*). Ask individual children to suggest actions for 'wriggle giggle' or 'jiggle wriggle'. Generate rhymes for the following 'le' words: wobble, hobble, guzzle, bubble, sizzle (some could have invented words as their rhyme, e.g. wibble wobble).

INDEPENDENT WORK

In pairs, ask the children to think of five more ways to travel, e.g. slide, jump, crawl, wobble. They need to decide how to write each word and how to present the poem.

GUIDED READING — CORE

Ask the children to identify any 'action' words in a text. Compile a list and discuss the effect of choosing a particular word to describe an action, e.g. to convey the character's emotion ('stomped off' instead of 'wandered away').

PLENARY

Display and discuss the targets for this unit and talk about the type of things the class will be doing to help them achieve the target.

Share one or two ideas for presenting the *Ten Ways to Travel* poem. Talk about the effect of adding actions to the performance.

SESSION 2

FOCUS
- Can you show ways that words can convey actions?

RESOURCES
- *Cats Can* Fiction Skills Big Book page 12
- Resource Sheets 1 'Tigers can…' and 2 'Animals in the Wild'

SENTENCE WORK

Write the following sentences on the board: *Yesterday I had a cheese sandwich for my lunch. Today I am having a tuna sandwich. Tomorrow I will have an egg sandwich.* Ask the children to identify the verbs in the sentences. Explain that some verbs have more than one word, e.g. 'am having' 'will have'. *Which verb tells us of something that happened in the past?* (had) Explain that this is called the 'past tense'. Do the same with the other verbs. Tell the children that most present tense verbs form the past tense by adding 'ed', e.g. walked. Verbs that end in 'e' drop the 'e' before adding 'ed', e.g. love loved. Tell the children to write on their whiteboards the past tense of the following 'le' verbs: tickle, wriggle, giggle, chuckle, grumble, cuddle.

SHARED READING AND WRITING

Read the poem *Cats Can* to the class and discuss how the poet has used the writing of the words to convey the actions of the cat.

Talk for writing Explain to the class that they are going to write a similar poem on a wild animal, e.g. Tigers can … Snakes can … Eagles can … Brainstorm words and phrases that describe the animal and which can be written visually, e.g. Snakes can: hiss, wriggle, squirm, strike, slither, bite.

Demonstration writing Choose one example to demonstrate. Talk about your decisions on how to arrange the words to create a picture of the tiger hunting. You may wish to use RS1 as a prompt.

INDEPENDENT WRITING

Ask the children to choose one of the animals discussed in the shared work and write their own shape poem on RS2.

GUIDED READING — SUPPORT

Reread *Cats Can* with the group. Think about how cats move. Can the children describe the way a cat moves?

Ask the group to think of different animals to represent in their poems. They should share ideas and discuss ways of representing the words to convey the actions of the animal.

PLENARY

Ask the children to share their poems and to mime the actions where possible.

SESSION 3

FOCUS
- How can you represent weather in a shape poem?

RESOURCES
- *The River* Essential Fiction page 23

SHARED READING AND WRITING
Read the *The River* and discuss the significance of the layout. Encourage the children to explain why the poem is the shape it is. Direct the class into a choral reading of the poem, e.g. one child to start and others to join in until the whole class is reading 'The Sea'.

Talk for writing Introduce the idea that you could write a similar shape poem about a thunderstorm. Ask the children to recall the stages of a summer storm, e.g. a few drops of rain, down-pour, thunder and lightning, rain slows down, sun comes out again. For each stage of the storm brainstorm words and phrases to represent the sounds and actions of a storm, e.g. trickle, drizzle, rumble, flashed, roared, howled.

Time out for discussion In small groups, ask children to plan ways of presenting each of the words from the brainstorm.

Demonstration writing Introduce the overall shape of the poem (and talk about how you are presenting particular words to evoke the sights and sounds of a thunderstorm). Demonstrate to half way through the poem and explain that the children will be able to complete this shape poem or write their own version.

INDEPENDENT WRITING
Ask the children to write their own shape poem describing the storm and using ideas from the whole class plans. A thesaurus may help to generate further weather words.

GUIDED WRITING — SUPPORT
Give each member of the group a word or phrase describing part of the storm, e.g. thunder claps, zigzags of lightning, rain splashing, rain dripping, clouds clearing. Talk about how each word could be presented and where it fits into the overall shape of the poem. Put it all together and read the poem aloud. *Do the words convey the build up of the storm?*

PLENARY
Share the completed storm shape poems. Choose one completed versions to read aloud. Discuss the effect of presenting the words in a particular way and the way that this affects performance of the poem.

SESSION 4

FOCUS
- Are there other types of shape poem that you can use as a model for your own writing?

RESOURCES
- *Spider* Fiction Skills Big Book page 13
- Resource Sheets 3 'The Bee', 4 'The Butterfly' and 'The Snail'

SENTENCE WORK
Explain that young children often make mistakes with past tense verbs. They add 'ed' to verbs which do not form the past tense with 'ed', e.g. went (wented) make (maked) go (goed). Ask the children for the correct form of each past tense verb.

Time out for writing Ask the children to work with a partner and to write the irregular past tense of the following present tense verbs: eat, ride, drive, blow, hid, run, say. (Remind them that they could think of the past tense if they put the verb in a sentence, e.g. Yesterday I … .)

SHARED READING AND WRITING
Read the poem *Spider* and discuss how the poet has used the shape poem concept differently. Explain how each of the eight strands of the web describes the spider and is a noun.

Demonstrate how to write a kenning shape poem of a bee. Write the hyphenated descriptions on the body stripes, e.g. *honey-maker, pollen-gatherer, flower-visitor, nest-builder, striped-stinger, egg-layer.* Explain that the second description is usually a two-syllable word ending in 'er'. You may wish to use RS3 as a prompt.

INDEPENDENT WRITING
In pairs, ask the children to choose either a butterfly or a snail (using RS4) and write a kenning shape poem using hyphenated nouns to describe the creature, e.g. crooked-flier, flower-lover, fluttery-winger, slime-trailer, plant-eater, house-carrier.

GUIDED WRITING — SUPPORT
Support the group as they brainstorm knowledge about the earthworm. Help them to turn the words into hyphenated noun descriptions, e.g. leaf-eater, soil-helper, earth-turner, blind-wriggler, earth-muncher, worm-caster.

PLENARY
Ask pairs of children to read out one of their descriptions and invite the rest of the class to guess which creature is being described.

41

SESSION 5

FOCUS
- **What is the best way of presenting shape poems?**

RESOURCES
- Resource Sheets 2 'Animals in the Wild', 4 'The Butterfly' and 'The Snail'

SHARED WORK
Presentation of poems Reread the shape poems shared this week from the Big Book and Essential Fiction. Remind the children of the shape poems they have created ('The Storm', 'Animals in the Wild', 'The Butterfly', and 'The Snail'). Tell the children they are each going to choose the poem they like best and then they are going to present it in a class anthology of shape poems. Discuss different ways they could set out and depict their poem, e.g. using IT, cutting out shapes, using different coloured paper.

INDEPENDENT WORK
Ask the children to choose a poem and present it in their best hand-writing for inclusion in the class poetry book.

GUIDED WRITING — CORE
Support the group as they decide on their poem and its presentation. Discuss the final layout of the book and illustration and title for the cover.

PLENARY
Share the finished poems and arrange in the class book.

Refer to the targets for the unit. Which aspects are they particularly pleased with?

On the Literacy World Interactive CD for Stage 1 Fiction, you will find the following resources for this unit:
- Copies of all the Fiction Skills Big Book pages for interactive work (*Cats Can* page 12 and *Spider* page 13)
- Interactive word and sentence work for Sessions 1 and 4
- All the Resource Sheets for independent work for you to customise
- Comprehensive Teaching and Planning Guides for the unit are also available on the CD.

PROMPT: **Writing exemplar**

Tigers can ...

Tigers can slink

And tigers can prowl

Tigers can pounce

And tigers can sssnarl

Tigers can purr

And tigers can ROAR!

Name								Date

Animals in the Wild

Choose one of the following animals and create a picture with the words.

SNAKE	EAGLE
hiss, wriggle, squirm, strike, slither, bite, squeeze	*glide, soar, sip, swoop, seize, hover, snatch*

STAGE 1 | TERM 1 | For use with Unit 3 Session 2 as independent work.
© Harcourt Education Ltd. 2004. Copying permitted for purchasing school only. The material is not copyright free.

PROMPT: **Kenning shape poem**

The Bee

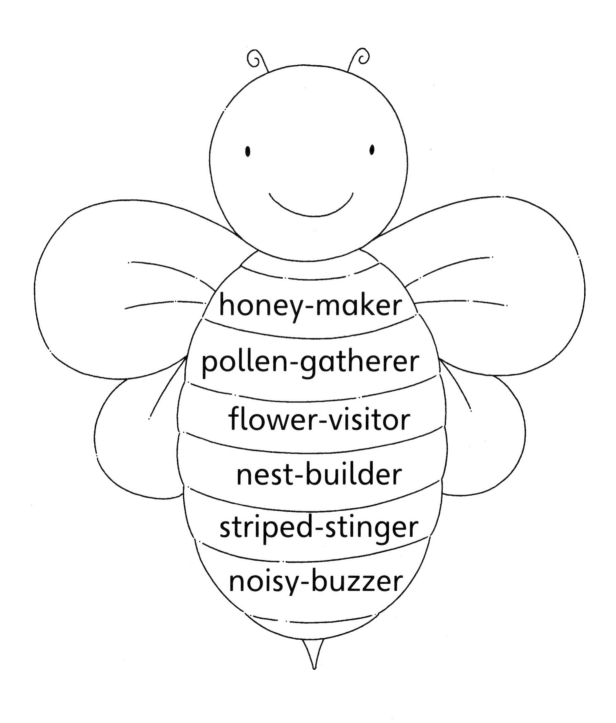

The Butterfly

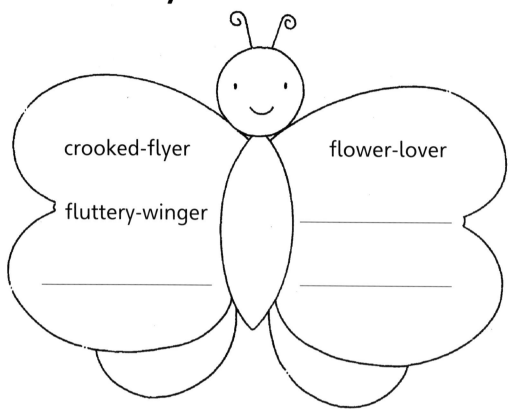

The Snail

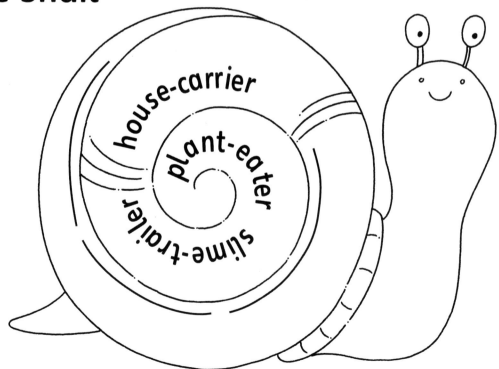

1 1 4 Poetry: Observation

KEY INFORMATION

TEACHING OBJECTIVES

TEXT LEVEL

T1 T6 read aloud and recite poems comparing different views of the same subject; discuss choice of words and phrases that describe and create impact

T1 T7 distinguish between rhyming and non-rhyming poetry and comment on the impact of layout

T1 T8 express their views about poems identifying specific words and phrases to support their viewpoint

T1 T9 generate ideas relevant to a topic by brainstorming and word association

T1 T13 collect suitable words and phrases in order to write poems and short descriptions; design simple patterns with words; use repetitive phrases; write imaginative comparisons

SENTENCE LEVEL

T1 S3 explore the function of verbs in sentences

T1 S5 use the term 'verb' appropriately

T1 S6 secure knowledge of question marks and exclamation marks in reading, understand their purpose and use appropriately in own writing

WORD LEVEL

T1 W2 identify phonemes in speech and writing; blend phonemes for reading; segment phonemes for spelling

T1 W9 investigate and learn to use the spelling pattern 'le'

T1 W16 understand the purpose and organisation of the thesaurus and make use of it to find synonyms

UNIT SUMMARY

RESOURCES

- **Essential Fiction Anthology** *Listen; Bed in Summer* pages 10–11
- **Fiction Skills Big Book** *Wings; The Lake* pages 14–15
- **Resource Sheets** 1–6
- **Literacy World Interactive** Unit 4 (optional)

In this 1- or 2-week unit children read, perform and respond to a range of poems. They create their own observational poems based on models from reading.

The second week is optional and it provides consolidation and reinforcement of the key teaching points covered in Week 1.

5–14 GUIDELINES

Reading level B
- Awareness of genre
- Reflecting on writer's craft
- Reading aloud

CHILDREN'S TARGETS

READING
I can recite my own poem for an audience.

WRITING
I can create a poem which rhymes.

WORD
I am learning to use a thesaurus.

SPEAKING AND LISTENING
I can work with others to generate ideas for poems.

OUTLINE PLAN

SESSION	WHOLE CLASS WORK		INDEPENDENT WORK	GUIDED GROUPS	WHOLE CLASS WORK plenary
1 Monday	**Word work** Revision of phonemes to prepare class for vocabulary of five senses – counting phonemes **W2**	**Oral language work** Introduce focus of unit Discuss the five senses using objects: seeing; touching; smelling; tasting; hearing **T13**	**Independent work** Guess object using senses Write description on whiteboard without disclosing object	**Guided writing** support Describe object orally before writing	Share descriptions of objects Introduce targets
2 Tuesday	**Shared reading** Introduce *Wings* in BB Discuss the different senses and the form of the poem **T6 T7 T8**	**Sentence work** Cover the verbs in the poem Discuss function of verbs in sentences (Links to Unit 1 of GfW) **S3 S5**	**Independent writing** Complete the sentences on RS1, using a thesaurus **W16**	**Guided writing** core Complete sentence using powerful verbs	Share independent work 'Guess my verb' activity
3 Wednesday	**Shared writing** Demonstrate using *Wings* as model to write own poem for two stanzas about 'touch' and 'taste' **T13**		**Independent work** Write three further stanzas using senses of hearing, touch, taste	**Guided writing** support Group compose three further stanzas	Invite children to perform own poems **T6**
4 Thursday	**Shared reading** Read *Listen* in EF Look at punctuation and discuss form and pattern of poem especially rhyme pattern **T13 S6**		**Independent work** Identify rhyme that describes things to hear Extension – create words and phrases to compose rhyming couplets	**Guided writing** support Brainstorm rhyming phrases	Start collection of rhyming words and keep for reference
5 Friday	**Shared writing** Model writing first verse of *Look!* using *Listen* poem **T13**		**Independent writing** Write three more stanzas for the poem called *Look!* Use notes collected in previous sessions on RS4	**Guided reading** support Learn a stanza from *Listen* by heart	Invite pairs to perform their poems – check on correct format Revise poems reading during week **T8**
6 Monday (optional)	**Word work** Spelling of words containing 'le' **W9**	**Shared reading** Read and discuss *Bed in Summer*. Explore form of poem in EF	**Independent work** Find examples of words containing 'le' or practise *Bed in Summer*	**Guided writing** extension List descriptive words and phrases about bedtime	Groups to prepare and perform stanzas from *Bed in Summer*
7 Tuesday (optional)	**Sentence work** Play 'Quickwrite' (links with Unit 1 of GfW)	**Shared reading** Read poem *The Lake* from BB, talking about personification	**Independent work** Create spidergram to describe scene in different weather – sea in winter/summer	**Guided reading** core Create words and phrases for personification	Collect in ideas from spidergrams Create descriptive phrases
8 Wednesday (optional)	**Shared reading and writing** Reread *The Lake* Talk about personification and share ways of using this to describe the sun		**Independent work** Personify nouns on RS5	**Guided writing** support Help group to personify nouns	Share examples of personification Look at effect of personification
9 Thursday (optional)	**Shared writing** Demonstrate writing verse of *The Tree* using personification		**Independent work** Write two stanzas about *The Tree* on RS6 using personification	**Guided writing** support Help group write stanzas for autumn and winter	Invite children to share poems Have they followed the pattern and is the personification effective?
10 Friday (optional)	**Oral language work** Discuss ways of presenting poems using voices, sounds, volume, etc. Discuss most effective ways of presenting their own poems on *The Tree*		**Independent work** Copy out own stanzas in neat hand-writing or use IT	**Guided reading** core Children decide and give reasons about which poems in unit they like best	Evaluate poems and review targets

Abbreviation key
- **BB** Fiction Skills Big Book
- **EF** Essential Fiction Anthology
- **GfW** Grammar for Writing
- **SPB** Spelling Bank
- **RS** Resource Sheet

TEACHING NOTES

SESSION 1

FOCUS
- How can you collect ideas for writing based on descriptions of the five senses?

RESOURCES
- An orange, cut in half and placed in a cloth bag
- A piece of cucumber, a piece of kitchen foil, a tomato, a rattle, a kiwi fruit, and a piece of textured material, e.g. velvet, each placed in a separate box

WORD WORK
Ask the children to think about how they can use their phonic knowledge to help them spell words. Say the following words: *see, smell, touch, taste, hear*.

Time out for discussion Tell the children to work with a partner and to count on their fingers the number of phonemes they can hear in each word s/ee (2), s/m/e/ll (4), t/ou/ch (3), t/a(-e)/s/t (4), h/ea/r (3)

Ask the children to think of other words that contain the same spelling of the long vowel phoneme, e.g. bee, waste, near.

ORAL LANGUAGE WORK
Limbering up Demonstrate each of the five senses using actions, e.g. making spectacles with fingers around the eyes (look).

Explain that in this unit the children are going to read and write poems based on close observation. Invite four children to come out to the front. Ask one child to put their hand in the bag and to describe the object they feel, e.g. *The shape is half a sphere. It feels soft and the middle is squidgy.* Ask the remaining children to describe what the object smells, tastes and looks like (by peeping into the bag). Write their descriptions on the board.

INDEPENDENT WORK
Give each group a whiteboard and one of the objects (in its box). Ask each child to choose one of the senses and write a sentence on the whiteboard about their object, e.g. kitchen foil (*it makes a crinkling noise; it has no taste; it looks bright and shiny; it has no smell; it feels smooth*).

GUIDED WRITING — SUPPORT
Help the group to describe their objects by composing sentences orally before they write.

PLENARY
Each group challenges the rest of the class to guess their object based on their 'sense' descriptions.

Read through the targets for this unit. *What will we need to do to achieve these targets?*

SESSION 2

FOCUS
- How does the poet use the five senses?

RESOURCES
- *Wings* Fiction Skills Big Book page 14
- Thesauruses (one per group)
- Resource Sheet 1 'Powerful verbs'

SHARED READING
Read the poem *Wings* to the class. Reread it and ask the children to demonstrate the appropriate sense for each verse by making the relevant actions.

Discuss with the class what the poet would touch, taste, listen to etc.

Discuss the effect of the repetition (it provides a rhythm and a pattern). Each sense is introduced in the same way. Because the poem does not rhyme, the rhythm and repetition are even more important.

SENTENCE WORK
Cover each verb in the poem (e.g. 'touch', 'glide', 'taste', 'listen', 'graze') with a mini Post-it note. Ask the children to recall the verbs and discuss the function of each verb.

Suggest the children move in ways implied by the following action verbs, e.g. staggered, crept, tiptoed. Draw out the idea of 'powerful verbs' and talk about the effect of changing the verb in a sentence to create a different atmosphere, give a clue about character etc. (Links with Unit 1 of *Grammar for Writing*.)

INDEPENDENT WORK
Ask the children to complete the sentences on RS1 using powerful verbs. They could use a thesaurus to help them.

GUIDED WRITING — CORE
Write the following sentence on a whiteboard: *The man _____ across the room.* Ask the children to supply a verb for the gap. Discuss how the verb alters the picture of the man as he moves, e.g. the verb 'stormed' describes the man in an angry mood. Ask the children to write five different sentences, each conveying a different mood or character.

PLENARY
Ask individual children to select one of their sentences and to move across the classroom demonstrating their verb. Others should guess which verb is being mimed. Record the verbs on the board. Ask the guided group to explain what they have been exploring with verbs.

49

SESSION 3

FOCUS
- How do you write a new poem using a poem you have read as a model?

RESOURCES
- *Wings* Fiction Skills Big Book page 14
- Resource Sheet 2 'A senses poem'

SHARED WRITING
Reread the poem *Wings* to the class. Explain that you are going to write a poem based on the senses and using *Wings* as a model. It will have the same structure with each stanza starting 'If I had wings' followed by a description based on one of the senses.

Time out for discussion Ask the children to think of three things that will be helpful when writing a non-rhyming poem. (Using repetition, having a patterned rhythm, using powerful verbs, using each of the senses) Share the children's suggestions and make a list: 'Good ideas when writing a poem'.

Demonstration writing Write the first two stanzas on 'touch' and 'taste'. Talk through the choice of vocabulary and how to improve it. Stress the strategy of reading and rereading as you write to check that it sounds right. (An annotated text can be found on RS2.)

INDEPENDENT WRITING
Working in pairs, ask the children to write the next three stanzas of the poem covering the senses: sound (hear), smell and sight (see).

Extension Children can attempt a final stanza in which they sum up what would be most wonderful about having wings. When the poems are completed the children practise reading them aloud and adding mimed actions in preparation for a performance.

GUIDED WRITING — SUPPORT
Tell the children they are going to write three stanzas of a senses poem with your support. Draw five boxes on the board and label them with each of the senses. Give the children time to talk about flying and what they would be able to see, hear, taste, touch and smell. Note vocabulary and encourage them to add more description. Support them as they write a sentence for each one using the structure: *If I had wings I would…*

PLENARY
Invite pairs of children to perform their poems. One child should mime the action for the appropriate sense while the other child reads the stanza. Finally discuss the poems of the extension group doing the independent work, asking the more able children to write their summing up stanza. Refer back to the 'Good ideas when writing a poem' list and support the children in checking which features they have included in their own work.

SESSION 4

FOCUS
- How can you use rhyme in a poem?

RESOURCES
- *Listen* Essential Fiction page 11

SHARED READING
Read the poem *Listen* to the class. Which sense was the poet thinking about? Look at the layout and talk about the effect of the punctuation, use of brackets, use of ellipses etc. Discuss why the word 'everything' is written differently.

Ask the children to work in pairs and to decide how to divide up the reading of each stanza. For example, Child 1 might read the first line and Child 2 might ask the question before Child 1 gives the answer. These roles could be reversed in the next stanza.

Share some of the children's prepared readings and discuss the 'clues' from the poem about how to perform, e.g. the first line is an exclamation, the second line is spoken quietly because it is in brackets.

Identify the rhyming words and the rhyming pattern. Demonstrate how to generate rhyming words for a common letter string by scanning through the alphabet, e.g. 'crashing sea' rhymes could be buzzing **b**ee, angry **f**lea, rusty **k**ey, all around **m**e, as far as I can **s**ee, like a gallon of **t**ea, like a creaking **tr**ee.

INDEPENDENT WORK
Working in pairs, ask the children to generate phrases which describe interesting things to hear and which rhyme with the following letter strings (-ay, e.g. donkey bray, children at play; -ing, e.g. a bossy king, a doorbell ring, a choir who sing, a fluttering wing; -ick, -at).

GUIDED WRITING — SUPPORT
Brainstorm with the children some rhyming phrases of things you can hear, e.g.
The familiar sound
Of a ticking clock.
The scraping sound
Of a key in a lock.
Remind them that lines 3 and 5 should rhyme.

PLENARY
Make a collection of the class rhyming words drawn from the independent and guided work. Keep these for reference for the next session.

SESSION 5

FOCUS
- How can you use a pattern to create a new poem?

RESOURCES
- Resource Sheet 3 'A poem for seeing'
- Resource Sheet 4 'Look! What can you see?'

SHARED WRITING

Limbering up Do the actions to represent each of the five senses and ask the children to identify them. Finish with the action for 'to see' (fingers as glasses).

Talk for writing Explain that you are going to write a poem about the sense of sight based on the pattern of the poem *Listen*. (You may wish to use RS3 as a prompt.) Ask the children to imagine that they are looking around outside. Make notes about what they might see: in the sky, the weather, the trees and plants, traffic and animals. Think about how to describe what the thing looks like and select powerful verbs to describe what it is doing.

Teacher scribing Select ideas to use in the first stanza and involve the children in suggesting how to make changes to the original model so that it is about what you can see. Remind them of the rhyming pattern and collect their suggestions for a pair of rhyming words that would work in this stanza. Involve them in checking that you have used the same punctuation as the original.

INDEPENDENT WRITING

Invite the children to write three more stanzas for a poem called *Look!* closely based on the framework of *Listen*. Encourage them to refer to the notes collected in the shared session. They can use the writing frame on RS4 to support them if necessary.

GUIDED READING — SUPPORT

Reread the poem *Listen*, encouraging the children to join in. Challenge them to each learn a stanza off by heart. Talk about strategies for remembering the poem, e.g. a line at a time, adding actions.

PLENARY

Invite pairs of children to perform their poems. Discuss how they managed to follow the pattern of the model poem.

Review the poems that you have read during the week. Ask the children to reflect on which they preferred and challenge them to justify their points of view.

SESSION 6 OPTIONAL

FOCUS
- When you read poems can you understand and explain what they are about?

RESOURCES
- *Bed in Summer* Essential Fiction page 10

WORD WORK

Brainstorm words ending in 'le' and create a class list. Sort the words and categorise them under the headings: -ckle, -able, double letter +le, -cle, -dle, -ble, -ible and -ple. Look out for any patterns that would help when remembering spellings. Invite the children to add to these during the week. (Links with *Spelling Bank*, page 5.)

SHARED READING

Limbering up Ask the children to talk to a partner about what time they go to bed and what time they get up in the morning.

Read the poem *Bed in Summer* and encourage the children to respond by asking questions, e.g. *Why does the author say 'I get up at night'? Why does the author say 'I have to go to bed by day'? What can he see after he's gone to bed? What can he hear?*

Look at the form and pattern of this poem. *Which words rhyme? Is this the same as other rhyming poems you have read?*

Reread the poem with the children joining in. Discuss things to remember when performing poetry, e.g. pace, intonation, attention to punctuation and the difficulties of reading in unison.

INDEPENDENT WORK

Ask the children to work in pairs and to scan through a selection of fiction looking for 'le' words. They should record these under the headings of the class list.

OR:

Divide the children into groups of 3. Ask them to share out the stanzas between them and to practise reading aloud. Encourage them to begin learning their stanza off by heart.

GUIDED WRITING — EXTENSION

Ask the children to think about what they hear and see when they have to go to bed whilst it is still light. They should list words and phrases, selecting descriptive vocabulary and looking for alternatives in a thesaurus.

PLENARY

Ask one or two groups to perform the poem. Talk about ways that they enhanced their performance, e.g. miming actions, their use of intonation, their pace and use of punctuation.

SESSION 7 OPTIONAL

FOCUS
- How can you explore the language and form of a poem?

RESOURCES
- *The Lake* Fiction Skills Big Book page 15

SENTENCE WORK
Play 'Quickmake' using the sentence 'The stormy sea crashed onto the rocks.' Invite the children, one at a time, to change each word in turn, e.g. 'That stormy sea … That raging sea … That raging giant '. When each word in the sentence has been changed once, record the sentence on the board and work through the new sentence changing each word at a time. Be explicit about the word classes, e.g. *First we must change the determiner 'The'. Next, we will change the adjective 'stormy'.* (Links with Unit 1 of *Grammar for Writing*)

SHARED READING
Read *The Lake* to the class. Ask the children to describe what the lake is like in different weathers. Talk about personification. *Why is the lake smiling, hunching its shoulders and hiding? Does the poem rhyme? Does it have a repeated pattern?*

INDEPENDENT WORK
Tell the children to work in pairs and to create a spidergram of words to describe the sea in different weather. They should write the phrase 'Sea in winter' and brainstorm adjectives to describe it, e.g. freezing, chilly, cold, icy, grey. Then they should do the same with 'Sea in summer'. They could use a thesaurus to help them, looking up the words 'cold' and 'hot'.

GUIDED READING — CORE
Reread the poem and ensure all the children understand the vocabulary. Ask them which words and phrases created the most vivid pictures in their minds. Talk about personification. Tell the children to imagine that they are a car. What sort of car will they be? *For example, I am a Mini. I am small but quite cool. I can fit in small spaces.*

PLENARY
Draw on the board the spidergram *Sea in winter* and collect in the different descriptions the children have written. Do the same for *Sea in summer*. Join the adjectives to make phrases, e.g. *the cold, grey sea; the calm, lapping waves.*

SESSION 8 OPTIONAL

FOCUS
- Can you recognise personification and explain what effect it has on a poem?

RESOURCES
- *The Lake* Fiction Skills Big Book page 15
- Resource Sheet 5 'Personification'

SHARED READING AND WRITING
Reread *The Lake* to the class. Talk again about personification. Tell them to imagine that the sun is a person. So every movement the sun does will be described in the actions that a person might do, e.g. The Sun peeped over the rim of the Earth. It slowly crept across the sky.

💬 **Time out for discussion** Work with a partner and think of one further personification for the sun, e.g. 'eating' 'smiling', 'glaring' or 'touching'.

Look at the structure of the poem. Explain that there is a pattern in each stanza which answers the following questions: When? (One a calm day); What? (The lake); Personification (Imagines it's a mirror); Further personification (Smiles back).

Challenge the children to find the same structure in stanzas 2 and 3.

INDEPENDENT WORK
Ask the children to complete the sentences on RS5 where nouns are personified. Encourage them to read each sentence through and check that it makes sense.

GUIDED WRITING — SUPPORT
Discuss with the children how they would personify the nouns using the verbs on RS5. Scribe their answers. Ask them to choose one personified noun from the list and draw a cartoon-type picture to illustrate what this would look like, e.g. a tree with arms and a face, arms wrapped around itself to keep warm.

PLENARY
Share the examples of personification, particularly those created in the guided group. Ask the children to try and explain the effects of using personification, e.g. it can be funny, it helps you to imagine something.

SESSION 9 OPTIONAL

FOCUS
- Can you write your own poem based on a model from reading?

RESOURCES
- *The Lake* Fiction Skills Big Book page 15
- Resource Sheet 6 'Personification in poetry'

SHARED WRITING

Reread the poem. Explain to the class that they are going to help you to write a poem based on the form of *The Lake* and using personification as the main literary device. Write up the model derived from the original poem: When?, What?, Personification, Further personification.

Introduce the theme of the new poem, *The Tree*, and ask the children to talk about how a tree changes during the year. Note useful words and phrases. *Does the tree remind you of any sort of human behaviour?* e.g. new leaves in the spring are like someone waking up after a long sleep.

Use the children's suggestions to help you compose the first and second stanzas. Involve them in decisions about starting new lines and using punctuation in the same way as the original. (You may wish to use RS6 as a prompt.)

INDEPENDENT WORK

Ask the children, in pairs, to write the next two stanzas of the poem about the tree, describing it in autumn and winter. Remind them of the pattern of the original poem.

GUIDED WRITING — SUPPORT

Support the group as they work out the stanzas for autumn and winter. Talk about the When?, What? and Personification pattern.

PLENARY

Invite the children to share their verses. Encourage others to observe if the poem's pattern has been followed. Comment particularly on the effectiveness of the personification.

ORAL LANGUAGE WORK

Discuss with the children different ways that poems can be performed, e.g. different voices, sounds effects, volume. Talk about ways in which the poem *The Lake* could be performed, e.g. one voice per verse, different voices speaking different lines, adjusting the pace according to the words. Agree on performance details and perform.

Reread the class poem *The Tree*, using stanzas written by the children to complete it. Discuss ways in which the class poem could be displayed, e.g. on different trees representing each season for a wall display, on separate pages, with illustrations and included in a scrapbook.

INDEPENDENT WORK

Ask the children to copy out their stanzas in neat handwriting or use IT to enhance the presentation of their poem.

GUIDED READING — CORE

Look back at all the poems read in this unit. Ask the children to reread them and make a decision about which they have enjoyed reading the most. They need to explain why and refer to examples in the text to back up their points.

PLENARY
REVIEW AND EVALUATION

Read through the targets for the unit and ask the children to reflect on their progress. Ask them to reflect on what they have learned about poems from this unit. Which aspect did they most enjoy? What have they learned about performing and presenting a poem?

On the Literacy World Interactive CD for Stage 1 Fiction, you will find the following resources for this unit:

- Copies of all the Fiction Skills Big Book pages for interactive work (*Wings* page 14 and *The Lake* page 15)
- Interactive word and sentence work for Sessions 1, 2 and 6
- Extra reading (*Why Y Tree*, *Jack Frost*)
- All the Resource Sheets for independent work for you to customise
- Comprehensive Teaching and Planning Guide for the unit are also available on the CD.

SESSION 10 OPTIONAL

FOCUS
- What have you learnt about poetry?

RESOURCES
- *The Lake* Fiction Skills Big Book page 15
- Children's poems from previous session

Name _____ Date _____

Powerful verbs

Add in powerful verbs to complete the sentences.

You could use a thesaurus to help you.

The baby _____ across the room.

The angry toddler _____ across the room.

The excited girl _____ across the room.

The unhappy boy _____ across the room.

The busy mother _____ across the room.

The sneaky thief _____ across the room.

The old lady _____ across the room.

The hairy spider _____ across the room.

The disobedient dog _____ across the room.

The tiny kitten _____ across the room.

PROMPT: Writing exemplar

A senses poem

If I had wings ...

sense of touch

> I'm going to write a different stanza for each of the five senses. I think I'll start by copying the same order of senses as the poet used in *Wings*, so my first sense is 'touch'. Now I'll keep the opening of each stanza the same as the poem so I'll start ...

If I had wings
I would touch the top
of ~~a~~ the tallest skyscraper
and float above the city.

> Now, I need to add an adjective such as 'tallest'. I like that because of the repetition of the 't' sound at the beginning of 'top' and 'tallest' ... now I'll just cross-reference with our checklist to make sure that I am including all the features for a non-rhyming poem. Yes, I've got repetition and a pattern and I've used powerful verbs. So, for the second stanza I'll start in the same pattern about the sense of taste ...

sense of taste

If I had wings
I would taste a mouthful
of white cloud as light
as candyfloss.

> *Can I improve on that stanza?* I could say more about the cloud and link it with the candyfloss if I described it as 'fluffy' ... and candyfloss is usually pink not white ...

If I had wings
I would taste a mouthful
of ~~white~~ billowing cloud as
~~light~~ fluffy as candyfloss.

STAGE 1 | TERM 1 | For use with Unit 4 Session 3 as a prompt for shared writing.
© Harcourt Education Ltd 2004. Copying permitted for purchasing school only. The material is not copyright free.

PROMPT: Writing exemplar

A poem for seeing

Instead of the word 'Listen' what is going to be the word on the first line of the poem? ... 'Look'. *And what punctuation do I need?* ... I'll add an exclamation mark.

Look

What would the next line be? I mustn't forget the punctuation.

Look!
(What can you see?)
The curving arc
of a rainbow bright.

Now I need my descriptive phrase of something interesting to see. I'll write about a rainbow ...

the word 'bright' is a good word for the end of the line because we can think of lots of words that rhyme with 'bright'.

A twinkling star
Setting the sky alight ...

Can you come up with a descriptive phrase of something exciting to see that rhymes with 'bright'?

Now I'll just check that I've got the same pattern for my punctuation. *Have I remembered the question mark and the brackets and the ellipsis?*

STAGE 1 | TERM 1 | For use with Unit 4 Session 5 as a prompt for shared writing.
© Harcourt Education Ltd. 2004. Copying permitted for purchasing school only. The material is not copyright free.

Name _____ Date _____

Look! What can you see?

Write three more verses for the poem.

Look!
(What can you see?)

The _____

of a _____

A _____

_____

Look!
(What can you see?)

The _____

of a _____

A _____

_____

Look!
(What can you see?)

The _____

of a _____

A _____

_____

STAGE 1 | TERM 1 | For use with Unit 4 Session 5 as independent work.
© Harcourt Education Ltd. 2004. Copying permitted for purchasing school only. The material is not copyright free.

Name _____   Date _____

Personification

Make up some sentences using personification.
The first one has been done for you.

1 tree   shivered
   In the autumn the tree shivered and the leaves fell off.

2 wind   howled
   _____

3 computer   hiccupped
   _____

4 bus   squealed
   _____

5 moon   gazed
   _____

6 fire   grabbed
   _____

7 river   gurgled
   _____

PROMPT: **Writing exemplar**

Personification in poetry

I'm going to call my poem *The Tree* because that will allow me to describe the changes that occur in each season. I'll start with a description of the tree in spring. I'm going to follow the pattern of 'When', 'What', 'Personification' and 'Further Personification' we discovered in *The Lake* …

The Tree

same capital letters as original poem

When — On a cool day in spring

What — The tree

Personification — Wakes up and smiles at the sun

And stretches its limbs — *Further personification*

Coaxing the baby leaves to unfurl

To clothe the bare branches in green.

same punctuation as original poem

Now we'll write the second stanza. We've got our pattern and we know the subject – the tree in summer. Let's brainstorm ideas for personification of the tree in summer: stands tall and proud, shades the children as they play, holds out its arms to tempt children to climb, tosses its head.

1 1 5 Plays

KEY INFORMATION

TEACHING OBJECTIVES

TEXT LEVEL		SENTENCE LEVEL		WORD LEVEL	
T1 T3	be aware of the different voices in stories using dramatised readings	T1 S6	secure knowledge of question marks and exclamation marks	T1 W10	recognise and spell common prefixes
T1 T4	read, prepare and present playscripts	T1 S9	notice and investigate a range of other devices for presenting texts	T1 W11	use knowledge to generate new words from root words
T1 T5	recognise the key differences between prose and playscripts	T1 S10	identify boundaries between separate sentences in reading and own writing	T1 W12	use the term prefix
T1 T15	write simple playscripts based on own reading and oral work				

UNIT SUMMARY

RESOURCES

- **Essential Fiction Anthology** *Rumpelstiltskin* pages 12–17
- **Fiction Skills Big Book** *Rumpelstiltskin* playscript; *Dick Whittington* pages 16–19
- **Resource Sheets** 1–12
- **Literacy World Interactive** Unit 5 (optional)

In this 2-week unit the children will read playscripts, compare them to prose and become familiar with the main features. They will use what they have learned to write a pantomime, based on a familiar story, for the class to perform.

As this 2-week unit focuses on pantomimes it might be appropriate to undertake this unit towards Christmas.

5–14 GUIDELINES

Reading level B/C
- Awareness of genre
- Reflecting on writer's craft
- Reading aloud

CHILDREN'S TARGETS

READING

I can take part in a play reading.

WRITING

I can write a play for several characters.

SENTENCE

I know when to use question marks and exclamation marks.

DRAMA

I can act out dialogue between two characters.

GUIDED READING LINKS

- *Magic Sticks* (Core)
- *Mad Trad Tales* (Satellites)
- *Goat-skin Lad and other Tales* (Comets)

OUTLINE PLAN

STAGE 1 · TERM 1 · UNIT 5

SESSION	WHOLE CLASS WORK		INDEPENDENT WORK	GUIDED GROUPS	WHOLE CLASS WORK plenary
1 Monday	**Shared reading** Introduce focus. Share prior knowledge about *Rumpelstiltskin* and then read and discuss *Rumpelstiltskin* from EF. Perform dramatised reading of story **T3**		**Independent work** Choose a scene and complete speech bubbles for the characters using RS1	**Guided writing** support Highlight dialogue using RS2	Share some speech bubble dialogues *What will we need to do in this unit?*
2 Tuesday	**Word work** Select high frequency words and discuss ways to remember how to spell them	**Shared reading** Read play version of *Rumpelstiltskin* from BB. Discuss key differences between prose and playscript **T4 T5**	**Independent work** Mark words spoken and read as a play RS3	**Guided writing** support Using different colours, underline words spoken by different characters	Invite children to read dialogue using marked text. Discuss differences between prose and playscripts
3 Wednesday	**Word work** Explore common prefixes – un, dis, re **W10 W11 W12**	**Shared reading** Create class checklist of features of playscripts **T5**	**Independent work** Find specific examples of each feature of playscripts on checklist	**Guided reading** core Group to complete RS4	Discuss differences between playscript and prose
4 Thursday	**Sentence work** Investigate questions. Demonstrate how to turn statements into questions (links with Unit 3 of GfW)	**Shared writing** Choose some of the completed RS1 speech bubble text and present as playscript	**Independent work** Use completed speech bubble text on RS1 to present as a playscript	**Guided writing** extension Create dialogue between King and Miller's daughter	Invite children to hot seat Rumpeltiltskin; the rest of the class should ask questions as to motive and behaviour
5 Friday	**Sentence work** Look at exclamations and function of exclamation marks (links with Unit 3 of GfW)	**Shared writing** Cross-referencing with the checklist, demonstrate how to present another section of *Rumpelstiltskin* as a playscript	**Independent writing** Use extracts from *Rumplestiltskin* to write a playscript scene	**Guided writing** support Use RS6 writing frame for support to write a play	Invite groups of children to perform their scripted versions of *Rumpelstiltskin*
6 Monday	**Shared reading** Discuss pantomimes. Tell the story of Dick Whittington	**Word work** Common prefixes – un, dis, re **W10**	**Independent work** Complete the words adding prefixes un, dis, and re on RS7 **W10 W11 W12**	**Guided writing** extension Use a dictionary to find new words with prefixes un, dis and 're'	Prefix challenge game
7 Tuesday	**Plan for writing** Identify key events in story of *Dick Whittington* using BB. Demonstrate writing initial incident in picture 1 as a play, adding character actions		**Independent writing** Complete the dialogue for picture 2 using RS9 **S9**	**Guided writing** support Orally rehearse dialogue for picture 2	Invite groups to read and perform playscripts to class. Talk about typical pantomime dialogue
8 Wednesday	**Shared writing** Choose events in picture 3 and, with advice from the class, write as a playscript incorporating some typical pantomime dialogue		**Independent work** Write Scene 4. Remind class of the story using RS8 if necessary **T15**	**Guided writing** support Compose song for character to sing	Discuss playscripts and the song from the support group, asking children to suggest changes where necessary
9 Thursday	**Shared writing** Prepare the class for writing the final two scenes from the BB pictures. Remind them about characteristics of a pantomime	**Extended writing** Allocate groups to write dialogue for Scenes 5 and 6		**Guided writing** core Discuss typical endings to pantomines	Share some of the playscripts, checking content against class checklist
10 Friday	**Oral language work** Allocate parts for each scene of the play and do a performance of the play. Discuss ways to improve performance		**Review and evaluation** Complete the self-evaluation using RS12		*Have you reached your targets? What do you need to work on?* Discuss opportunities for performing the pantomime

Abbreviation key
BB Fiction Skills Big Book
EF Essential Fiction Anthology
GfW Grammar for Writing
SPB Spelling Bank
RS Resource Sheet

TEACHING NOTES

SESSION 1

FOCUS
- How do you identify dialogue in a story?

RESOURCES
- *Rumpelstiltskin* Essential Fiction pages 12–17
- Resource Sheet 1 'Speech bubbles 1' and 2 'Speech bubbles 2'

SHARED READING

Limbering up *Guess the story from the following clues: a miller's daughter marries a king; the miller boasts about his daughter; she has to give away a necklace and then a ring; she might have to give away her baby daughter; the name of the story is very important in the plot. What story is it?* (Rumpelstiltskin)

Read the story and discuss the following questions:
- *Who is good and who is bad in the story?*
- *Do you feel sorry for Rumpelstiltskin?*
- *What examples of 'the rule of three' can be found in the story?* (three times told to spin straw to gold; three rewards promised; three days in which to find name etc.)

Ask the children to listen as you read and to notice what you read and what you leave out. Read page 12 up to line 14, saying only the words of dialogue. Ask the children how you knew which words were spoken (speech punctuation). Point out that this makes it sound like a play rather than a story.

Time out for reading Ask them to work in threes (King, daughter/Queen and Rumpelstiltskin) and to read lines 19 to the end as a playscript.

INDEPENDENT WORK

Ask the children to choose a scene and to complete the speech bubbles for the characters using RS1.

GUIDED WRITING — SUPPORT

Use RS2 to help the children to distinguish between narration and dialogue. The children can decide which bits actually need to appear in the speech bubbles and cut out those words. They need to decide which character is speaking on each line and then they need to read through to check that the dialogue makes sense.

PLENARY

Ask pairs of children to act out their speech bubble dialogue. Ask the rest of the class to identify the speakers from their dialogue. Introduce the targets for this unit and talk about the sort of things that they will be doing to help them to achieve the targets.

SESSION 2

FOCUS
- What are the key differences between prose and playscripts?

RESOURCES
- *Rumpelstiltskin* Fiction Skills Big Book pages 16–17
- *Rumpelstiltskin* Essential Fiction pages 12–17
- Resource Sheet 3 'Text marking'

WORD WORK

Select appropriate high frequency words from the Big Book playscript, e.g. 'who', 'always', 'about', 'instead', 'clever'. Devise suggestions for remembering how to spell these words, e.g. *always remember there's only one 'l' in 'always'; look for the little word 'out' in 'about'.*

SHARED READING

Look together at the version of *Rumpelstiltskin* in the Big Book written as a playscript. Talk about the purpose of this type of writing, i.e. written for actors to read the different parts; make the story come to life by acting it out. Look at the layout and talk briefly about how you know when to say your lines and which parts you read aloud.

Ask three confident readers to read the parts of the Narrator, the Miller and the King. Read the scenes from the Big Book.

Time out for discussion Ask the children to work in pairs and to find two differences between the dialogue in the story of *Rumpelstiltskin* and the dialogue in the play version (layout, no speech marks, no 'she said/he said').

Discuss the differences they found and talk about the layout of a play. Explain that this is how characters in film and television read their lines. Ask the children to work in threes and to read the extract imagining they are making a recording for the radio. One group could record their version for others to hear in the plenary.

INDEPENDENT WORK

Ask the children to highlight or underline the actual words spoken on RS3. Then they should read the text as dialogue with a partner.

GUIDED WRITING — SUPPORT

Support the children in underlining the words that are actually spoken and using a different colour for each character.

PLENARY

Invite pairs of children to read their marked text as a play. The rest of the class should follow their own marked version and check that it is accurate. Recap on the differences between prose and playscripts.

SESSION 3

FOCUS
- What are the features of a playscript?

RESOURCES
- *Rumpelstiltskin playscript* Fiction Skills Big Book pages 16–17
- Resource Sheet 4 'Features of a playscript'

WORD WORK
Write the following words on the board: *happy, lucky, appear, obey, play, write*. Talk about the meaning of these words. Then write the prefixes *un, dis* and *re* on the board.

💬 **Time out for discussion** Ask the children to work in pairs and to link the prefixes to the words.

Talk about the effect on the meaning of the word by adding the prefix. Discuss the fact that the spelling of the 'base' word is not altered when the prefix is added. Note that 'appear' can take the prefix 'dis' and 're'. (Links with *Spelling Bank*, page 6) What prefixes could be added to the following words? (like, fill, agree, pay)

SHARED READING
Look again at the playscript in the Big Book. Start a class checklist about features of playscripts. Ask the children to identify the features from the example in the Big Book (e.g. layout, character speaking listed down the left-hand side of the page, stage directions, guidance for the actors about how to say their lines). Talk about other features, such as a cast list, and discuss their purpose.

INDEPENDENT WORK
Ask children to complete RS4. Refer them to the class checklist and label specific examples of each feature of the playscript.

▶ **Extension** In pairs, children can devise the dialogue for the part of the play when the Queen is guessing the strange little man's name.

GUIDED READING — CORE
Support the children as they complete RS4. Help them identify the stage directions and the speakers.

PLENARY
Ask the children to think about the differences between a playscript and a piece of prose in a story. Leave them to discuss in pairs and then take feedback. Draw a simple table to use for noting the children's ideas.

SESSION 4

FOCUS
- How do you present dialogue as a playscript?

RESOURCES
- Completed examples of RS1
- *Rumpelstiltskin* Essential Fiction pages 12–17
- Resource Sheet 5 'Text for playscript'

SENTENCE WORK
Tell the children that they are going to investigate turning statements into questions, e.g. choose some statements from Rumpelstiltskin and demonstrate how to transform them into questions. For example: The King was very fond of gold. *Who was fond of gold? What was the king fond of? What did the King think about gold?* Write the following statements on the board:
The poor girl began to cry.
The little man set to work.
When the King saw the gold he was very pleased.

💭 **Time out for thinking** Ask the children to work in pairs and to devise two questions from each of the above statements.

SHARED WRITING
Teacher demonstration Choose some of the speech bubble text created by the children using RS1 in Session 1. Demonstrate how to present this as a playscript. (See annotated text on RS5 as a prompt.) Talk about the setting for the scene, the conventions for indicating who is speaking and the layout of the playscript.

INDEPENDENT WORK
Give the children back their completed resource sheets (RS1) from Session 1 and ask them to present the speech bubble dialogue in playscript format. They should refer to the class checklist to ensure they include all the features.

GUIDED WRITING — EXTENSION
Tell the children to look again at *Rumpelstiltskin* on page 14 lines 56–59 when the King is pleased with all the gold. They should imagine the dialogue that might have taken place between the King and the Miller's daughter and to present it in playscript format.

PLENARY
Invite children to be in the hot seat and play *Rumpelstiltskin* at the point in the story when he challenges the Queen to guess his name. The rest of the class should think of questions to ask him regarding his motives and behaviour, e.g. *Why did you spin the straw into gold for a gold necklace when you could have spun straw into gold for yourself? Why did you want the Queen's baby daughter?*

SESSION 5

FOCUS
- How do you change prose into a playscript?

RESOURCES
- *Rumpelstiltskin* Essential Fiction pages 12–17
- Resource Sheet 6 'Frame for a playscript'

SENTENCE WORK

Play the 'collect and classify' activity to investigate the function of exclamation marks. Search through some text and identify the explanation notes, then classify them into categories: surprise, fear, loudness, humour etc. (Links to Unit 3 of *Grammar for Writing*.)

Write the following sentences on the board and ask the children what punctuation they need:
- *I don't believe it*
- *Help Help*
- *Rumpelstiltskin is my name*
- *You'll never guess my name he shouted*

Talk about using exclamation marks to suggest fear, surprise, loudness or humour.

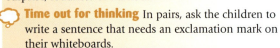 **Time out for thinking** In pairs, ask the children to write a sentence that needs an exclamation mark on their whiteboards.

SHARED WRITING

Teacher scribing Ask the children to look at page 16 of Essential Fiction. Explain that the author has not given any details of the conversation between the Miller and his daughter after the Miller has discovered Rumpelstiltskin's name.

Time out for thinking Ask the children to work in pairs. Spend a few minutes imagining what the Miller and his daughter might say to one another.

Write a script for this scene, asking the children to suggest ideas based on their discussion. Involve them in recalling the layout and features of a playscript. Refer to the checklist and show them how to refine the suggestions they make to ensure that it sounds like a playscript.

INDEPENDENT WRITING

Tell the children to look at line 95 where Rumpelstiltskin comes back for the third time. They should write the scene as a playscript incorporating all the features.

GUIDED WRITING — SUPPORT

Provide the children with the writing frame on RS6 to help them set their work out as a playscript, using lines 95–104 from *Rumpelstiltskin* in the Essential Fiction Anthology.

PLENARY

Invite the children to work in pairs and to read aloud the script they have written in independent work. *Does it work when you are performing it? Is there anything you need to add or change?*

SESSION 6

FOCUS
- Can you retell a story from pictures?

RESOURCES
- *Dick Whittington* Fiction Skills Big Book pages 18–19
- Resource Sheet 7 'Hidden words'

SHARED READING

Limbering up Find out what the children know about pantomimes: *Have you ever seen a pantomime? What type of stories are performed?*

Show the class *Dick Whittington* from the Big Book. Ask the children if they have ever heard the story or seen the pantomime of Dick Whittington. Retell the story using the pictures. Explain that they are going to write part of a playscript about Dick Whittington. Talk about the key events in turn. Jot down the names of the main characters.

WORD WORK

Write the following words on the board: *tidy, usual, appoint, honest, turn, cycle*. Talk to the class about the effect of adding a prefix to each word, e.g. un, dis, re. Add the prefixes to the words and talk about the unchanged spelling of the base word and the changed meaning. Rub out the prefixes. Challenge the children to write on their whiteboards the correct prefix for each word as you point at it. (Links with *Spelling Bank*, page 9.)

INDEPENDENT WORK

Ask children to use RS7 and complete the word search looking for base words and then adding the relevant prefix.

GUIDED WRITING — EXTENSION

Ask the children to look through the dictionary for words beginning 're', 'pre' and 'un'. Remind them of the meaning of each prefix. Ask the children to decide if a word which starts with those letters is an example of a prefix or not.

PLENARY

Play the 'Prefix Challenge' game. Write the following 10 base words on the board: *well, infect, popular, qualify, do, honest, zip, allow, trust, unusual*. Tell the children that the prefixes 'un' or 'dis' can be added to each word. Divide the class into two teams. Invite two children from Team A to come out to the board. One child should add the correct prefix to the word and the other child should give the meaning of the word. If both are correct the team scores 2 points. Then invite two children from Team B to do the same.

SESSION 7

FOCUS
- How do you plan a playscript?

RESOURCES
- *Dick Whittington* Fiction Skills Big Book pages 18–19
- Resource Sheets 8 '*The story of Dick Whittington*' and 9 'Playscript for *Dick Whittington*'

PLAN FOR WRITING

Explain to the class that you are going to organise the story of Dick Whittington into the structure and features of a play. (You may wish to use RS8 as a prompt.)

Look again at the Big Book illustrations for the story. Refer to the class checklist of play features and show how to map the oral story into the play structure, e.g. remind the children of the characters (cast) and explain that the play will need a narrator to move the story on. Decide on a setting for each scene: a country road leading to London.

Time out for discussion Divide the class into pairs and ask one child to take the part of Dick and the other the part of the cat. Ask them to imagine the dialogue for the first picture.

Share some of the suggestions and write good examples on the acetate in the form of speech bubbles. (Keep these suggestions for the final playscript.)

Teacher demonstration Tell the children you are going to write the episode when Dick is working in the kitchen and they are going to continue the dialogue in independent work. Write the words *Cook*, *Dick* and *Cat* on the board. Explain that you need to give some indication about how the characters might say their words so you'll write: *Cook (looking furious)*. Ask the children to suggest what the cook might say, e.g. "Hurry up, you lazy boy!"

INDEPENDENT WRITING

Ask the children to complete the dialogue for the next scene based on the second picture using RS9.

GUIDED WRITING — SUPPORT

Orally rehearse the dialogue between Dick, the cook and Alice. Scribe some of their suggestions. Draw attention to the fact that only the actual words spoken are written in the play. Encourage the children to write some of the utterances themselves.

PLENARY

Invite two groups to perform their playscripts to the rest of the class. Ask the children to suggest stage directions to give guidance to the actors. Look again at the checklist of play features. Ask the children if they know any specific features of pantomimes (audience participation – 'Oh no it isn't'/'Oh yes it is'; talking animals; principal 'boy' is a girl; acting, singing and dancing are often included; usually performed at Christmas and New Year; based on a traditional tale).

SESSION 8

FOCUS
- Can you write your own playscripts?

RESOURCES
- *Dick Whittington* Fiction Skills Big Book pages 18–19
- Shared writing from previous sessions
- Resource Sheets 10 'Song for *Dick Whittington*' and 11 'Song for our favourite citizen'

SHARED WRITING

Teacher scribing Explain that you are now going to write the playscript for Scene 3 of the story of *Dick Whittington*. Look again at the third picture in the Big Book and recall the action in the plot it represents. (Dick and the cat leaving London when he hears the bells calling him back.)

Time out for discussion Ask the children to work in pairs and prepare the dialogue between Dick Whittington and the cat as they leave London. Remind them that Dick is feeling very unhappy and the cat is trying to cheer him up.

Take in some suggestions and discuss how these should be presented as a playscript. What does the narrator need to say to move the action forward? Does it need directions to the actors? (unhappily) (trying to cheer up Dick).

Explain that you are going to write the dialogue for Scene 3 and you are going to try to include some pantomime features discussed in the plenary in Session 7. Using the children's suggestions, write the scene as a playscript on a large sheet of paper up to the point when the cat first hears the bells. (Keep these suggestions for the final playscript.) Then share with children the song *Turn again Whittington, Thou worthy citizen, Lord Mayor of London*. (You may use RS10 as a prompt, if you wish.) Ask them how you should round off the scene.

INDEPENDENT WORK

Tell the children to work with a partner and write Scene 4 in which Dick, Mr Fitzwarren and the cat set off in the boat to sell their goods. Tell them to look again at the picture in the Big Book and reread the story summary for Scene 4. Write the following narrator's part to get them started: *A few years passed and Dick set sail on Mr Fitzwarren's boat. They were off to sell their goods in far countries. Of course, Dick's cat went with him.*

GUIDED WRITING — SUPPORT

Explain that their task will be to prepare a song for Scene 4. Use a well-known song as a model (see RS11) and make up new words for the characters to sing. Explain that the audience also join in with pantomime songs so it needs to be easy to learn, e.g. lots of repetition.

PLENARY

Read through the playscript and songs that have been written so far. *Could you use them for a performance? Does the story make sense and does the text follow the points on the checklist?* Ask the children to suggest any changes or additions to improve the play.

SESSION 9

FOCUS
- What have you learnt about writing playscripts?

RESOURCES
- *Dick Whittington* Fiction Skills Big Book pages 18–19
- Resource Sheets 6 'Frame for a playscript' and 8 'Dick Whittington'

SHARED WRITING
Teacher scribing Look at the last two pictures in the Big Book. Discuss with the class where these scenes take place and list the characters for each scene. Write for the class the narrator's opening for each scene based on the story on RS8. Talk about the fact that the final scene needs to bring the play to a close and round it all off with a satisfactory conclusion (all ends happily with a final song).

EXTENDED WRITING
Divide the class in half. Ask one half, working in pairs, to write the dialogue for Scene 5 and the other half to write the dialogue for Scene 6. Remind the children to identify the boundaries between separate sentences.

Support Children can use the frame for a playscript on RS6. Encourage the children to compose lines orally before writing them down and to keep rereading to check for sense.

GUIDED WRITING — CORE
Discuss typical ways to end a pantomime, e.g. happy ending (with villain getting just deserts), whole cast on stage for a grand finale. Support them as they write their own final scene and praise examples of 'pantomime endings' with songs etc.

PLENARY
Share some of the playscripts the children have written. Check the content against the class checklist. Discuss the effectiveness of the dialogue. Does it need extending or reducing? Would stage directions help the actors? Demonstrate how to delete unnecessary words and how to indicate where more words are needed. Discuss how successfully the sentence boundaries have been marked.

SESSION 10

FOCUS
- Can you use your own scripts to help you to perform a play?

RESOURCES
- One complete version of the play compiled from teacher-led shared work and children's independent work. (Ideally this should be typed up as a continuous playscript.)
- Resource Sheets 11 'Song for our favourite citizen' and 12 'My evaluation sheet'

ORAL LANGUAGE WORK
Divide the class into 6 groups (one for each Scene). Allocate the parts asking two children to share the part of the narrator to ensure every child has a speaking part. Tell the groups to practise their scenes so the dialogue runs smoothly.

Introduce the song for the finale ('What shall we do with a drunken sailor?' with alternative words). You may wish to use RS11 as a prompt.

Do a performance of the play so that each group has a chance to perform their own scene. Encourage children to view it critically. *Can the dialogue be heard? Do people come in on cue? Do they sing the songs enthusiastically?*

REVIEW AND EVALUATION
Read through the self-evaluation sheet (see RS12) and talk about the evidence that children will need to look for when they are evaluating their own achievements.

PLENARY
Refer to the original targets for the unit. Discuss how each target has been achieved. Highlight any areas where further work may be necessary. Discuss further opportunities for performing the play.

On the Literacy World Interactive CD for Stage 1 Fiction, you will find the following resources for this unit:

- Copies of all the Fiction Skills Big Book pages for interactive work (*Rumpelstiltskin* pages 16–17 and *Dick Whittington* pages 18–19)
- An audio recording of *Rumpelstiltskin*
- Interactive word and sentence work for Sessions 2, 3, 5 and 6
- All the Resource Sheets for independent work for you to customise
- Comprehensive Teaching and Planning Guides for the unit are also available on the CD.

Name _____ Date _____

Speech bubbles 1

What are they saying to each other?

Name Date

Speech bubbles 2

Can you turn this conversation into speech bubbles?

"This is your last chance," he said.

"Is it Herbert?" asked the Queen.

"No," said the little man.

"Is it Humphrey?" asked the Queen.

"No," said the little man, "you will never guess my name."

STAGE 1 | TERM 1 | For use with Unit 5 Session 1 as guided writing.
© Harcourt Education Ltd. 2004. Copying permitted for purchasing school only. The material is not copyright free.

Text marking

Highlight or underline the dialogue.

One day the Queen was in the nursery with her baby daughter when the door burst open and there was a strange little man.

"I have come for the baby," he said. "Remember you promised that I could have your first born child."

The Queen began to cry. "Please do not take my baby away," begged the Queen. "I'll give you anything else, but not my baby."

The little man felt sorry for the Queen so he said, "I will give you three days. If in that time you can guess my name, you can keep your child."

"But how can I ever guess your name?" sobbed the Queen.

"Ha! Ha! Ha! You never will," laughed the strange little man as he skipped out of the room.

Name _____ Date _____

Features of a playscript

Label the features of this playscript.

Rumpelstiltskin

Act 1 ← _First part of the play_

Outside a mill below the castle walls ← _____

Narrator There was once a miller who was always boasting about his clever daughter. But one day, when the King came to call, he made one boast too many.

Miller *(bowing low)* Sire, my daughter is the cleverest girl in the world. Why, she can even spin straw into gold.
← _____

King Is that right? Well, I would like to have gold instead of straw. If your daughter is as clever as you say all will be well. If not …

Miller *(stepping back in alarm)* I didn't mean …

King Silence! We'll soon find out if you have been telling the truth or not. *(The soldiers arrest the miller's daughter. The miller sinks to his knees and puts his head in his hands.)*

Act 2 ← _____

Inside the castle ← _____

Narrator The King put the miller's daughter in a room full of straw.

King *(threateningly)* Now we'll see if you're as clever as your father said. Spin this straw into gold, or I'll chop off your head.
← _____
(Turns on his heels and leaves the room, locking the door behind him.)

STAGE 1 | TERM 1 | For use with Unit 5 Session 3 as independent work.
© Harcourt Education Ltd. 2004. Copying permitted for purchasing school only. The material is not copyright free.

PROMPT: Writing exemplar

Text for playscript

To turn these speech bubbles into a playscript I would have to decide whether the dialogue comes at the beginning, the middle or the end of the story. This comes from near the beginning so I'll write …

Act 1

Set the scene to show where the action is taking place

Outside the mill

No speech marks needed in a playscript

King   (*haughtily*) We'll see about that!

Miller   My daughter can spin straw into gold.

These are the words that are spoken

King   (*haughtily*) We'll see about that!

Clue for the actor in brackets to show how to say the words

STAGE 1 | TERM 1 | For use with Unit 5 Session 4 as a prompt for shared writing.
© Harcourt Education Ltd. 2004. Copying permitted for purchasing school only. The material is not copyright free.

Name _____ Date _____

Frame for a playscript

Use this frame to write a playscript.

**RUMPELSTILTSKIN
ACT 5
In the Palace**

Narrator   The next morning the nursery door burst open and in came the strange little man.

Rumpelstiltskin   (*sharply*) _____

_____

Queen   (   ) _____

Rumpelstiltskin   _____

Queen   _____

Rumpelstiltskin   (   ) _____

Queen   (   ) _____

Name _____   Date _____

Hidden words

Find 12 base words hidden in this word search.

```
Z G Y N T U R N
A G R E E A C U
L P A D E X O K
H A P P Y Q V I
L Y P Z B C E N
U A O B E Y R D
C W I N T C P X
K S N F I L L Q
Y H T A D E F G
Z T G H Y W X T
```

Decide which prefix could go with each word and write the word in the correct list.

un   dis   re

_____   _____   _____

_____   _____   _____

_____   _____   _____

_____   _____   _____

   STAGE 1 | TERM 1 | For use with Unit 5 Session 6 as independent work.
© Harcourt Education Ltd. 2004. Copying permitted for purchasing school only. The material is not copyright free.

PROMPT: Text for the picture story

The story of *Dick Whittington*

Scene 1

Once upon a time there was a poor boy called Dick Whittington. One day he decided to set off to London to seek his fortune for he had been told that everyone in London was rich and that even the streets were paved with gold. On the way he met a cat. Together they set off on the long walk to London.

Scene 2

When Dick arrived in London he found that the streets were not paved with gold. He got some work in the kitchen of a rich merchant, Mr Fitzwarren. The cat turned out to be very good at catching mice but the cook gave Dick all the worst jobs to do and he was very unhappy. The only person who showed Dick any kindness was Alice, the rich merchant's daughter.

Scene 3

One morning Dick could stand it no longer. He decided to leave London and return home. The cat faithfully followed him. Then Dick heard the bells of the churches of London. He listened to the chimes. They seemed to be saying "Turn again Whittington, Lord Mayor of London. Turn again Whittington, thrice Mayor of London." Dick thought this was a sign. "The bells are telling me to turn back," said Dick to the cat. So he turned around and headed back to London.

Scene 4

Some years passed and Dick no longer worked in the rich merchant's kitchen. He was now an assistant to Mr Fitzwarren and he travelled with him on board his ship taking valuable cargo to far countries. Once again the cat proved to be a useful companion. She killed all the rats on board the ship.

Scene 5

When the ship came to a beautiful island Mr Fitzwarren was keen to sell all his cargo. The king was delighted with the cloth and gold and traded spices and jewels in return. He invited Mr Fitzwarren and the crew to dine with him at a great feast. But no sooner had the food been set out on the table when a horde of rats swarmed in and began to gobble up the food. The king declared "If only someone could rid me of these rats. I would give them a huge reward." Dick's cat looked at Dick and Dick looked at the cat. Then Dick spoke up, "My cat can do that, your majesty," he said. And with that the cat began to pounce on the rats. Within ten minutes there was a pile of dead rats in the corner of the room and all the other rats scampered off never to return. The king was true to his word and he gave Dick great riches.

Scene 6

When the ship returned to London Dick was a wealthy man. He married Alice, Mr Fitzwarren's daughter and, just as the bells had said all those years before, he became Lord Mayor of London, not just once but three times.
And the cat? Well she never left Dick's side and he made sure that her life was very comfortable for he never forgot how she had brought him his fortune.

Name _____ Date _____

Playscript for *Dick Whittington*

Complete the playscript to go with Scene 2.

Characters

      Cook   Cat   Dick   Alice

Narrator   Dick got a job in a rich man's kitchen. The cook was very cross and Dick had to work very hard. He was glad to have the cat as his companion.

Cook   (*looking furious*) _____

_____

Dick   (*nervously*) _____

_____

Cat   (*quietly*) _____

Narrator   Alice, the merchant's daughter, often came down to the kitchen to talk to Dick.

Alice   _____

_____

Dick   _____

_____

Cat   _____

_____

PROMPT: Pantomime features

RESOURCE SHEET 10

Song for *Dick Whittington*

In Pantomimes a good way to involve the audience is to have a song.

In Scene 3 the cat tells Dick he can hear the bells but Dick is not interested. The cat insists that the bells have a message for Dick. Then the cat asks the audience to sing along with her to help Dick hear the message. Everybody sings the round for Scene 3. Dick agrees that the bells have a message and he turns back for London.

This traditional rhyme can be sung as a round.

	doh	doh – doh	doh – doh – doh
	Turn	*again*	*Whitt – ing – ton*
(Top)	doh	ti – la	so – fa – me
	Thou	*worth – y*	*cit – i – zen*
	La	fa so	me – doh
	Lord	*Mayor of*	*Lon – don.*

STAGE 1 | TERM 1 | For use with Unit 5 Session 8 as a song for the whole class.

PROMPT: **Pantomime features**

Song for our favourite citizen

In Scene 5 Dick becomes assistant to Mr Fitzwarren and travels with him to countries abroad. It is here that the cat earns riches for Dick by killing the unwanted rats aboard Mr Fitzwarren's ship. Mr Fitzwarren starts the song to the tune of *What shall we do with a drunken sailor?*

Mr Fitzwarren What can we do about all these big rats?
What can we do about all these big rats?
What can we do about all these big rats?
Early in the morning.

Dick We'll get my cat to chase and kill them.
We'll get my cat to chase and kill them.
We'll get my cat to chase and kill them.
Early in the morning.

Cat I'll soon get rid of all those big rats.
I'll soon get rid of all those big rats.
I'll soon get rid of all those big rats.
Early in the morning.

In Scene 6 Dick returns a wealthy man and marries Alice. And just as the bells had predicted, he becomes Lord Mayor of London. The cat asks the audience to join in this time and they sing the finale continuing the tune of *Turn again Whittington*.

Audience Hurrah for Dick Whittington!
Our favourite citizen,
Lord Mayor of London.

Name _____ Date _____

My evaluation sheet

The focus for this unit was _____
_____

My Reading target was _____
_____

My Writing target was _____
_____

The best piece of writing I did was _____
_____

The things I still need to work on are _____
_____

My Sentence level target was _____
_____

I have learned to _____
_____

My Word level target was _____
_____

I now know how to _____
_____

The part of the unit I enjoyed most was _____
_____

STAGE 1 | TERM 1 | For use with Units 1, 2 and 5 Session 10 as review and evaluation.
© Harcourt Education Ltd. 2004. Copying permitted for purchasing school only. The material is not copyright free.

1 2 6 Oral and performance poetry

KEY INFORMATION

TEACHING OBJECTIVES

TEXT LEVEL

T2 T4	choose and prepare poems for performance identifying appropriate expression, tone, volume and use of voices and other sounds
T2 T5	rehearse and improve performance taking note of punctuation and meaning
T2 T11	write new or extended verses for performance based on models of 'performance' and oral poetry read

SENTENCE LEVEL

T2 S8	other uses of capitalization for reading e.g. names, headings, special emphasis, new lines in poetry

WORD LEVEL

T2 W3	read and spell correctly high frequency words
T2 W4	discriminate syllables in reading and spelling
T2 W6	use independent spelling strategies ... spelling by analogy
T2 W13	recognise and spell common suffixes and how these influence word meanings
T2 W14	use their knowledge of suffixes to generate new words from root words
T2 W16	use the term 'suffix'

UNIT SUMMARY

RESOURCES

- **Essential Fiction Anthology** *If You Want To See An Alligator; Fisherman Chant; Gran, Can You Rap?; The Travellin' Britain Rap* pages 30–31, 38–41
- **Fiction Skills Big Book** *With My Hands; The School Kids' Rap* pages 20–23
- **Resource Sheets** 1–6
- **Literacy World Interactive** Unit 6 (optional)

In this 2-week unit, the children read a selection of oral and performance poems. They consider what makes an effective performance and use this knowledge to prepare and perform poems for an audience.

- The children write new verses for a poem.

There are five optional sessions that provide consolidation and reinforcement of the key teaching points for this unit, if required.

5–14 GUIDELINES

Reading level B
- Awareness of genre
- Reflecting on writer's craft
- Reading aloud

CHILDREN'S TARGETS

READING
I can prepare a poem for performance.

WRITING
I can write a new verse for a poem.

SENTENCE
I know when to use capital letters for effect.

WORD
I know how suffixes change word meanings.

SPEAKING AND LISTENING
I can perform poems using my voice and other sources.

DRAMA
I can comment on dramatic features.

OUTLINE PLAN

SESSION	WHOLE CLASS WORK		INDEPENDENT WORK	GUIDED GROUPS	WHOLE CLASS WORK plenary
1 Monday	**Word work** Recognise and spell common suffixes (ly, ful, less) and how these influence word meanings. (Links to SPB page13) **W13**	**Shared reading** Introduce focus: performance poetry Read and discuss *With My Hands* from BB **T4**	**Independent work** Mark suggestions for performing poem on RS1	**Guided reading** support Reread poem and discuss how to perform it	Share suggestions and start class list of ideas for performance
2 Tuesday	**Shared reading** Reread *With My Hands* Groups perform a verse Invite pupils to comment **T5**	**Word work** Think of words with suffixes (ly, ful, less) **W13**	**Independent work** Scan text for suffixes	**Guided reading** core Select another poem for performance	Create class list of words with suffixes and discuss effects on word meanings
3 Wednesday	**Shared writing and sentence work** Other uses of capitalization. Start class checklist of occasions when capital letters are used (Links to Unit 12 of GfW) **S8** Discuss poster for advertising performance of *With My Hands* reminding children about punctuation in presentation		**Independent work** Devise poster for advertising performance of poem	**Guided writing** support Group plan their poster	Discuss different uses of capitalization Individual children to make capital letters using their bodies
4 Thursday	**Word work** Building words from roots using suffixes **W13 W14 W16**	**Shared reading** Read and discuss *If You Want To See An Alligator* Discuss ways of performing poem Direct class to perform poem	**Independent work** Add suffixes to words on RS2	**Guided writing** core Use cards from RS3 to play a suffix game	Perform *If You Want To See An Alligator* Judge performance against criteria
5 Friday	**Shared reading** Reread poem *If You Want To See An Alligator* Model how to write a poem about a tiger using same pattern Brainstorm ideas for completing poem, discuss ways to enhance performance and emphasise capital letters **S8**		**Independent writing** Use writing frame for own poem on RS4	**Guided reading** extension Read and prepare a performance of *Fisherman Chant*	Guided group to perform poem Class to assess performance against class checklist
6 Monday	**Word work** Discuss rhyming words and letter patterns **W6**	**Shared reading** Introduce focus: rap poems Read and discuss *The School Kids' Rap* in BB **T4**	**Independent work** Brainstorm further rhyming words using the poem as example	**Guided writing** support Generate and spell more rhyming words	Collect rhyming words from independent work Listen to rap poem Create checklist of things to include in a rap performance
7 Tuesday	**Shared reading** Read and discuss *Gran, Can You Rap?* and *The Travellin Britain Rap* from EF Decide how to perform poem **T5**		**Independent work** Practise performance of chosen poem **T5**	**Guided reading** support Group to perform chosen poems	Groups to perform chosen poem Class evaluate performance
8 Wednesday	**Word work** Practise spelling high frequency words from KS1 **W3**	**Shared writing** Demonstrate writing new verse for *The School Kids' Rap* **T11**	**Independent writing** Write new fourth stanza for rap poem	**Guided writing** support Generate rhyming words about school	Share problems about rhyming words Invite others to suggest solutions
9 Thursday	**Word work** Revise suffixes – adding 'y' **W13 W16**	**Independent writing** Reread *The School Kids' Rap* to class Children add own verses to rap poem on RS6 frame **T11**		**Guided focus** extension Compose new rap poem	Share verses and discuss performance of poem
10 Friday	**Performance** Groups select favourite poem and prepare and perform **T4 T5**		**Review and evaluation** Children complete self-evaluation on RS10 (Unit 8)	**Guided reading** support Rehearse chosen poem	*Have you reached your target?*

Abbreviation key
- **BB** Fiction Skills Big Book
- **EF** Essential Fiction Anthology
- **GfW** Grammar for Writing
- **SPB** Spelling Bank
- **RS** Resource Sheet

TEACHING NOTES

SESSION 1

FOCUS
- How can you make a poem come alive?

RESOURCES
- *With My Hands* Fiction Skills Big Book pages 20–21
- Resource Sheet 1 '*With My Hands* by Steve Turner'

WORD WORK
Write the following words on the board: *hopeful hopeless*. Ask the children what is the same and what is different between the words. (The root is the same but the suffix changes the meaning of the word.) Ask the children to think of sentences using 'hopeful' and 'hopeless'.

Time out for thinking Write the following base words on the board: *pain, thought, love, care, help, lone*. Ask the children to add the suffixes 'ly', 'ful' and 'less' to the base words.

Ask the children to hold up their white boards and point at the word which means 'taking a lot of care'; 'on your own'; 'very nice'; 'not thinking of others'; 'no pain'; 'helping someone'.

Write the following base words on the board and ask the children to work with a partner and decide which suffix could be added to each word: *wish* (ful), *end* (less), *success* (ful), *head* (less), *forget* (ful), *home* (less), *brave* (ly). (Links with *Spelling Bank*, page 13.)

SHARED READING
Introduce the focus for this unit of work – performance poetry. Read and discuss the poem *With My Hands* in the Big Book. Talk about the rhyme and rhythm. Ask the children to suggest how the poem might be performed for an audience, e.g. how to perform each of the actions; how to say each of the action words. Using the acetate show the children how to mark the first stanza poem to give guidance for performance, e.g. how to make the hand actions; double underline for loud reading; crescendo mark (<) to show getting louder; 'ssh' to indicate quiet; sound effect marks in the margin to indicate how many voices reading.

INDEPENDENT WORK
Give each pair of children a copy of RS1 and ask them to mark the remaining stanzas of the poem to indicate suggestions for performance.

GUIDED READING — SUPPORT
Reread the poem with the group and give guidance on how to mark the performance ideas.

PLENARY
Start a class list of suggestions for poetry performance. Introduce the targets for this unit of work.

SESSION 2

FOCUS
- What do you need to include in a poetry performance?

RESOURCES
- *With My Hands* Fiction Skills Big Book pages 20–21
- Completed examples of RS1

SHARED READING
Look again at the poem *With My Hands* in the Big Book. Invite pairs of children to share their suggestions for performing different lines from RS1 and mark them on the acetate.

Divide the class into 4 groups and allocate a verse to each group. Explain that you will be the conductor and you will indicate when each group is to perform their section of the poem. The acetate will indicate how the words are to be spoken and the notes in the margin will remind them of the hand actions.

Conduct a performance! Ask the children to reflect on any changes which might enhance the performance.

WORD WORK
Write the following suffixes on the board: *ly, ful, less*.

Time out for thinking Think of at least one word ending in each of the suffixes.

Collect in their words under the suffix headings. Check that all suggestions are suffixes and talk about those which are not, e.g. only, silly.

Pick examples of root words (help, thought, care, lone, beauty) and explore the effect of adding the suffix. Can they predict what happens to, e.g. root words ending in 'y' or 'e'?

INDEPENDENT WORK
Give each child a fiction text. Tell them to scan the text for examples of words that have the suffixes on the board.

GUIDED READING — CORE
Select another poem suitable for performance. Read it through together and discuss performance. Mark suggestions using the conventions agreed in the whole class session and reread as a performance.

PLENARY
Collect in the words the children have found in independent work and create a class list of words with suffixes. Group the words together under the headings 'ly', 'ful' and 'less'. Draw attention to those words which change 'y' to 'i' and those words that keep the 'e' before the suffix is added.

Stage 1, Term 2, Unit 6

SESSION 3

FOCUS
- When do you use capital letters?

RESOURCES
- Essential Fiction and Essential Non-fiction anthologies

SHARED WRITING AND SENTENCE WORK

Talk to the children about the use of capital letters. Remind them that they are not only used at the start of a sentence.

Time out for thinking Think of three uses of capital letters other than the start of a sentence. (days of the week; months of the year; pronoun 'I'; names of people and places; initials; titles, e.g. Mr. Mrs. Miss, Doctor; headings; postcodes; some abbreviations, e.g. Rd. Ave. P.M. Rev.

Give each child either an Essential Fiction or Essential Non-fiction Anthology and ask them to skim through to find further examples of the use of capitalization.

Discuss how some of these are arbitrary – at the author's discretion. Start a class checklist of 'Must use a capital letter' and 'Could use a capital letter'.

Plan for writing Tell the children that you want to devise a poster to advertise their performance of *With My Hands*.

Time out for thinking Ask the children to think of the information that will need to be included on the poster, e.g. times, venue.

Make notes from their suggestions. Talk about options for presenting the poster. *Where would you have to use capital letters? Should some whole words be in capitals?*

INDEPENDENT WORK

Tell the children to use the information collected in the shared time and to devise a poster advertising the performance of their poem.

GUIDED WRITING — SUPPORT

Help the group to plan their poster before they start writing. Discuss the use of capital letters – the times when it is essential and the occasions when it is optional.

PLENARY

Display the posters and discuss the different uses of capitalization. Invite the children to defend their decisions to use or not to use capital letters. Refer to the class 'Must/Could use a capital letter' checklist. Have the children included capitals from the 'could' category? e.g. to add emphasis.

Ask individual children to form a capital letter using their bodies. The rest of the class guess which letter is being represented.

SESSION 4

FOCUS
- How can you best perform a poem to bring out its meaning?

RESOURCES
- *If You Want to See An Alligator* Essential Fiction page 30
- Resource Sheets 2 'Things I know about suffixes' and 3 'Suffix cards'

WORD WORK

Ask the children to tell you what a suffix is and what purpose it plays.

Write the word *stripe* on the board. Ask the children how you might describe a tiger's coat using the word *stripe* (stripy). What has happened to the end of the word? (drop the 'e' and add 'y') Explain that 'y' is a suffix like 'ly', 'ful' and 'less'. Demonstrate with the following words which end in 'e', e.g. smoke, spike, stone.

Write the words *grease*, *bone* and *noise*. Remind the children of the spelling generalisation and ask them to write the words as adjectives on their whiteboards. (greasy, bony, noisy)

SHARED READING

Read and discuss the poem *If You Want To See An Alligator*. Draw attention to the line of capitals at the end of the poem and talk about why the poet has chosen to write the words in this way. Look again at the class checklist of advice when performing a poem (devised in Session 1). Using the acetate, ask the children to mark the text to show how they would perform certain lines or stanzas.

INDEPENDENT WORK

Ask the children to add suffixes to the base words on RS2.

Support Children can read the root words aloud and try adding each suffix in turn. They then need to decide whether to write the word down: *Do they sound like real words? Have they heard the words before?*

GUIDED WRITING — CORE

Give out a suffix card from RS3 to each child. Hold up the base words. If the children think they are holding a suffix that could be added to that word they should add their suffix and then write the new word on their whiteboards.

EXTENDED PLENARY

Divide children into four groups and ask each group to prepare a lively rendition of the poem based on the annotations made in shared reading. Others should judge the effectiveness of the performance against the class checklist.

SESSION 5

FOCUS
- Can you write your own poem for performance?

RESOURCES
- *If You Want To See An Alligator; Fisherman Chant* Essential Fiction pages 30 and 31
- Resource Sheet 4 'If you want to see a …'

SHARED WORK
Reread the poem *If You Want To See An Alligator*. Explain that you are going to write a poem about a tiger following the pattern of the original poem. Ask the children what the first stanza tells you (where you must go to see an alligator); the second stanza describes what the alligator is like. The third stanza repeats the first, the fourth explains how to call the alligator and the fifth describes what you must do once the alligator is roused.

Plan for writing Brainstorm the information needed to complete ideas for the poem about a tiger, e.g. where you must go to see a tiger, e.g. *You must go down to the misty steamy bamboos of the hot Bengali jungle.* Make notes based on the children's ideas. Do the same for the other stanzas.

Teacher demonstration Make an enlarged copy of the poetry frame on RS4. Using the ideas from the brainstorm, complete the poem. As you write, remind the children of the way that capital letters were used in the original version. Use this as a model for the new poem, involving children in decisions about how and when to use capitals for effect.

Read through the finished poem together and then discuss ways to enhance the performance of the poem (using the class checklist).

INDEPENDENT WRITING
Give each child a copy of RS4. This is a frame for them to write their own poem 'If you want to see a …' Tell them to think of a wild animal and write the poem based on the original. Encourage them to refer to the notes made in the class brainstorm and add new ideas of their own.

GUIDED READING — EXTENSION
Read with the children the poem *Fisherman Chant*. Talk about the repetition and pattern of the language. Work together to prepare a performance of the poem.

PLENARY
Ask the guided group to perform their prepared poem and the rest of the class to assess it against the class checklist. Invite other children to share the poems they wrote in independent work and discuss the ways that they have made use of the original.

SESSION 6

FOCUS
- What do you know about rap poems?

RESOURCES
- Completed Resource Sheet 1 'With My Hands'
- *The School Kids' Rap* Fiction Skills Big Book pages 22–23
- Recorded performance of *The School Kids' Rap*

WORD WORK
Give each child a copy of completed RS1 ('With My Hands'). Tell the children to work with a partner and underline the rhyming words. Collect in some of the rhyming examples. Generate more rhymes and draw attention to the fact that the rhyming words have the same letter pattern, e.g. 'stroke and poke' but some rhyming words could use different letter patterns, e.g. 'soak, folk'. Generate more rhymes for the 'oak', 'olk' and the 'oke' words, e.g. oak, joke, yolk. Do the same with 'pay' and 'pray' (grey, they, weigh, sleigh).

SHARED READING
Time out for discussion Ask the children to turn to a partner and to share what they know about rap.

Share their knowledge with the class and explain that at the end of the unit they will be writing and performing a rap poem.

Read *The School Kids' Rap* poem. Discuss the poem with the class and take suggestions about how you should read it in rap style. Ensure the children understand about the importance of rhythm and rhyme. Draw attention to the internal rhyme in lines 11 and 12 ('school', 'cool', 'grace', 'ace'). *What does the poem tell you about rap poems?*

INDEPENDENT WORK
Write the rhyming words from the poem on the board. Divide the class into groups of six and give each group two rhyming pairs from the poem, e.g. chalk/talk and time/rhyme. Tell them to generate as many further rhyming words as they can.

GUIDED WRITING — SUPPORT
Help the children to generate more rhyming words. Encourage them to spell the words using Look Say Cover Write Check.

PLENARY
Collect in the rhyming words from the independent work. Ask the groups how many different spellings for the rhymes they found (beat: feet, Pete; toes: grows, nose, doze, foes; ace: chase, plaice). Read the rap poem then listen to a recorded performance of the poem.

Discuss the effects that the performer used. Make a checklist of things to include when performing a rap poem.

STAGE 1 · TERM 2 · UNIT 6

SESSION 7

FOCUS
- How can you perform rap poems?

RESOURCES
- *Gran, Can You Rap?*; *The Travellin' Britain Rap* Essential Fiction pages 38–39 and 40–41

SHARED READING

Read and discuss *Gran, Can You Rap?* What is the rhyme pattern of the poem? What language shows that this form of poetry is Afro-Caribbean? What do they notice about the rhythm and rhyme? What words has the poet made up? Why do you think he did this?

Read and discuss *The Travellin' Britain Rap*. Why do you think the poet has repeated 'Traffic noise, traffic noise'? Why do you think the poet has written some words on a single line?

Which poem is easier to read in 'rap' style? Why might this be?

Divide the class into groups of 6. Ask each group to choose one of the rap poems and to decide how to perform the poem. Which lines could be accompanied by rhythmical sounds?

INDEPENDENT WORK

Let the groups practise the performance of their poem.

GUIDED READING — SUPPORT

Support the group in deciding how they will perform their chosen poem. Refer to the poems that they have heard being performed and decide how to work in particular effects. Help them to evaluate their own performances and think about ways to improve them.

PLENARY

Invite the groups to perform their chosen poem. The rest of the class should comment on particularly successful lines or effects.

SESSION 8

FOCUS
- How can you write your own rap poem?

RESOURCES
- *The School Kids' Rap* Fiction Skills Big Book pages 22–23
- 1–6 dice
- Resource Sheet 5 'Writing a rap poem'

WORD WORK

Select ten words from the high frequency word list that are causing the class some spelling problems. Write these on the board and talk about the 'tricky' parts of each word. Suggest ways for children to remember correct spellings. Erase the words from the board.

Divide the class into pairs. Combine pairs to make teams of 12 children. Roll a dice. Give each pair a number from 1 to 6. The pairs of children whose number corresponds to the number on the dice should write the tricky word on their whiteboards. They should hold up their whiteboards and you should give marks for correct spellings. The teams should keep a tally of their score.

SHARED WRITING

Teacher demonstration Look again at stanzas 1–3 of *The School Kids' Rap*. Explain that you are going to write two new lines to replace lines 11 and 12 in stanza 3 and then write a whole new stanza to come before the final stanza. (Use RS5 as a prompt, if you wish.) Demonstrate how to use the rhyme structure and rhythm of the original as you compose the new stanza. Compose alternative lines, rehearse orally and involve the children in deciding which is best.

INDEPENDENT WRITING

Ask the children to think of something about school and to write one new fourth stanza. It could be about playtime, P.E. in the hall or even dinner time. They should work in pairs and brainstorm words for their stanza and generate rhymes for those words. Remind them that the words they choose for the ends of their lines are the ones that must rhyme.

Extension Children can add a further verse.

GUIDED WRITING — SUPPORT

Help the children choose an aspect of school and to generate rhyming words. Support their spelling.

PLENARY

Ask the children to share any problems they had with finding rhyming words. Invite other children to suggest ways round the problem, e.g. by rephrasing: 'In our school the team comes first' which is difficult to rhyme and could become 'The football team likes to win. And the spectators all make a din.'

STAGE 1 — TERM 2 — UNIT 6

SESSION 9

FOCUS
- How can you use a model to help you write a rap poem?

RESOURCES
- *The School Kids' Rap* Fiction Skills Big Book pages 22–23
- Resource Sheet 6 'Frame for rap poem'

WORD WORK
Remind the children about suffixes. What do they remember about words ending in 'e' before 'y' is added (noise/noisy)? Explain that some words which have a short vowel sound, e.g. fun or sun, double the consonant before the suffix 'y' is added: funny, sunny. Ask the children where else a short vowel affects the consonant before an ending, e.g. run, running; clap, clapping. (Links to Speling Bank, page 9.)

Time out for thinking Ask the children to add the suffix 'y' to the following words: mud, fur, fat.

Plan for writing Read through *The School Kids' Rap* and the additional stanzas written in the previous session. Ask the children to read through the stanza they wrote themselves. Discuss the idea of a performance of the poem. What would they include? How could they use the tips they have picked up in previous sessions?

EXTENDED WRITING
Give each child a copy of RS6. This has the first two verses of the original poem and space for the children to add in the lines you created in Session 8. After this they should add their own one or two verses created in independent work in Session 8. Then, working with a partner they should add some performance notes as a guide to how best to perform their poem.

Support Move around the groups helping where necessary.

GUIDED WRITING — EXTENSION
Challenge children to compose a new rap poem using *The School Kids' Rap* as a model, e.g. *The Teachers' Rap* or *The Toddlers' Rap*. Support them as they discuss ideas and collect rhymes. Encourage them to work collaboratively to produce two stanzas that they are all happy with.

PLENARY
Invite children to come out and perform the two verses of their rap poem. The rest of the class can make suggestions about enhancing the performance, e.g. sound effects, finger clicking.

SESSION 10

FOCUS
- Can you use what you have learnt to perform a poem for an audience?

RESOURCES
- *With My Hands; The School Kids' Rap* Fiction Skills Big Book pages 20–21 and 22–23
- *Gran, Can You Rap; The Travellin' Britain Rap* Essential Fiction pages 38–39 and 40–41
- Resource Sheet 10 from Unit 8 'My evaluation sheet'

SHARED READING
Performance of poems Reread all the poems in the unit. Ask the children which poem they liked best and divide them into performance groups according to their choice. Each group should prepare a performance of their chosen poem using the performance notes created during the unit. Groups should perform their poems to the class. If possible, tape record and/or video the performances for others to enjoy. Involve the audience in evaluating the performances.

GUIDED READING — SUPPORT
Work with the less confident readers, supporting them in selecting their poem, reading it through together and discussing the performance. Give feedback as they rehearse their performance, reminding them of the checklists for performance that they compiled in previous sessions.

REVIEW AND EVALUATION
Give each child a copy of RS10 (Unit 8). Talk about each of the questions and help children to decide how they should complete the information.

PLENARY
Take feedback from the children on the unit: *What have you learnt from the unit? What do you need to work on?*

On the Literacy World Interactive CD for Stage 1 Fiction, you will find the following resources for this unit:
- Copies of all the Fiction Skills Big Book pages for interactive work (*With My Hands* pages 20–21 and *The School Kids' Rap* pages 22–24)
- Copies of all the Essential Fiction pages for interactive work (*If You Want To See An Alligator* page 30)
- An audio recording of *The School Kids' Rap*
- Interactive word and sentence work for Sessions 1, 4 and 6
- All the Resource Sheets for independent work for you to customise
- Comprehensive Teaching and Planning Guides for the unit are also available on the CD.

Name　　　　　　　　　　　　　　　　Date

With My Hands by Steve Turner

Add directions for performing the remaining verses. The first one has been done for you.

<u>Shake hands with a partner</u>　Grasp another hand (*shake*)

<u>Group 1</u>　Stick two bits of wood (*make*)

<u>Group 2</u>　Squeeze an empty can (*crunch*)

<u>Everyone</u>　Fingers in a fist (*punch*)

_____　Slip a silver coin (*pay*)

_____　Push them palm to palm (*pray*)

_____　Test the water's heat (*dip*)

_____　Hang on for your life (*grip*)

_____　Push or pull a chair (*shift*)

_____　Raise a weight up high (*lift*)

_____　Press the button down (*click*)

_____　Finger up your nose (*pick*)

_____　Grab an arm or leg (*catch*)

_____　Give an itch a bash (*scratch*)

_____　Knock on someone's door (*rap*)

_____　Thank you very much (*clap*)

Name _____ Date _____

Things I know about suffixes

1 _____

2 _____

Make as many words as you can by adding a suffix to the following base words.

Remember, some base words can take more than one suffix.

	ly	ful	less	y
help		helpful	helpless	
loud				
hair				
quick				
ice				
quiet				
use				
love				
hope				
stripe				
noise				
care				

Name   Date

Suffix cards

Cut out the words and play the game.

care	slow	ease
real	pain	friend
juice	nose	play
y	y	ly
ly	ful	ful

STAGE 1 | TERM 2 | For use with Unit 6 Session 4 as guided work.
© Harcourt Education Ltd. 2004. Copying permitted for purchasing school only. The material is not copyright free.

Name _____ Date _____

If you want to see a …

Think of a wild animal. Write your own poem in the same way as *If You Want To See An Alligator* by Grace Nichols.

If you want to see a _____

you must _____

_____

I know a _____

who's living down there _____

He's _____

_____

Yes, if you really want to see a _____

you must _____

_____

Go down _____ and say,

" _____

_____

_____ "

And _____

But _____

_____

PROMPT: Writing exemplar

Writing a rap poem

It's halfway through the third stanza so I'll begin the same way as the poet …

That's right children, keep in time.

Now we've got rhythm,
  all we need is rhyme.

I'll rhyme this time because the beat is neat.

So come on kids, stamp your feet.

use internal rhyme …

and a word that rhymes with 'neat'.

There's one thing about _____

The teachers are great and the kids are cool.

We all work hard, we do our best.

Then in the summer we have a rest.

I'll fill in our school name.

Name _____ Date _____

Frame for rap poem

Add your own verses.

The School Kids' Rap

Miss was at the blackboard writing with the chalk,
When suddenly she stopped in the middle of her talk.
She snapped her fingers – Snap! Snap! Snap!
"Pay attention children and I'll teach you how to rap."

She picked up a pencil, she started to tap.
"Altogether children, now Clap! Clap! Clap!
Just get the rhythm, just get the beat.
Drum it with your fingers, stamp it with your feet.

_____
_____
_____
_____
_____
_____

Snap those fingers, tap those toes.
Do it like they do it on the video shows.
Flap it! Flap it! Clap! Snap! Clap!
Let's all do the school kids' rap!"

STAGE 1 | TERM 2 | For use with Unit 6 Session 9 as extended writing.
© Harcourt Education Ltd. 2004. Copying permitted for purchasing school only. The material is not copyright free.

1 2 7 Narrative: Traditional tales

KEY INFORMATION

TEACHING OBJECTIVES

TEXT LEVEL

- **T2 T1** investigate the styles and voices of traditional story language – collect examples e.g. story openings and endings
- **T2 T2** identify typical story themes
- **T2 T6** plan main points as a structure for story writing ... discuss different methods of planning
- **T2 T8** write portraits of characters using story text to describe behaviour and characteristics
- **T2 T9** write a story plan for own traditional tale

SENTENCE LEVEL

- **T2 S4** extend knowledge and understanding of pluralisation
- **T2 S5** use the term singular and plural appropriately

WORD LEVEL

- **T2 W6** use independent spelling strategies
- **T2 W7** practise new spellings regularly by Look Say Cover Write Check strategies
- **T2 W8** how words change when 'er' 'est' and 'y' are added
- **T2 W9** investigate and identify basic rules for changing the spellings of nouns when 's' is added
- **T2 W11** use the terms 'singular' and 'plural' appropriately
- **T2 W24** explore opposites

UNIT SUMMARY

RESOURCES

- **Essential Fiction Anthology** *The Gifts at the Bottom of the Well* pages 24–25
- **Fiction Skills Big Book** *Traditional Tales* pages 20–35
- **Resource Sheets** 1–8
- **Literacy World Interactive** Unit 7 (optional)

In this 2-week unit the children read traditional stories and identify common features in this type of writing. They use these features to tell stories and then go on to plan and write their own traditional stories.

5–14 GUIDELINES

Reading level B
- Awareness of genre
- Reading for enjoyment
- Knowledge about language

CHILDREN'S TARGETS

READING
I can read aloud and observe the punctuation.

WRITING
I can write a traditional story in paragraphs.

SENTENCE
I know how to make nouns plural.

WORD
I can add the suffixes 'er', 'est' and 'y.'

SPEAKING AND LISTENING
I can tell a story out loud, using expression.

GUIDED READING LINKS

- *Goat-skin Lad and other Tales* (Comets)
- *Mad Trad Tales* (Core)
- *Nutty as a Noodle* (Satellites)

OUTLINE PLAN

STAGE 1 · TERM 2 · UNIT 7

SESSION	WHOLE CLASS WORK		INDEPENDENT WORK	GUIDED GROUPS	WHOLE CLASS WORK plenary
1 Monday	**Oral language work** Brainstorm features of traditional stories Make class checklist **T1**	**Word work** Investigate spelling of nouns when 's' added. Listing typical nouns from traditional stories and turning into plural nouns **S4 S5**	**Independent reading** Identify different ways of opening a traditional story **T1**	**Guided reading** core Read and discuss story openings	What will we need to do in this unit? Share openings from independent work
2 Tuesday	**Shared reading** Read *The Gifts at the Bottom of the Well* to line 35 from EF Predict what happens next	**Sentence work** Collect and classify plural words (links to Unit 11 of GfW) **S4 S5**	**Independent reading** Find plural and singular nouns from *The Gifts at the Bottom of the Well*	**Guided reading** support Discuss spellings of nouns and how to form plurals	Brainstorm endings to well-known traditional stories
3 Wednesday	**Shared reading** Reread *The Gifts at the Bottom of the Well* Identifying features on the checklist and features that deviate. Mapping story onto 'Characters, Setting, Problem, Solution' frame **T2**	**Word work** Select words from traditional stories and discussing ways to help remember how to spell them **W6**	**Independent work** Choose a traditional tale to map onto story grid	**Guided reading** extension Identify features of traditional tales	Discuss phrases collected by extension group. Invite class to suggest when they might be used
4 Thursday	**Shared writing** Use *Traditional Tales* from BB to create a story from the pictures with 'Characters, Setting, Problem, Solution' frame **T6**	**Word work** Suggest opposites to character descriptions and linking these to events in well-known stories **W6**	**Independent work** Find opposites of characters and events in *The Gifts from the Bottom of the Well*	**Guided writing** support Spell high frequency words from NLS (Years 1–2) **W7**	Play 'Who am I?' Select a well-known character and give details under headings 'Characters, Setting, Problem, Solution'. Class guess character
5 Friday	**Word work** Form the plural with words ending in 'y' **W9**	**Shared writing** Create story (orally) from 'Characters, Setting, Problem, Solution' cards	**Independent work** Using BB and complete character poster on RS3 **T8**	**Guided writing** support Writing a character poster	Play traditional story 'consequences'
6 Monday	**Shared writing** Use *Traditional Tales* from BB to demonstrate how to map story onto story grid. Writing opening paragraph with 'Setting and Character' **T9**		**Independent writing** Write opening paragraph of own traditional story using own character from poster	**Guided writing** core Develop story grids and posters	Share opening paragraphs and use of three camera shot opening
7 Tuesday	**Word work** Look at adjectives of comparison – adding suffixes 'er' and 'est' **W8**	**Shared writing** Demonstrate how to write the 'problem' section of own traditional tale	**Independent work** Select own problem for characters to overcome. Writing next episode of own story	**Guided writing** support Improve character posters	Look at partners, stories and cross reference story to checklist of features
8 Wednesday	**Word work** Revise plurals and adding suffixes 'er' and 'est' **W8**	**Shared writing** Discuss the ending of own traditional story and reaching satisfactory conclusion	**Independent work** Write ending to own traditional story	**Guided writing** extension Develop language features of traditional tale	Share titles of stories. Invite others to guess the theme of the story from the title
9 Thursday	**Shared reading and writing** Discuss typical language patterns and features and identifying paragraphs **T1**	**Extended writing** Discuss own stories with reference to 'good story' writing features. Produce fair copy of traditional story Using IT where appropriate		**Guided writing** support Perfect stories, editing and proofreading	'Hot seat' main character from different children's stories
10 Friday	**Word work** Identify problem spellings. Discussing strategies for learning spelling **W6 W7**	**Review and evaluation** Complete RS12 (Unit 5) Discuss how to display own stories Complete own fair copies and add illustrations	**Independent writing** Make fair copies of work and add illustrations	**Guided writing** support Work to complete own work	Read unconventional traditional story and identify where story deviates from class checklist

Abbreviation key
BB Fiction Skills Big Book
EF Essential Fiction Anthology
GfW Grammar for Writing
SPB Spelling Bank
RS Resource Sheet

TEACHING NOTES

SESSION 1

FOCUS
- What are the features of a traditional story?

RESOURCES
- Short version of traditional tale, e.g. *Jack and the Beanstalk*
- Resource Sheet 1 'Traditional story (openings)'
- Selection of traditional story books

ORAL LANGUAGE WORK
Introduce the focus for the unit. Explain to the children that they are going to learn about the features of traditional stories and use these to write their own traditional story.

Time out for discussion Put the children into pairs and ask them to think of as many titles of traditional stories as they can.

Collect in the different story titles. Tell or read a brief version of one, e.g. *Jack and the Beanstalk*. Ask the children what features in that tale are common to other traditional stories, e.g. 'Once upon a time', 'happily ever after'; three repeated events. Start a class list under the heading 'Features of traditional tales' and add to the list during the unit.

WORD WORK
Remind the children of the terms 'singular' and 'plural'. Make a list of nouns, e.g. king, queen, dragon, palace, forest, wish, prince. Use a magnetic letter 's' and add it to each noun in turn. *Is this the correct spelling of the plural?* Begin to hypothesise about which words just add 's' for the plural.

Challenge pairs of children to choose one plural noun and write it in a sentence on their whiteboards.

INDEPENDENT READING
Give each group a selection of traditional stories and ask them to find five different openings for such stories.

GUIDED READING — CORE
Using RS1, read and discuss the story openings. Ask the children what elements in the openings are common to all tales.

PLENARY
Collect in a range of story openings from the independent work. Choose one of the newly created openings written by the guided group and ask the children to explain how they kept the pattern of a traditional tale opening.

Present the targets for this unit and talk about how the children will achieve them.

SESSION 2

FOCUS
- What happens in traditional stories?
- Can you predict events?

RESOURCES
- *The Gifts at the Bottom of the Well* Essential Fiction pages 24–25

SHARED READING
Read to the class the first part of *The Gifts at the Bottom of the Well* up to line 35.

Time out for thinking Ask the children predict what will happen next in the story. Ask them the following questions:
- What will happen to the bad sister?
- How many doors will she knock at?
- How do you know the answers to these questions?

Read to the end of the story to see how accurate the children's predictions were. Look again at the class checklist of features started in Session 1. *How did it help with answering the predictions? Are there any new features to add?* (characters not named, such as step-daughter, youngest son etc.)

SENTENCE WORK
Explain that nouns are naming words and that they can be singular or plural.

Time out for thinking Ask the children to jot down on their whiteboard the plural form of the following nouns: *cat, boy, tree, door, girl*.

What did you do to the word to make it plural? (add an 's')
What is the plural of box? Explain that in words ending in 'sh', 'ch', 'x' and 'ss' you have to add 'es'.

Ask the children for the plural of: *fox, lunch, glass*.

INDEPENDENT READING
Ask the children to look through the story *The Gifts at the Bottom of the Well* and find six words that are plural nouns and six words that are singular nouns.

GUIDED WRITING — SUPPORT
Ask the children to write down the objects they can see and then discuss the spellings. Explain that all the words are nouns. Demonstrate how to form the plurals of the nouns by adding 's', 'es' or 'ies'.

PLENARY
Brainstorm endings to traditional tales, e.g. *What happens at the end of Cinderella? Sleeping Beauty?* Summarise these, e.g. Prince marries Princess. Add to the checklist of 'features'.

SESSION 3

FOCUS
- How can you map the story on to a grid?

RESOURCES
- *The Gifts at the Bottom of the Well* Essential Fiction pages 24–25

SHARED READING
Reread *The Gifts at the Bottom of the Well* to the class.

Time out for thinking Look at the class checklist of features. Find three features that tell you that this is a traditional story (good versus bad; characters not named; tasks to be completed; three doors; opening and ending; good rewarded)

Plan for writing Draw a story grid on the board (four boxes: 'Characters, Setting, Problem, Solution'). Ask the children to help you to map the details of the story on to the grid, e.g. two sisters and a fairy; set down a well. Help the children identify the problem for the good sister (loses her bucket) and the solution (completes task for fairy and is given back her bucket, plus reward). Ask them to do the same for the bad sister. Write their answers on to the story grid.

WORD WORK
Select typical words from traditional tales, e.g. once, kingdom, giant, wicked, reward, fairy, beautiful, handsome, castle, and discuss strategies for learning the spellings (Look Say Cover Write Check; syllabification; identifying phonemes; common letter strings).

INDEPENDENT WORK
Ask the children to work in pairs and to choose two traditional tales they know well, e.g. *Little Red Riding Hood*, *Rumpelstiltskin*, *The Gingerbread Man*, *Jack and the Beanstalk*. They should map these on to the story grid: Characters, Setting, Problem, Solution.

GUIDED READING — EXTENSION
Provide a selection of traditional tales. Prompt the children to refer to the class checklist of features and to skim through the tales to find examples of traditional story language, e.g. 'Years passed,' 'A little further on', 'Before long' and examples of phrases repeated three times. Write these up for the rest of the class to refer to.

PLENARY
Discuss the phrases collected by the group. Share some of the story grids and enter these on a grid for all the class to see. Invite the children to suggest when some of the phrases might fit into the story grids, e.g. A little further on Jack met a funny little old man. Years passed and the princess was very lonely in her garden.

SESSION 4

FOCUS
- What are the essential ingredients for planning a traditional story?

RESOURCES
- *Traditional Tales* Fiction Skills Big Book pages 24–25
- *The Gifts of the Bottom of the Well* Essential Fiction pages 24–25

SHARED WRITING
Look at the pictures in the Big Book. Explain that these will provide the essential ingredients for devising a new story. Talk through the Characters, Settings and Problems suggested by the pictures.

Time out for thinking Tell the children to work in pairs and to choose a Character, a Setting and a Problem. Collect in some of the suggestions. Circle the relevant items in the Big Book (e.g. Prince, Castle, Dragon). Invite other pairs of children to choose a solution to the problem.

WORD WORK
Remind the children that traditional tales often involve opposites, e.g. 'good sister' and 'bad sister'. Ask them to suggest opposites to a list of words: kind, selfish, greedy, rude, etc. Write the opposites next to the words. Ask the children to think of examples of characters from traditional tales who portray these characteristics.

INDEPENDENT WORK
Ask the children to look through *The Gifts at the Bottom of the Well* and to find as many examples of opposites as they can. They should list opposites of character as well as opposites of actions.

GUIDED WRITING — SUPPORT
Choose a selection of high frequency words, e.g. from NLS Years 1–2. Demonstrate how to spell these words and ask the children to suggest the opposites, e.g. down (up), in (out), do (don't), first (last).

PLENARY
Play 'Who am I?' Draw the story grid on the board. Ask the children to think of a traditional story. Invite some to share something about the setting, e.g. *I live in a mill*; something about the problem in their story, e.g. *I have to turn straw into gold*; and something about the solution, e.g. *I guess the name of a funny little man*. (Rumpelstiltskin)

SESSION 5

FOCUS
- How can you combine the ingredients to make a traditional story?

RESOURCES
- Resource Sheets 2 'Traditional story (features)', 3 'My character poster'

WORD WORK

Time out for thinking Ask the children what they know about how plurals are formed. (Most add 's'; for words ending 'sh', 'ch', 'x', 'z' and 'ss' add 'es').

Explain that words ending in 'y' form the plural by changing the 'y' into 'i' and adding 'es'. Demonstrate with the words 'baby' and 'lady'.

Ask the children to work with a partner and to write the plurals: *city, puppy, party, fly, jelly, berry, army*. Then invite individuals to spell the plurals of: *watch, baby, sister, tree, wish, lady*. (Links to *Spelling Bank*, page 10.)

SHARED WRITING

Copy RS2 onto thin card. Give each group a Character, Setting, Problem and Solution. Tell the group to create a traditional story based on their ingredients. Each group should perform their story for the rest of the class.

INDEPENDENT WORK

Tell the children to choose a character from the Big Book pages. They should complete RS3 for their chosen character, filling in the character details, ready to use in the traditional story they are going to write.

GUIDED WRITING — SUPPORT

Support the group to complete their character poster on RS3. Orally rehearse the writing before helping them with spelling.

PLENARY

Divide the class into groups of six. Play traditional story 'Consequences'. Each child needs a sheet of paper. Write the following frame on the board:
(Character) met (Character) in (Setting)
He said (…), She said (…)
In the end (…)

Ask the children to complete the first section and fold over the paper and pass it to the child on their right. Continue until all sections have been completed. Open out the sheets and share the story outlines. Collect and share some of the best examples.

SESSION 6

FOCUS
- How can you set the scene for a traditional story?

RESOURCES
- *Traditional Tales* Fiction Skills Big Book pages 24–25
- Resource Sheet 4 'Traditional story (characters/opening)'

SHARED WRITING

Explain to the children that they are all going to start writing their own traditional stories in this session.

Teacher demonstration Demonstrate how to select story ingredients from the chart in the Big Book. Explain that you are going to choose a Prince as your main character and that you're going to set your story in the castle.

The problem for the Prince, is that he only cares about gold. A magic elf grants him great riches. The solution will be that the Prince realises that wealth is not everything.

Supported composition Give each child a story grid and their character posters from the previous session. Remind them that they have already chosen their main character. They now need to select the other ingredients of their story and note it on the grid. Offer support as they do this and encourage them to use and adapt ideas from the Big Book if necessary.

Teacher demonstration Go on to demonstrate how to write the opening paragraph of your story. Remind them that the opening paragraph should introduce the main character and the setting. Think aloud about the personality of your character: rich or poor, selfish or kind etc. Look again at RS1 and adapt one of the openings to make it suitable for your character and setting. Remind the children of the three camera shot approach, used in Term 1, to describe the setting. (You may wish to use RS4 as a prompt.)

INDEPENDENT WRITING

Ask the children to write their own opening paragraph (using the three camera shot approach for the setting).

GUIDED WRITING — CORE

Discuss their character posters and planning grids. Ensure that the 'problem' they have chosen will prompt a good story line. Support them as they write their opening paragraph on OHTs.

PLENARY

Share the opening paragraphs created by the core group in the guided writing work. Discuss the success of the traditional opening, the three camera shot setting and the personality of their character. Tell the children that they are going to write the middle section of their story in the next session so they should be thinking about how the character's problem can become a story.

SESSION 7

FOCUS
- How can you link the problem to the theme in your traditional story?

RESOURCES
- *Traditional Tales* Fiction Skills Big Book pages 24–25
- Resource Sheet 5 'Traditional story (problem)'

WORD WORK
Select three tall children in the class. Explain that __ is tall, but is __ taller and is __ tallest of them all.

Write the words on the board and ask the children what changes you have made to each adjective (added 'er' for comparison between two, and added 'est' for comparison for more than two.)

Time out for thinking Ask the children to use their whiteboards and add 'er' and 'est' to the following words: *cold, high, rich, small*.

Explain that the base word in the adjectives does not change when the suffixes are added. This is true of most adjectives. Ask the children what they think happens to words with a short vowel before a single consonant such as 'big' (double the consonant).

Ask the children to use their whiteboards and add 'er' and 'est' to the following words: *fat, thin, hot, sad*. (Links to *Spelling Bank*, page 8.)

SHARED WRITING
Teacher demonstration Reread the opening paragraph of your story. Ask the children what part of the story should come next (Problem). Remind them of the plan you completed before writing the opening and discuss how you can move your story on to introduce the problem. Talk about how you are able to give clues about the character through the way they speak or behave. (you may wish to use RS5, as a prompt.)

INDEPENDENT WORK
Tell the children to reread their stories so far and to refer to their completed story posters and to the class checklist of features, and to consider how they can incorporate some of these into their stories, e.g. repeated actions, introduction of a magical creature. They should write the next section of their stories.

GUIDED WRITING — SUPPORT
Support the group as they look back at their posters and discuss their chosen 'problem' for their character. Do their solutions link to their problems?

PLENARY
Ask the children to swap their stories with a partner. The partner should cross-reference the story with the class checklist and find specific examples of traditional story features. Share these with the class. Talk about language patterns that make the story sound authentic.

SESSION 8

FOCUS
- Can you keep the reader interested in your story by developing the plot?

RESOURCES
- *Traditional Tales* Fiction Skills Big Book pages 24–25
- Resource Sheets 6 'Traditional story (middle)' and 7 'Traditional story (end)'

WORD WORK
Write the following words on the board: *cold* and *hot*. Ask two children to come out and to write the words adding 'er'. They should explain their spelling choices.

Write the words *baby* and *babies*. Ask the children how the word changes in the plural. Write the word *happy* on the board. Ask them how the word would change when adding 'er' or 'est'. Write *happiest* on the board. *Can you come up with a spelling rule to explain this change?*

SHARED WRITING
Teacher scribing Reread your modelled story so far. Explain that in the opening of the next paragraph you need to introduce the magic elf.

Time out for thinking Ask the children to work with a partner and write a sentence introducing the elf. Collect in their ideas and select an appropriate sentence for the story.

Continue to demonstrate how to develop your traditional story. (You may wish to use RS6 and RS7 as prompts.) Stop after Ivan wishes the gold away.

Ask the children to help you tie up the loose ends of your story. *Will the funny little man help Ivan? Will Ivan regret his wish for gold? Will Ivan's behaviour change after this?* Talk about conclusions of traditional stories referring to the Big Book. Write the conclusion of your traditional story. Talk about choosing a title for the story. Discuss options, e.g. *The Foolish Wish, Too Much Gold, Real Treasure*.

Ask the children to work with a partner and to plan the ending for their traditional story.

INDEPENDENT WORK
Ask the children to reread their stories so far and to write the ending (solution). They should refer to the class checklist of features and to the suggestions in the Big Book. They should also choose a title for their story.

GUIDED WRITING — EXTENSION
Ask the children to read through their stories so far and to check that they contain the language features of traditional tales.

PLENARY
Share some of the titles children have chosen for their stories. Invite others to guess the theme of the story from the title.

SESSION 9

FOCUS
- Can you recognise the language and features of a traditional story?
- Can you improve your own writing?

RESOURCES
- Resource Sheet 8 'Traditional story'

SHARED READING AND WRITING
Give each pair of children a copy of either the modelled story (RS8) or a copy of the story you have demonstrated for the class. Recap on the key text and language features of traditional stories. Ask the children to tell you how to mark the story, identifying the relevant text and language features. Use two colours: one to mark typical language patterns, e.g. Long ago, or any repeated phrases; another colour should mark typical text features, e.g. deals with kings, queens, opposites etc. Also mark the paragraphs as *Character* and *Setting*, *Problem* and *Solution*. Finally, the children should rate the success of the story and identify any areas where they think the story could be improved, e.g. more repetition, more examples of the rule of three. They should give the story a mark out of ten and justify their grade.

EXTENDED WRITING
Tell the children to look through their own finished stories and check that they have included as many language features as possible. They should identify any spellings they are not sure about and check these in a dictionary. They should look particularly carefully at correctly demarcating speech.

When their work has been checked, the children should make a fair copy of their story in their best handwriting or using a word processor.

GUIDED WRITING — SUPPORT
Support the children in reading through their work, checking spellings and punctuation and making changes. Help them to identify words that they frequently misspell and think about strategies for learning and remembering them.

Take it in turns to read finished stories aloud and encourage the rest of the group to respond to the stories, e.g. *Were the characters described effectively? Did they include features of traditional tales? Was there a good solution?*

PLENARY
Demonstrate how to explore the story and characters further by putting a main character in the hot seat. Ask questions such as: *What did you learn from this experience? Do you ever wish you had done things differently?*

Invite children to be in the hot seat for the main character from their story.

SESSION 10

FOCUS
- What is the best way to present your work?
- What have you learnt from this unit?

RESOURCES
- Resource Sheet 10 from Unit 8 'My evaluation sheet'
- An example of a alternative traditional tale where the conventions are inverted, e.g. *Ten in the Bed* Allan Ahlberg, *Topsy Turvy* Dick King-Smith

WORD WORK
Identify problem spellings from the children's draft stories. Write approximately ten words on the board and choose appropriate strategies for learning how to spell these words. (syllabification, counting phonemes, words within words, mnemonics, 'Look Say Cover Write Check', highlighting the tricky part etc.)

> **Time out for thinking** Ask the children to work with a partner. One should sit with her/his back to the board. The other partner selects a spelling and challenges her/his partner to write it. They should change places and roles after each word.

REVIEW AND EVALUATION
Encourage the children to review and evaluate their work using RS10 from Unit 8. When they have completed this ask them to discuss which parts of the unit they enjoyed most and where they still feel there is scope for improvement. As a class, review progress towards the unit targets. Children should discuss how their completed stories should be displayed.

INDEPENDENT WRITING
Ask the children to complete their fair copies, paying particular attention to spelling corrections and adding an illustration.

GUIDED WRITING — SUPPORT
Focus on individuals identified as needing support as they work to complete their fair copies.

PLENARY
Read the class a story (where traditional conventions are given a twist). Encourage children to look at the class checklist of features and ask them to listen for deviations from these.

On the Literacy World Interactive CD for Stage 1 Fiction, you will find the following resources for this unit:

- Copies of all the Fiction Skills Big Book pages for interactive work (*Traditional Tales* pages 24–25)
- Audio recordings of *Jack and the Beanstalk* and *Ten in the Bed*
- Interactive word and sentence work for Sessions 2, 4, 5 and 8
- All the Resource Sheets for independent work for you to customise
- Comprehensive Teaching and Planning Guides for the unit are also available on the CD.

Traditional story (openings)

Find some common features in these story openings.

Cock-a-doodle-doo Mr Sultana **Michael Morpurgo**	*Grey Wolf, Prince Jack and the Firebird* **Alan Garner**	*Rumpelstiltskin* **Kit Wright**
In a far off land a long long time ago there once lived a great and mighty Sultan.	Once long ago, not near, not far, not high not low, at the place where the seven rivers meet there lived a king.	There was once an old miller who lived deep in a forest by a winding river.
The Frog Prince **Rose Impey**	*The Sleeping Beauty* **Rose Impey**	*Snow White* **Rose Impey**
In the olden days when wishing still did some good there was a king and he had a string of daughters.	In the days when there were still fairies there lived a king and queen who were immensely rich.	It was the middle of winter, a long time ago, and a young queen sat sewing by an open window.
Beauty and the Beast **Rose Impey**	*The Twelve Dancing Princesses* **Rose Impey**	*The Storyteller* **Anthony Minghella**
There was once a man who set out on a journey full of hope, but returned in complete despair.	Long ago, in another time, in another country, there lived a king who had twelve daughters, all equally beautiful and yet entirely different.	Not so long ago, in the deep north – where it can be so cold, just very cold is considered quite warm – two dark hearts ruled the land.

STAGE 1 | TERM 2 | For use with Unit 7 Session 1 as guided reading.
© Harcourt Education Ltd. 2004. Copying permitted for purchasing school only. The material is not copyright free.

WORD WORK: **Cards**

Traditional story (features)

Characters

| Prince | Princess | Poor girl |
| Poor boy | King | Queen |

Settings

| palace | forest | cave |
| poor cottage | castle | mill |

Problems

| a dragon | a wolf | a giant |
| a wicked uncle | no money | lose magic charm |

Solutions

| get married | rescue | find wealth |
| trick evil character | solve riddle | return home |

STAGE 1 | TERM 2 | For use with Unit 7 Session 5 as shared writing.
© Harcourt Education Ltd. 2004. Copying permitted for purchasing school only. The material is not copyright free.

Name _____ Date _____

My character poster

Choose and draw your character.

Then fill in the details.

Name: _____
_____

Appearance: _____
_____

Age: _____

Personality: _____
_____

Address: _____
_____
_____

Best known for: _____
_____
_____

Problem: _____
_____
_____

Literacy World | STAGE 1 | TERM 2 | For use with Unit 7 Session 5 as independent work.
© Harcourt Education Ltd. 2004. Copying permitted for purchasing school only. The material is not copyright free.

PROMPT: **Writing exemplar**

Traditional story (characters/opening)

> I'll look again at some of the openings studied before and adapt one for the opening of my story …

Long, long ago in a far away land there lived a Prince called Ivan.

> and use the three camera shot approach so I'll describe the palace from three views.

He lived in a magnificent palace set high in the mountains. The walls of the palace were made of white marble and each room was decorated with gold. But Prince Ivan was not happy. He wanted more gold.

> The end of the first paragraph makes us want to read on …

STAGE 1 | TERM 2 | For use with Unit 7 Session 6 as a prompt for shared writing.
© Harcourt Education Ltd. 2004. Copying permitted for purchasing school only. The material is not copyright free.

PROMPT: Writing exemplar

Traditional story (problem)

> My next paragraph introduces the problem.

> In my plan Ivan cares only about gold so I'll write about that …

> "mug" doesn't seem very suitable for my story so I'll write "goblet" instead.

One day Prince Ivan was counting all his gold. He was sitting on his gold throne and drinking from his gold ~~mug~~ goblet. His mother asked him if he would like a friend to come and play but Ivan said. "I don't need any friends. I have my gold to play with."

> The reader must understand how awful Ivan is, so I've tried to show this by describing how he is only interested in his gold and by repeating his reply.

> Now that's the end of that paragraph so I need to link it with the next paragraph and introduce the magic elf …

So Ivan sat alone in his gold room, on his gold throne, counting out the gold in ten enormous sacks and as he counted he muttered to himself, "I love gold. I wish I had all the gold in the world."

> … I've set up the arrival of the magic elf who will come when he hears Ivan's wish.

STAGE 1 | TERM 2 | For use with Unit 7 Session 7 as a prompt for shared writing.
© Harcourt Education Ltd. 2004. Copying permitted for purchasing school only. The material is not copyright free.

PROMPT: **Writing exemplar**

Traditional story (middle)

> You had lots of good ideas for introducing the magic elf but I think I'll write …

Just then the door burst open and a funny little man appeared by Ivan's side. Ivan was so shocked he forgot whether he had counted five million gold coins or four million gold coins.

> I've deliberately exaggerated how much money Ivan is counting because that's more like the language of traditional tales.

The little man said, "Do you really want all the gold in the world?"

"Of course, I do," said Ivan.

"Close your eyes and count to three," said the elf. "When you open your eyes, your wish will have come true."

Prince Ivan did as he was told. He closed his eyes and counted **one** … *(Ivan heard coins tumbling down the chimney)* **two** … *(Ivan heard coins rattling up the stairs)* **three** … *(Ivan heard coins clattering in the courtyard)*. He opened his eyes. There were gold coins pouring out of the fireplace. There were gold coins blocking the doorway and out in the courtyard mounds of gold coins covered the grass and flowers.

"Stop! Stop!" shouted Ivan.

STAGE 1 | TERM 2 | For use with Unit 7 Session 8 as a prompt for shared writing.
© Harcourt Education Ltd. 2004. Copying permitted for purchasing school only. The material is not copyright free.

PROMPT: Writing exemplar

Traditional story (end)

> If we look at our story grid we see the solution follows the problem …

Then Ivan realised how foolish he had been. Gold coins did not bring him friends or happiness.

"I wish I had never set eyes on any gold coins," shouted Ivan.

> I'll look back at the story grid. Ivan must realise that gold is not everything. Maybe he should wish the gold away …

"Are you sure?" said a voice by Ivan's ear. Ivan turned and saw the strange little man sitting on top of the mounds of gold.

"Yes," said Ivan. At once the gold and the funny little man vanished. Ivan found himself alone, sitting on a wooden stool looking at ten empty sacks.

Did Ivan miss all his gold? No, not one bit. He spent his time playing with his friends and helping his parents in the palace. But Ivan always kept one gold coin in his pocket to remind him of the funny little man and how he had helped him to see what real treasure is.

> The last paragraph rounds off my story.

Name												Date

Traditional story

Use two colours and mark:
- typical language features
- typical language patterns

Divide the story into paragraphs:
Character; Setting; Problem; Solution.
Where could the story be improved?

Long, long ago in a far away land there lived a Prince called Ivan. He lived in a magnificent palace set high in the mountains. The walls of the palace were made of white marble and each room was decorated with gold. But Prince Ivan was not happy. He always wanted more gold.

One day Prince Ivan was counting all his gold. He was sitting on his gold throne and drinking from his gold goblet. His mother asked him if he would like a friend to come and play but Ivan said, "I don't need any friends. I have my gold to play with."

So Ivan sat alone in his gold room on his gold throne counting out his gold in ten enormous sacks and as he counted he muttered to himself, "I love gold. I wish I had all the gold in the world."

Just then the door burst open and a funny little man appeared by Ivan's side. Ivan was so shocked he forgot whether he had counted five million gold coins or four million gold coins.

The little man said, "Do you really want all the gold in the world?"

"Of course, I do," said Ivan.

"Close your eyes and count to three," said the elf. "When you open your eyes, your wish will have come true."

Prince Ivan did as he was told. He closed his eyes and counted **one** ... (*Ivan heard coins tumbling down the chimney*) **two** ... (*Ivan heard coins rattling up the stairs*) **three** .... (*Ivan heard coins clattering in the courtyard.*) He opened his eyes. There were gold coins pouring out of the fireplace. There were gold coins blocking the doorway and out in the courtyard mounds of gold coins covered the grass and flowers.

"Stop! Stop!" shouted Ivan.

Then Ivan realised how foolish he had been.

"I wish I had never seen a gold coin," shouted Ivan.

"Are you sure?" said a voice by Ivan's ear. Ivan turned and saw the strange little man sitting on top of the mounds of gold.

"Yes," said Ivan. At once the gold and the funny little man vanished. Ivan found himself alone, sitting on a wooden stool looking at ten empty sacks.

Did Ivan miss all his gold? No, not one bit. He spent his time playing with his friends and helping his parents in the palace. But Ivan always kept one gold coin in his pocket to remind him of the funny little man and how he had helped him to understand what real treasure is.

STAGE 1 | TERM 2 | For use with Unit 7 Session 9 as shared work.

© Harcourt Education Ltd. 2004. Copying permitted for purchasing school only. The material is not copyright free.

1 2 8 Myths, fables and parables

KEY INFORMATION

TEACHING OBJECTIVES

TEXT LEVEL

T2 T2	identify typical story themes
T2 T3	identify main and recurring characters, evaluate their behaviour and justify views
T2 T6	plan main points as a structure for story writing, considering how to capture points in a few words that can be elaborated later
T2 T7	describe and sequence incidents in a variety of ways
T2 T9	write a story plan for own myth, fable or traditional tale
T2 T10	write alternative sequels to traditional stories, ... using typical phrases and expressions from story

SENTENCE LEVEL

T2 S1	use awareness of grammar to decipher new or unfamiliar words
T2 S2	the function of adjectives in sentences
T2 S3	use the term adjective appropriately
T2 S6	note where commas occur in reading and to discuss their functions in helping the reader
T2 S7	use the term comma appropriately
T2 S10	understand the differences between verbs in the first, second and third person
T2 S11	understand the need for grammatical agreement in speech and writing

WORD LEVEL

T2 W12	recognise and generate compound words
T2 W15	use the apostrophe to spell shortened forms of words
T2 W24	explore opposites

UNIT SUMMARY

RESOURCES

- **Essential Fiction Anthology** *Birth of the Stars; Baira and the Vultures Who Owned Fire; The Crowded House; The Dog and the Bone; The Stag and His Spindly Legs* pages 26–29, 32–37
- **Fiction Skills Big Book** *Why The Moon Shines At Night; The Sly Builder; The Bear and the Travellers* pages 26–31
- **Resource Sheets** 1–9
- **Literacy World Interactive** Unit 8 (optional)

In this 3-week unit the children read a range of myths and legends, parables and fables. They recognise the features of each genre. They write an alternative sequel to a well-known fable.

5–14 GUIDELINES

Reading level B
- Awareness of genre
- Reading for enjoyment
- Knowledge about language

CHILDREN'S TARGETS

READING
I can recognise the main features of a myth, legend, parable and a fable.

WRITING
I can plan and write my own version of a fable.

SENTENCE
I can add adjectives to make my writing more interesting.

WORD
I am learning to use the apostrophe to show a letter is missing.

GUIDED READING LINKS

- *Steggie's Way* (Core)
- *Fair's Fair* (Satellites)
- *Jane Blond Schoolgirl Superspy* (Comets)

OUTLINE PLAN

STAGE 1 · TERM 2 · UNIT 8

SESSION	WHOLE CLASS WORK		INDEPENDENT WORK	GUIDED GROUPS	WHOLE CLASS WORK *plenary*
1 Monday	**Shared reading** Introduce focus Read and discuss *Birth of the Stars* from EF **T2**	**Sentence work** Select words and check meanings from context **S1**	**Independent work** Draw three speech bubbles for tortoise, first moth and wizard. *What did they say?*	**Guided reading** support Discuss punctuation of sentences **S6 S7**	*What will we need to do in this unit?* Discuss purpose for myths
2 Tuesday	**Shared reading and sentence work** Read *Why the Moon Shines at Night* from BB Discuss with class and identify features of a myth **T2**		**Independent work** Create list of ten titles for myths, e.g. Why the sun is hot	**Guided reading** core Collect titles for myths	Share the titles from the independent work
3 Wednesday	**Shared reading** Read *Baíra and the Vultures* from EF Look at characteristics of a legend **T3**		**Independent work** Draw story plan for Baíra – look at problems	**Guided reading** support Map story of Baíra in sequence	Freeze-frame some of the problems and solutions
4 Thursday	**Shared reading and writing** Reread *Why the Moon Shines at Night*. Plan new myth Scribe first part of story **T6**		**Independent writing** Complete the story from class plan	**Guided writing** support Retell story and look at ending	Look at class checklist. *How well does the story meet the criteria?*
5 Friday	**Sentence work** Look at function of adjectives **S2 S3**	**Shared writing** Discuss the endings of the story	**Independent writing** Make fair copies of conclusion to own myths	**Guided writing** support Use IT to present work	Re-enact the myth of *Why There is Only One Sun* in the sky
6 Monday	**Sentence work** Look at the addition of prefixes to root words. Discuss the need for pronouns and verbs to agree **S10 S11**		**Independent writing** Change the writing from the third person to the first person	**Guided writing** support Orally rehearse sentences in the first person	Ask individual children to retell their escape as Baíra
7 Tuesday	**Shared reading** Read *The Crowded House* from EF to the class Look at what makes a parable?	**Sentence work** How adjectives add detail to nouns **S2 S3**	**Independent work** Using RS Change the adjectives	**Guided writing** extension Create a parallel parable	Ask extension group to share parable and class to suggest a moral
8 Wednesday	**Drama work** Reread parable of *The Crowded House*. Ask groups to freeze-frame episodes	**Word work** ook at compound nouns **W12**	**Independent writing** Sketch characters and write thought bubbles for each	**Guided writing** core Look at the Rabbi's point of view	Share wok from independent activity and discuss
9 Thursday	**Shared reading and word work** Read *The Sly Builder* from BB. Discuss the morals of a parable. Look at opposites used in the parable. Link to class checklist **W24**		**Independent work** Using *Parable of the Crowded House*, find all the opposites	**Guided writing** core Predict what might happen next in the story	Share the opposites from the independent work
10 Friday	**Shared reading and writing** Reread the parable of *The Sly Builder*. Identify features. Demonstrate how to write a sequel to the story **T9 T10**		**Independent work** Suggest a suitable resolution to the parable	**Guided writing** support Link story to moral	Share independent work *What do you know about parables?*

Abbreviation key
- **BB** Fiction Skills Big Book
- **EF** Essential Fiction Anthology
- **GfW** Grammar for Writing
- **SPB** Spelling Bank
- **RS** Resource Sheet

SESSION	WHOLE CLASS WORK		INDEPENDENT WORK	GUIDED GROUPS	WHOLE CLASS WORK plenary
11 Monday	**Word work** Look at contractions and when they indicate the omission of a letter or letters **W15**	**Shared reading** Read the fable *The Dog and the Bone*. Discuss the morals of the story	**Independent work** Find 15 different contractions using class fiction books	**Guided writing** core Categorise contractions	Categorise the contractions from independent work Make class list and invite children to add to this during the week
12 Tuesday	**Word work** Look at contractions and find matching pairs	**Shared reading** Read *The Stag with his Spindly Legs* and look at the morals of fables	**Independent work** Complete the missing sections on RS6 and add the moral	**Guided writing** extension Write story outline for *Stag and his Spindly Legs*	Share the work from independent time
13 Wednesday	**Shared reading and writing** Demonstrate writing from pictures in *The Bear and the Travellers* Discuss language choices and vocabulary decisions. Draw attention to commas **S6 S7**		**Independent work** Work out the dialogue for *The Bear and the Travellers* from BB	**Guided writing** support Retell the story and include dialogue between two characters	Invite children to mime the story *The Travellers and the Bear*
14 Thursday	**Plan for writing** Orally rehearse opening sentence of their fable. Talk about paragraphs and plan		**Extended writing** Children write fable based on shared story plan. They should evaluate each other's story	**Guided writing** support Orally rehearse sentences before writing	Revise strategies for spelling unknown words. Look at suggestions for final presentation of fable
15 Friday	**Review and evaluation** Share edits and explain reasons for these	**Independent writing** Class make fair copy of their fable: some can use IT		**Guided writing** support Make fair copies of their fable	*Have you reached your targets? What do you need to work on?*

Abbreviation key
- **BB** Fiction Skills Big Book
- **EF** Essential Fiction Anthology
- **GfW** Grammar for Writing
- **SPB** Spelling Bank
- **RS** Resource Sheet

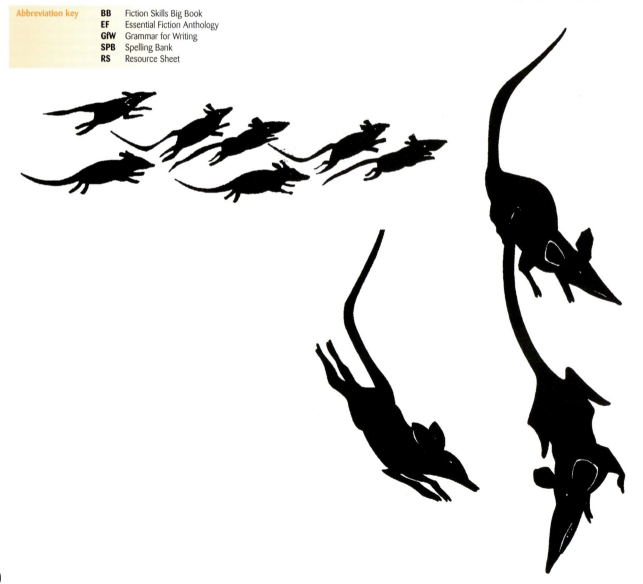

TEACHING NOTES

SESSION 1

FOCUS
- What is a myth?

RESOURCES
- Resource Sheet 1 'Animal silhouettes'
- *Birth of the Stars* Essential Fiction pages 32–33

SHARED READING

Introduce the unit by explaining to the children that you are going to read some myths and legends.

Limbering up Ask the children what they know about myths. Have they ever heard any stories such as: *Why the Sun is Hot, Why the Bear has a Stumpy Tail*. Tell them that myths are ancient stories which explain events.

Show the children the silhouettes (on an overhead projector) from RS1 and ask them to guess which animals are which.

Read *Birth of the Stars*. Ask the following questions:
- *What is this story trying to explain?*
- *Do you think this myth really explains why there are stars in the sky?*

Start a class checklist with the heading 'Features of myths and legends'.

SENTENCE WORK

Pick out some less familiar words from the story, e.g. 'casting', 'reveal', 'distant'. Look at the words in context. Show the children how to predict the meaning of the word based on its context and word class (verb, adjective etc.).

INDEPENDENT WORK

Ask the children to sketch pictures of the tortoise, the moth, and the wizard. They should draw a speech bubble for each character and imagine what each character might have said at the following points in the story: Tortoise (line 22), First moth (line 37), Wizard (line 51).

GUIDED READING — SUPPORT

Reread the first paragraph of *Birth of the Stars* ignoring all punctuation. Ask the children what you have omitted. Ask them to identify when each full stop occurs. Draw attention to the commas. Discuss with the group what purpose the comma plays in helping the reader to make sense of the writing.

PLENARY

Introduce the targets for the unit and talk about what they will be doing to achieve them.

SESSION 2

FOCUS
- What are the characteristics of a myth?

RESOURCES
- *Why the Moon Shines at Night* Fiction Skills Big Book pages 26–27

SHARED READING AND SENTENCE WORK

Read the myth *Why the Moon Shines at Night*. Discuss the story and ask the following questions:
- *What is this myth trying to explain?*
- *Is any of it based on what we know about the Moon and the Sun?*

Draw attention to the commas in the story. Ask the children what function they have in the sentences. *When do we use commas?* (to separate clauses in a sentence before direct speech; in a list; to mark off adverbs or adverbial phrases).

Time out for thinking Draw a basic story plan on the board: 'Characters/Setting/Problem/Solution'. Ask the children to draw the same plan on their whiteboards and map the events of the myth onto the plan.

Take in the children's suggestions. *What is different about the story plan for a myth and for a contemporary story?* (characters not people; no particular setting; problem is to do with the natural world; solution explains some natural phenomenon)

Look again at the checklist started in the previous session and add some more features based on the discussion.

INDEPENDENT WORK

Ask the children to work in pairs to create a list of ten titles for myths which are an attempt to explain why the world is as it is. Each title should start *Why the …*, e.g. *Why the squirrel's tail is bushy, Why the sea is salty*.

Extension Children can select one of their titles and think about a possible answer that could form the basis of a myth. They should make notes.

GUIDED READING — CORE

Tell the group to look through a range of myths from a library or class collection and to collect titles from published myths. Discuss how classical myths do not always explain a natural phenomenon but sometimes focus more on characters, e.g. *The Labours of Hercules*.

PLENARY

Share the titles from the independent work. Take in suggestions about how some of these titles might be answered, e.g. The squirrel has a bushy tail because he likes to keep his drey very clean and uses his tail to sweep and dust.

SESSION 3

FOCUS
- What is a legend?

RESOURCES
- *Baíra and the Vultures Who Owned Fire* Essential Fiction pages 34–37

SHARED READING

Look again at the class checklist 'Features of myths and legends'. Tell the class that myths and legends are very similar. Usually myths tell a story about some event in nature and are ancient while legends often tell stories about heroic characters from history. Ask them if they have heard of the legend of King Arthur (*The Sword in the Stone*).

Read to the class the story of *Baíra and the Vultures Who Owned Fire*.

Listening focus Ask the children to decide, as you read, whether it has more in common with a myth or a legend.

Explain that this story has characteristics of both genres – it explains a natural phenomenon but it has a main character like a legend. Ask the following:

- Why is fire so important to humans?
- What main event does the story explain?
- What features about animals are also explained by the story?
- Is Baíra a hero? How can you tell?

INDEPENDENT WORK

Ask the children to work in pairs and to draw a story plan (Characters/Setting/Problem/Solution) and to enter the story details onto the plan. Tell the children to look carefully at the number of problems. (Six problems: raw food; vultures chase Baíra; can't cross the river; river snake scales are burning; prawn's tail is burning; cururu-frog's mouth is burning.) When they have recorded each problem they should choose one and decide how to represent it in a freeze-frame.

GUIDED READING — SUPPORT

Use a large piece of paper to map the story plan. Ask the group to tell you who the characters are and what the setting is. Ask the children to help you to sequence the story after Baíra snatches the fire from the vultures. Help them to see these events in terms of problems and solutions. Write these on the story plan.

PLENARY

Display the completed story plan from the guided reading work and ask them to read out each problem and solution for the rest of the class to compare.

Invite pairs of children to come out and perform their freeze-frame. The rest of the class should guess which part of the story is being dramatised.

SESSION 4

FOCUS
- What must you remember when writing a myth?

RESOURCES
- *Why the Moon Shines at Night* Fiction Skills Big Book pages 26–27
- Resource Sheet 2 (plan for myth), 3 (story for myth) 'Why there is only one sun in the sky'

SHARED READING AND WRITING

Reread the story of *Why the Moon Shines at Night*. Look again at the class checklist 'Features of myths and legends'. Explain that you are going to plan a myth. Remind the children that myths usually explain natural phenomenon and so your myth is going to explain why there is only one sun in the sky. Tell the class the story and demonstrate how to complete a story plan. (You may wish to use RS2 as a prompt.)

Time out for thinking Ask the children to work with a partner and to think of a suitable sentence for the opening of the myth about the sun.

Teacher scribing Take in a few suggestions from the children and write the first part of the story for the class. Demonstrate how to take words and phrases from the planning notes and turn them into complete sentences. Read through the story so far together and talk about the language patterns of myths, eg. impersonal tone, people. (You may wish to use RS3 as a model for writing a myth.)

INDEPENDENT WRITING

Tell the children to refer to your completed plan and to write the rest of the story. Select some examples of the children's work for discussion in Session 5.

GUIDED WRITING — SUPPORT

Retell the story to the group and encourage them to talk through the ending. Look at the plan and support the group as they write the conclusion to the myth.

PLENARY

Look again at the class checklist of features of myths and see how well the story has met the criteria of myths. *Are there any other features to add here?* The class should assess how successful the 'explanations' are.

SESSION 5

FOCUS
- Does your ending have the features of a myth?

RESOURCES
- Children's work from Session 4
- Resource Sheet 2 'Why there is only one sun in the sky (plan for myth)', 3 'Why there is only one sun in the sky (story of myth)'

SENTENCE WORK

Talk to the children about adjectives and their function. *What do adjectives add to a sentence?* Look at RS3 and underline the key nouns.

Time out for thinking Ask the children to work in pairs and to think of suitable adjectives for each of the key nouns. Discuss the effect the adjectives have upon the writing.

SHARED WRITING

Show the class enlarged copies of the examples of the children's work from Session 4. Discuss how well the endings tie up the loose ends of the story. *Have the writers stuck to the original or have they made some changes?* Refer to the class checklist to see how many of the features of a myth are evident in the story.

Time out for thinking Tell the children to turn to a partner and to read their myth endings to one another. They should comment on the effectiveness of the endings and offer suggestions for improvement.

Draw attention to any particular spelling challenges posed by the task, e.g. quiver, eagle, arrow, earth.

INDEPENDENT WRITING

Ask the children to make a fair copy of their conclusions to the myth, incorporating any changes suggested by their partners. They should illustrate the final part of their story.

GUIDED WRITING — SUPPORT

Support the children to present their work using IT. They should use the spell check and discuss their choices for correct spellings. They could consider different fonts for effective presentation.

PLENARY

Stage-manage a re-enactment of the myth explaining why there is only one sun in the sky. Divide the children into groups (one group could be the suns, one group could be the people) and choose one child to be the boy and one child to be the eagle. Act as a narrator to prompt the dialogue for each group.

SESSION 6

FOCUS
- What happens to the verb in a sentence when the pronoun changes?

RESOURCES
- *Baíra and the Vultures Who Owned Fire* Essential Fiction pages 34–37

SENTENCE WORK

Invite three children (1 boy and 2 girls) to come to the front of the class. Point at yourself and say: *I am happy.* Point at the first child and say: *You are happy.* Point at one of the boys and say: *He is happy* and at one of the girls and say: *She is happy.* Point at all three children and yourself and say: *We are happy.* Point at the two girls and say: *You are happy.* Finally point at the whole class while talking to the three children and say: *They are happy.*

Ask the children what changes you had to make to the sentences.

Write the headings: *Pronoun (singular)* and *Pronoun (plural)* on the board. Ask the children to help you complete the chart using the initial sentence 'I am hungry.' Talk about the changes you have to make.

Write the sentence: *I am hungry.* and then change it to the past tense: *Yesterday, I was hungry.* Ask the children what has changed in the sentence. Go through the same pattern with the past tense: *You were, he was, you was/we was* errors.

Look again at the first paragraph of *Baíra and the Vultures Who Owned Fire* and ask the children to identify the pronouns and their linked verbs.

Explain that you are going to change the pronouns in the second paragraph from third to first person (i.e. from 'he' to 'I'). Model this for the first sentence (I was a young Indian and my name was Baíra.) Ask the children to do the same with the next sentence. *What effect does this have? What changes have to be made?* (Links to Unit 14 in Grammar for Writing.)

INDEPENDENT WRITING

Read *Baíra and the Vultures Who Owned Fire* from the first two paragraphs on page 36. Explain that a 'first person narrative' can sometimes seem more dramatic because we see things from the point of view of the main character. Tell the children that they are going to write the events from the point of view of Baíra.

GUIDED WRITING — SUPPORT

Tell the children to imagine they are Baíra. Ask them questions to help them see things from his point of view, e.g. *Where are you going to hide? What happens next?* Orally rehearse their sentences and scribe their suggestions.

PLENARY

Explain there is going to be a news conference in which Baíra is going to explain his dramatic escape from the vultures. Choose some children to be reporters and one child to be Baíra. Encourage him or her to give a lively account of their escape.

SESSION 7

FOCUS
- What is a parable?

RESOURCES
- *The Crowded House* Essential Fiction pages 26–27
- Resource Sheet 4 'Writing a parable'

SHARED READING

Explain that in this session you will be reading another type of traditional story – a parable.

Time out for thinking Tell the children to turn to a partner and to talk about what they know about parables. *What are they? Can you think of any parables you have heard?*

Collect in the children's suggestions. *Why might parables be told?* (a story with a moral)

Read *The Crowded House* and discuss the story based around the following questions:
- Why was Yitzak unhappy?
- What was the Rabbi's plan?
- In line 49, why was it called a 'huge little' house?
- How did the Rabbi's advice help Yitzak?

Explain that there is a lesson for life in this story and that is the purpose of a parable. The moral of this story could either be 'Be happy with what you have' or 'You don't know how lucky you are until things get worse'. Start a class checklist of features of parables.

SENTENCE WORK

Remind the children about how adjectives add detail to nouns. In this story the contrast between Yitzak's large family and his small house is an important part of the plot. Start a class list of adjectives of size.

INDEPENDENT WORK

Ask the children fill in the gaps on RS4 in the opening of the story, making the adjectives the opposite, e.g. not a 'poor' Jewish farmer but a 'wealthy' Jewish farmer. Explain that they will have to change some nouns too to keep the story consistent.

GUIDED WRITING — EXTENSION

Help the children to create a parallel parable in which a character is given so much of something they really like (e.g. sweets) that in the end they stop liking it.

PLENARY

Ask the guided writing group to share their parable and ask the rest of the class to suggest a moral for the story. Have they included some or all of the features of parables? Is there anything further to add to the checklist?

SESSION 8

FOCUS
- How do you know what the story characters are thinking?

RESOURCES
- *The Crowded House* Essential Fiction pages 26–27

DRAMA WORK

Reread the story of *The Crowded House*. Make a list of all the characters in the story (including the animals). Tell the children to choose to be one of the characters. They should take up a pose suitable for that character and then put it in a freeze frame. Move around among the children and select one child by tapping her/him on the shoulder. (The other children should relax their poses and listen.) Ask the child who he is and what he is thinking. (e.g. I am Yitzak and I am thinking that the Rabbi has gone mad.) Do the same with other children.

Remind the children that their 'think-alouds' are all first person narratives.

WORD WORK

Tell the children that compound words are words made up of two other words, e.g. sunlight, moonlight.

Ask the children to scan the lines of the story to find examples of compound words, e.g. line 11 inside; line 12 understand.

As you write each of these on the board, ask the children to generate other compound words based on the same words, e.g. understand: underground, underfoot, underarm, underclothes, underpass, undertake, underwater. What do they notice about the spelling when two words are put together? (neither word changes) (Links to *Spelling Bank*, page 12.)

INDEPENDENT WRITING

Ask the children to choose six characters from the story. They could sketch the characters and draw a thought bubble for each. They should write what each character is thinking at any point in the story. Remind them that they should write in the first person.

GUIDED WRITING — CORE

Discuss with the group the tale from the Rabbi's point of view. *How would the parable begin? How much of the Rabbi's plan would be revealed at the beginning?* Get the children to orally rehearse sentences before you write them. Discuss how the details of the story change when the focus is from a different point of view.

PLENARY

Share with the rest of the class the story generated in the guided writing work. Invite children to chip in with thought bubbles they created during independent work at the appropriate points in the narrative. Talk about the thought bubbles – explain to the children that they have been 'reading between the lines' to think about the story in more detail.

SESSION 9

FOCUS
- What are the features of a parable?

RESOURCES
- *The Sly Builder* Fiction Skills Big Book pages 28–29
- Resource Sheet 9 'Myths, legends, traditional tales, parables and fables'

SHARED READING AND WORD WORK

Limbering up Show the class the title of the next parable in the Big Book. Ask them to predict what sly thing the builder might do. Will he get away with it?

Read the story to the class and discuss the following questions:
- *How did the builder try to deceive the wealthy man?*
- *Why do you think he did this?*
- *Do you think the wealthy man realised the builder had tricked him?*
- *Has the builder been punished?*

Time out for thinking Tell the children to work with a partner and to decide on a moral for the parable. (Do as you would be done by; If a job's worth doing, it's worth doing well.)

Word work Tell the children that parables often deal with opposites of character and situation. Draw two columns on the board and ask the children to suggest opposites, e.g. generous man/mean man; rich/poor; beautiful house/shoddy house; honesty/dishonesty; best work/cutting corners; truth/lies.

Review and add to the class checklist of features of parables. (See RS9 for characteristics of myths, legends, traditional tales, parables and fables.)

INDEPENDENT WORK

Tell the children to look through the parable *The Crowded House* and to make a list of the opposites, e.g. large family/small house; wise/foolish; hut/mansion; huge/little; crowded/uncrowded; frustrated/content.

Extension Children can select some of the pairs of words and think about alternatives, e.g. further words meaning 'wise' and 'foolish'. Encourage them to make use of a thesaurus if possible.

GUIDED WRITING — CORE

Discuss with the group what the builder thought at the end of the story. *What do you think will happen next? Will the builder admit that he cut corners? Will he have to repair the house at his own expense?* Jot down some possible further endings to the story.

PLENARY

Share the opposites that the children have listed. Ask the core group to share their thoughts on how the story might develop.

SESSION 10

FOCUS
- What must you remember when writing a parable?

RESOURCES
The Sly Builder Fiction Skills Big Book pages 28–29
Resource Sheet 5 'Plan for a parable'

SHARED READING AND WRITING

Reread the parable of the sly builder and refer to the checklist of features of parables. Explain to the class that they are going to help you to complete a story ladder for a sequel to *The Sly Builder*. This time the builder behaves well and the moral of the parable will be: *If you give you will receive*. Explain that you are not going to write the whole story but you are going to sequence the incidents and jot down the main points. (Use RS5 as a prompt if you wish.)

INDEPENDENT WORK

Ask the children to work with a partner and to come up with a suitable resolution to the parable that links the complication with the moral. They should just write notes and complete RS5.

GUIDED WRITING — SUPPORT

Talk through with the group the various options for the builder after he has built the house for the old lady. *How can these link with the moral of the story?* Take in suggestions from the group and help children to structure their ideas and demonstrate how to write these as notes.

PLENARY

Share the suggestions from the children doing the independent work. Take a vote on the most suitable resolution which demonstrates the moral. Refer to the class checklist to see how many features of parables have been included.

115

SESSION 11

FOCUS
- What is a fable?

RESOURCES
- *The Dog and the Bone* Essential Fiction page 28
- Resource Sheet 9 'Myths, legends, traditional tales, parables and fables'

WORD WORK
Tell the children that some friends with a puppy visited you over the weekend and you had to keep giving instructions to the puppy, e.g. *Don't jump on that.* Write each contraction on the board as you say it. Ask the children what each word has in common (an apostrophe to show the letter 'o' is missing). Talk about why it is important to position the apostrophe in the correct place.

Write the full versions, e.g. *do not, can not, is not, does not.* Tell the children to write down the abbreviated words.

SHARED READING
Read the fable *The Dog and the Bone*. Discuss the fable through the following questions:
- *Why was he a silly dog?*
- *Was there really another dog with a bone?*
- *What is the moral of the story? Could it apply to people?*

Look at the class checklist created in Session 9. (You may use RS9 as a prompt, if you wish.) Ask the children how many of the characteristics are relevant to *The Dog and the Bone*. Ask the children if they know any other fables, e.g. *The Boy who cried Wolf*. What are the morals for these tales?

Time out for thinking Look again at the moral of the story. Ask the children to think of another way of expressing the same moral, e.g. *If you try to get too much you might lose everything.*

INDEPENDENT WORK
Ask the children to look through class fiction books and to make a list of 15 different contractions. Warn them to look carefully to ensure that the apostrophe is denoting a missing letter and not indicating possession, e.g. *the boy's cap*.

GUIDED WRITING — CORE
Ask the group to sort the contractions into categories, e.g. those which are negatives, such as *can't*; those which omit the letter 'i'; those which omit the letter 'o'.

PLENARY
Ask the group doing guided work to explain how they categorised the contractions. Invite the rest of the class to decide where their 15 words should be listed. *Are there any words that require a new category?*

Ask the children to bring in any versions of fables they have at home.

SESSION 12

FOCUS
- What do you know about fables?

RESOURCES
- *The Stag and His Spindly Legs* Essential Fiction page 29
- Resource Sheets 6 'Contractions' and 7 '*The Dog and the Bone* retold by Hiawyn Oram'

WORD WORK
Cut out the cards from RS6 and give one card to each child. Tell them to move around the classroom to find their 'partner' (i.e. the child with matching full or abbreviated form of the word). When they have found their partner they should sit down and write one sentence on a whiteboard using 'their' contraction.

Invite pairs to come to the front to show their sentence and to explain what letter is missing in their contraction.

SHARED READING
Read aloud to the class *The Stag and His Spindly Legs*.

Time out for thinking Tell the children to work with a partner and to choose one of the characteristics on the checklist about parables and fables and to find an example in this story.

Ask the children which fable they prefer. Which moral do they think best sums up its story?

From one of the books brought in by a child or from a school library book, choose a fable and read aloud the moral. Can the children speculate what events in a story would lead up to that moral? Read the fable aloud for children to judge how successful they were.

INDEPENDENT WORK
Give each child a copy of RS7. This is a summary of the story of *The Dog and the Bone* in note form. Ask the children to fill in the missing sections in note form and write the moral in their own words.

GUIDED WRITING — EXTENSION
Work with the group to divide the story of *The Stag and his Spindly Legs* into sequenced steps. Help them to write the events of the story in note form, e.g. 'A Stag was very proud of his magnificent antlers'.

PLENARY
Invite the children to share their notes for the missing sections of the action. If necessary help them to rephrase their words to be more note-like.

SESSION 13

FOCUS
- How can a plan help your writing?

RESOURCES
- *The Bear and the Travellers* Fiction Skills Big Book pages 30–31
- Resource Sheet 8 'The story of *The Bear and the Travellers*'

SHARED READING AND WRITING
Look at the pictures in the Big Book and use them to tell the fable of the *Bear and the Travellers*. (Use RS8 as a prompt if you wish.)

Talk about friendship and loyalty. *Was the first man a good friend? What would you have done in the same situation?* Ask the children to help you to write a moral for this fable. (You find your real friends when there's trouble about.)

Refer to the class checklist about fables and discuss where each feature appears.

Demonstration writing Explain to the children that you are going to write a plan for the story under the headings: Introduction, Problem, Complication, Resolution. Talk about how the plan needs only be in note form. (Use RS8 for reference.)

INDEPENDENT WORK
Tell the children to work in pairs and to work out the dialogue for each illustration in the Big Book. They should rehearse this and note some key sentences.

GUIDED WRITING — SUPPORT
Ask the children to retell the story and include some dialogue between the two characters. Scribe the story for them with the children supplying the dialogue.

PLENARY
Choose three children to take the roles of the bear and the two travellers. They should mime the actions. Act as narrator yourself to keep the drama on course. Talk about how the oral work they have done has helped them plan for their own writing in the next session.

SESSION 14

FOCUS
- What you must remember when writing a fable.

RESOURCES
- *The Bear and the Travellers* Fiction Skills Big Book pages 30–31
- Resource Sheet 8 'The story of *The Bear and the Travellers*'

SHARED WRITING
Plan for writing Explain to the children that they are going to write the first draft of the fable of the bear and the travellers. They are going to base it on the plan produced and the dialogue prepared in Session 13. Read through the plan together. (Use RS8 for reference.)

Time out for thinking Tell the children to turn to a partner and to orally rehearse the opening sentence for their fable.

Take in some suggestions and write some of the opening phrases on the board, e.g. *Once, long ago… There was once … Two travellers were once on a path through a forest …*

Look again at the plan and remind them about dividing their story into paragraphs based on the story divisions: Introduction, Problem, Complication and Resolution. Remind them to round off their fable with a moral.

EXTENDED WRITING
Ask the children to write their own version of the fable based on the shared story plan and incorporating features of fables.

After 35 minutes, ask the children to swap their fable with a partner and to read each other's stories. They should evaluate the work based on the following criteria: *Does the fable make sense? Is it divided into paragraphs? Are some good adjectives used?* Put a star next to the best sentence.

GUIDED WRITING — SUPPORT
Encourage them to rehearse sentences orally before writing and to keep checking that their story is following the plan.

PLENARY
Ask the class to identify any words they may not be sure how to spell. Talk through strategies for spelling the words, e.g. break into syllables, sound out the phonemes.

Discuss with the class how they would like to present the final copy of their story. Explain it will be on a page with some artwork on the border. Suggest they choose some small icons to go between the paragraphs, e.g. trees, bear's head.

Talk about different formats for the title and the moral of the fable.

SESSION 15

FOCUS
- How should you present your finished fable?
- What have you learned in this unit?

RESOURCES
- Resource Sheet 9 'Myths, legends, traditional tales, parables and fables'

REVIEW AND EVALUATION
Editing Talk to the class about some of the amendments/edits you have done to their work. Explain the reasoning for your suggestions. Draw attention to any particularly successful sections of children's work.

INDEPENDENT WRITING
Select some children to present their final copy on the computer using graphics and fonts as appropriate.

Ask the rest of the class to write out their fable in their best handwriting leaving space for illustrations between the paragraphs or for a decorative border.

GUIDED WRITING — SUPPORT
Help the children where necessary in making fair copies of their fable.

PLENARY
Revisit the targets discussed at the start of the unit. (Use RS9 as a prompt, if you wish.) Discuss how well these targets have been met. Discuss areas for improvement. *Do you prefer myths, parables or fables? Why? Which story did you enjoy most?*

On the Literacy World Interactive CD for Stage 1 Fiction, you will find the following resources for this unit:
- Copies of all the Fiction Skills Big Book pages for interactive work (*Why the Moon Shines at Night* pages 26–27, *The Sly Builder* pages 28–29 and *The Bear and the Travellers* pages 30–31)
- Copies of all the Essential Fiction pages for interactive work (*Birth of the Stars* pages 32–33)
- Interactive word and sentence work for Sessions 1, 2, 5, 6, 7, 8, 11 and 12
- Extra reading (*King Arthur*, *The Boy Who Cried Wolf*)
- An audio clip of *The Bear and the Travellers*
- All the Resource Sheets for independent work for you to customise
- Comprehensive Teaching and Planning Guides for the unit are also available on the CD.

PROMPT: **Guessing game**

Animal silhouettes

Cut around the outline of each creature and place each one on an overhead projector in turn and ask the children to guess what creature it is.

PROMPT: **Writing exemplar**

RESOURCE SHEET 2

Why there is only one sun in the sky
(story plan for myth)

Ideas

- there are seven suns in the sky
- each sun takes it in turn to warm the earth
- one day the suns shine at the same time
- the crops on earth die and rivers and ponds dry up
- the people on earth are starving
- a young boy climbs the highest mountain and shoots the nearest sun
- it falls to earth and becomes one of the great deserts on earth
- the people cheer but the earth is still too hot
- the boy shoots the suns, one by one
- the people tell the boy not to shoot the last sun
- the people send an eagle to snatch the last arrow from the quiver
- so the last sun is saved
- and that is why there is only one sun in the sky and six great deserts on earth

Structure

Character	Setting
boy	a kingdom long ago
Problems	**Solutions**
too many suns	shoots down each sun
boy will not stop	eagle snatches arrow
Explanation	
in the ending	

STAGE 1 | TERM 2 | For use with Unit 8 Session 4 as prompt for shared reading and writing.
© Harcourt Education Ltd. 2004. Copying permitted for purchasing school only. This material is not copyright free.

PROMPT: Writing exemplar

Why there is only one sun in the sky
(story for myth)

> In my first paragraph I will set the scene ... the opening needs to show the story is a myth ...

In the beginning when the world was young there were seven suns. Each day one of the suns would shine down onto the earth. The crops grew and the people were happy.

> then I'll look at the story plan for the first problem. I need to show the consequence/result of the first problem.

Then one day the seven suns decided they were tired of waiting their turn. They all wanted to shine at the same time and so they did. At once the crops shrivelled and died and the rivers and seas dried up. The people on earth were starving.

> ... then the solution to the problem ...

The people begged the suns to only shine one at a time but the suns refused. A young boy had an idea. Carrying his bow and seven arrows he climbed to the top of the tallest mountain. As the suns moved across the sky he took aim and shot the nearest sun. It fell to the earth and became the first great desert.

> ... this is a myth, so it must explain a natural phenomenon – I could use this to explain why there are six major deserts in the world.

The people cheered but the earth was still too hot. The boy was proud of his success and he drew another arrow from his quiver and shot down the next sun. Arrow after arrow he fired into the sky until there was just one arrow and one sun left. He drew out another arrow ...

> The story plan shows that this solution leads to a second problem, so that's what we will write next ...

STAGE 1 | TERM 2 | For use with Unit 8 Session 4 as prompt for shared reading and writing.
© Harcourt Education Ltd. 2004. Copying permitted for purchasing school only. The material is not copyright free.

Name _____ Date _____

Writing a parable

Complete the following sentences to make a different parable.

There once lived a _____ Jewish farmer

named Yitzak who had _____ and

lived in _____. Yitzak's house

was so _____ that his children

_____.

What will happen next in your new parable?
- _____
- _____
- _____

What will the moral of your parable be?

_____

_____

_____

_____

STAGE 1 | TERM 2 | For use with Unit 8 Session 7 as independent work.
© Harcourt Education Ltd. 2004. Copying permitted for purchasing school only. The material is not copyright free.

PROMPT: **Writing exemplar**

Plan for a parable

Story ladder

Resolution	Moral: If you give you will receive.
Complication	*(Explain that the children will be writing this section in independent work but that it must tie in with the moral.)*
Development	Builder decides to secretly build the old lady's house using good materials at his own expense.
Problem	Old lady approaches the builder and asks him to build her a new house. When the builder sees the materials the old lady intended him to use he realises the house will not be sturdy.
Introduction	There was once a builder who had cheated his master. Now he regretted his mean behaviour.

WORD WORK: **Cards**

Contractions

isn't	is not
there's	there is
I'd	I had
I've	I have
I'll	I will
he's	he is
she's	she is
hadn't	had not
haven't	have not
that's	that is
they've	they have
don't	do not
can't	cannot
doesn't	does not

Name _____ Date _____

The Dog and the Bone retold by Hiawyn Oram

Fill in the missing lines from this fable.

1 Once there was a greedy dog.

2 _____

3 He ran off over a bridge.

4 _____

5 He saw another dog with a big bone.

6 _____

7 He dropped his bone.

8 _____

The moral of this story is:

_____

_____

_____

_____

STAGE 1 | TERM 2 | For use with Unit 8 Session 12 as independent work.
© Harcourt Education Ltd. 2004. Copying permitted for purchasing school only. The material is not copyright free.

PROMPT: Writing exemplar

The story of *The Bear and the Travellers*

1 Once long ago two travellers were making their way through a forest. They heard the snap of twigs in the trees. They looked round and saw a huge brown bear. It stood up on its hind legs and chased them. The man and woman ran as fast as they could but the bear was gaining on them.	**2** The man decided that his only chance of escape was to climb a tree out of the reach of the bear. He chose the only tree with low branches and began to haul himself up. The woman traveller, realising her companion's plan, also ran towards the tree. But when she reached the tree the man roughly pushed her away.
3 Now the bear was getting very close. There was no time for the woman to look for another tree to climb so she curled up beside the path and pretended to be dead. The bear was curious at the sight of this figure on the ground. It approached the woman and sniffed at her. It put its huge nose right into the woman's face. The woman could feel its hot breath in her ear but she kept perfectly still. Eventually the bear decided that the woman was dead and it lumbered off into the forest.	**4** When the coast was clear, the man came down from the safety of his tree. He hurried over to his companion. "What was the bear saying to you?" he asked urgently. "I saw it whisper something in your ear." "It gave me some good advice," said the woman quietly, "It told me to choose my friends more carefully." And she walked off down the path on her own.

Plan

Introduction	Problem
Two travellers walking through forest see the bear.	Man climbs tree and pushes away woman.
Complication	**Resolution**
Woman pretends to be dead. Bear sniffs her and then goes off.	Woman realizes man is not a good friend.

PROMPT: **Checklist**

Myths, legends, traditional tales, parables and fables

Use these characteristics to establish class checklists for each category.

Myths
- Come from an oral tradition
- Ancient stories often told to explain natural phenomena
- Classic myths from Greece and Rome are about the gods and humans
- The setting is not specific, often moves between the earth and the heavens
- Characters not based on historical figures
- Myths from other cultures, e.g. Aboriginal, mainly about animals and gods
- Involve magical events
- Characters have super-human powers, e.g. Hercules, Odysseus
- In classical myths the gods are not always good. They may use humans as puppets for their own needs

Legends
- Ancient stories told about people, sometimes based on an historical figure, e.g. King Arthur
- Settings specified but take place on earth
- Characters often have super-human skills
- Characters often extremes, e.g. kings or poor boys

Traditional stories
- Old stories told to explain social behaviour, e.g. do not wander from the path
- Setting is specific to the origin of the story, e.g. miller/wood = Europe; spider/sandy beach = Caribbean
- Not based on historical figures
- Success often relies upon quick wit or trickery rather than super-human powers
- Based on magical events
- Story often involves good rewarded and evil punished
- Often involves the rule of three

Parables
- Not set in any specific time
- Deal with opposites
- Have a moral message
- Often very short stories
- Usually we do not know specific names of the characters

Fables
- Usually have animals for the main characters
- Usually very brief
- Always end with a moral

Name _____ Date _____

My evaluation sheet

The focus for this unit was _____
_____

My Reading target was _____
_____

My Writing target was _____
_____

The best piece of writing I did was _____
_____

The things I still need to work on are _____
_____

My Sentence level target was _____
_____

I have learned to _____
_____

My Word level target was _____
_____

I now know how to _____
_____

The part of the unit I enjoyed most was _____
_____

STAGE 1 | TERM 2 | For use with Units 6, 7 and 8 Session 10 as a plenary.
© Harcourt Education Ltd. 2004. Copying permitted for purchasing school only. The material is not copyright free.

1 3 9 Narrative: Plot

STAGE 1 • TERM 3 • UNIT 9

KEY INFORMATION

TEACHING OBJECTIVES

TEXT LEVEL

- **T3 T1** retell main points of story in sequence; to compare different stories
- **T3 T2** refer to significant aspects of the text e.g. opening, build-up atmosphere and to know how language is used to create these
- **T3 T10** plot a sequence of episodes modelled on a known story as a plan for writing
- **T3 T11** write openings for stories or chapters linked to or arising from reading; to focus on language to create effects e.g. building tension, suspense, creating moods, setting scenes

SENTENCE LEVEL

- **T3 S4** use speech marks and other dialogue punctuation appropriately in writing and to use the conventions which mark boundaries between spoken words and the rest of the sentence
- **T3 S6** investigate through reading and writing how words and phrases can signal time sequences

WORD LEVEL

- **T3 W1** the spelling of words containing each of the long vowel phonemes
- **T3 W5** identify misspelled words in own writing
- **T3 W9** recognise and spell the prefixes, mis, non, ex, co, anti
- **T3 W10** use their knowledge of these prefixes to generate new words from root words

UNIT SUMMARY

RESOURCES

- **Essential Fiction Anthology** *Stranded!* pages 58–61
- **Fiction Skills Big Book** *Quackers; Trapped!* pages 7, 32–35
- **Resource Sheets** 1–6
- **Literacy World Interactive** Unit 9 (optional)
- Screen version of *The Famous Five*

In this 2-week unit, the children learn about how authors develop a sequence of events into an exciting plot by reading different stories. They look at ways to create a tension in an adventure story. They move on to write an adventure story with a clear sequence of events and using language to create effects.

5-14 GUIDELINES

Reading level B/C
- Reflecting on writer's craft
- Reading for enjoyment
- Knowledge about language

CHILDREN'S TARGETS

READING
I can retell the main points of a story in sequence.

WRITING
I am learning to use language to create suspense in a story.

SENTENCE
I am learning to use speech marks.

WORD
I understand how a prefix changes the meaning of a word.

SPEAKING AND LISTENING
I can give reasons to explain my views.

DRAMA
I can use drama to explore stories.

GUIDED READING LINKS

- *Steggie's Way* (Core)
- *Emergency 999!* (Satellites)
- *Jane Blond Schoolgirl Superspy* (Comets)

OUTLINE PLAN

SESSION	WHOLE CLASS WORK		INDEPENDENT WORK	GUIDED GROUPS	WHOLE CLASS WORK plenary
1 Monday	**Oral language work** Introduce the unit – plot Retell story of *Jack and the Beanstalk*. Discuss sequence and look at problems and solutions Play sequence strips RS1 **T10**		**Independent reading** Add missing events in story on RS2	**Guided reading** support Sequence the events in the plot on RS1	Introduce targets, *What will we need to do in this unit?* Freeze frames action from *Jack and the Beanstalk*. Class to guess what is happening
2 Tuesday	**Word work** Recognise and spell prefixes: mis, non, ex, co anti **W9 W10**	**Shared writing** Add plot to simple story outline **T2**	**Independent writing** Add plot to the outline story on RS3	**Guided writing** support Add details to plot on RS3	Quiz: 'Guess my problems' Children give clues about problem and class guess the well known story
3 Wednesday	**Shared reading** Read *Stranded!* from EF. Map story onto story planner. Discuss the turning points in the plot		**Independent work** List the key turning points of *Stranded!* in sequence	**Guided reading** core Practise reading dialogue fluently	Discuss with the children times when they have been frightened. *What did you do? What did they say?*
4 Thursday	**Shared reading** Reread *Stranded!* How does the author create an atmosphere of fear? **T2**	**Word work** Write the linked phrases by letter patterns Words with similar spelling e.g. fear, near	**Independent writing** Write the speech dialogue of what Tim and his dad said to each other after the whale chased the shark away	**Guided writing** core Identify descriptive phrases and make into sentences	Share independent work. Present the dialogue as a radio play
5 Friday	**Sentence work** Demonstrate speech punctuation. Remind class about checklist of features (links to Unit 16 of GfW) **S4**		**Independent writing** Add reporting clauses to the speech on RS4	**Guided writing** extension Collect examples of reporting clauses	Play 'What if…' Children suggest changes to plot of *Stranded!*
6 Monday	**Oral language work** Look at picture for an adventure story *Trapped!* in BB Demonstrate story plan and emphasis tension/problem Look at the spelling of words the class might need	**Word work** Brainstorm words to use in adventure story	**Independent writing** Complete the story plan	**Guided writing** Support Complete story plans	Discuss features of adventure stories
7 Tuesday	**Shared writing** Look at opening of adventure story in BB Discuss how tension is created Demonstrate writing opening paragraph of own adventure story		**Independent writing** Write opening paragraph of own adventure story	**Guided writing** core Write dialogue which reveals personalities of characters	Share some opening paragraphs from the independent session
8 Wednesday	**Oral language work** Discuss ways children might continue adventure story Ask class to freeze-frame their action		**Independent writing** Class should write part of own story in which characters try and discuss various ways of escaping	**Guided writing** support Extend character descriptions	Look at solution to the problem *Has the writing followed the plan?*
9 Thursday	**Shared writing** Discuss possible endings. Demonstrate writing ending to own adventure story		**Extended writing** Write conclusion to own story	**Guided writing** extension make changes or additions to make plots more exciting	Look at checklist of items for editing their stories
10 Friday	**Shared writing** Discuss with the class ways of presenting their stories		**Independent work** Make fair copy of own work	**Guided writing** support Identify areas for improvement	*Have you reached your target?* Complete 'My evaluation' sheet' (Unit 12, RS6)

Abbreviation key
- **BB** Fiction Skills Big Book
- **EF** Essential Fiction Anthology
- **GfW** Grammar for Writing
- **SPB** Spelling Bank
- **RS** Resource Sheet

TEACHING NOTES

SESSION 1

FOCUS
- Why is sequence important in a story?

RESOURCES
- Resource Sheets 1 'Jack and the Beanstalk game' and 2 'The story of Jack and the Beanstalk'

ORAL LANGUAGE WORK

Introduce the unit and explain that the children are going to be looking at the key events in a story (plot). Then they will write their own adventure story for their peers.

Orally retell the story of Jack and the Beanstalk. (You may wish to use RS1 as a prompt.)

Remind the children of the key elements of stories: Characters, Setting, Problem and Solution.

Time out for thinking Tell the children to turn to a partner and to decide what should go into the 'Characters' and 'Setting' boxes for Jack and the Beanstalk.

Discuss the sequence of the problems facing Jack, e.g. Problem: poor; Solution: sells cow; Problem: mother's anger; Solution: beans are thrown away. Problem: giant comes home; Solution: Jack hides in oven and sees the giant's gold. Ask the children to help you to go through the story sorting out the sequence of problems. Talk about how one solution often creates another problem for the character.

Give out a story strip from RS1 to each group of three children. Help the children to sequence the story. *Who has the opening sentence of the story? How do you know?* Stick each strip on to the board.

From the sequenced sentence strips remove one strip without the class seeing which one. Read to the class the sentence before and the sentence after the gap. Tell them to write the missing sentence on their whiteboards.

EXTENDED INDEPENDENT WORK

Ask the children to look at RS2 which shows the story of Jack and the Beanstalk with key events missing. They can work out what is missing and write in the events.

GUIDED READING — SUPPORT

Using the sentence strips from RS1, challenge the group to read and sequence them into the correct order.

PLENARY

Introduce the targets for the unit. Tell the class that they are going to 'freeze-frame' the sequence of the story. Read each strip again and ask the children how many characters will be needed in that frame. Then invite the appropriate number of children to come out to be in the tableau.

SESSION 2

FOCUS
- What makes a good plot?

RESOURCES
- Resource Sheet 3 'Story skeleton'

WORD WORK

Remind the children about prefixes. Recall prefixes introduced in Term 1: *un*, *dis* and *re*.

Time out for thinking Give the children two minutes to think of words that start with any of those prefixes.

Write on the board the words: *understand* and *misunderstand*, *sense* and *nonsense*, *septic* and *antiseptic*, *port* and *export*. Ask the children to work out what each prefix might mean (mis = wrong, non = not, anti = against, ex = out).

Write the following base words on the board: *behave, fiction, trust, change, pel, fortune, stop, clockwise, print, smoking*, and ask the children to suggest a prefix for each base word.

SHARED WRITING

Demonstration writing Write on the board the following 'story': *A giant lived in a castle. He was hungry. He found some food. He went home.*

Explain that it is not a very successful story. It has no real tension because the problem (the giant was hungry) and the solution (he found some food) do not really link as we do not know what the giant found to eat.

Teacher scribing Ask the children to help you expand the problem and solution, e.g. *One day the giant was feeling very hungry. "I know what I fancy", said the giant in his thunderous voice, "three children on toast would be a tasty snack."*

INDEPENDENT WORK

Give each child a copy of RS3. Ask them to read it through, think about the plot and complete each part of the sheet.

GUIDED WRITING — SUPPORT

Look at RS3 and discuss how each section could be completed. Scribe their suggestions.

PLENARY

Play 'Guess my problem'. Give the class just the problem from a well-known story and ask them to identify the tale, e.g. My wicked step-mother tries to kill me. *(Sleeping Beauty)* Ask the children if they can select a problem from a well-known story and challenge the others to identify it.

SESSION 3

FOCUS
- What are the turning points of a plot?

RESOURCES
- *Stranded!* Essential Fiction pages 58–61

SHARED READING

Read the story *Stranded!* to the class.

🔊 **Listening focus** Identify the problem for the characters and the solution.

Ask the following questions:
- Was Tim frightened at the beginning of the story?
- How does the author let you know when Tim is really frightened?
- Did the author make you think Dad had been killed? How?
- What was the first problem for Tim and his Dad? (stranded) What was the next problem? (whale) Are there any other problems? (shark attacks boat, Dad overboard, Tim can't rescue Dad) What was the worst problem?
- Why does the author have so many linked problems? build up of tension, things seem bad but then they get worse. These problems are the turning points of the plot when characters have to react to events.
- What was the solution in the story? Do you believe the solution could happen?

INDEPENDENT WORK

Ask the children to list, in brief notes, the five problems in the story. They should write the solution next to each problem, e.g. Problem 1: Tim and his Dad are stranded. Solution 1: At the end of the story the wind picks up.

GUIDED READING — CORE

Tell the children to work in pairs and to read just the dialogue of the story. Give them a few moments to identify the spoken words and discuss how to say the words dramatically. They should practise their dialogue reading in their pairs and then ask different pairs to read different sections. Discuss how easy it was to create an atmosphere of fear with just the dialogue. *What else has the author done, apart from the dialogue, to build up dramatic tension?*

PLENARY

Ask the guided reading group to present their dramatisation of the story using just the dialogue. Discuss with the class how dialogue alone is not enough to create tension in the story.

Discuss with the class times when they have been frightened. Invite children to share things they said in their frightening episode. Add to this spoken language the description an author might include, e.g. Child: "I was dead frightened when I heard the noise downstairs." Teacher: Jo's heart thumped when he heard the noise downstairs.

SESSION 4

FOCUS
- How does an author create an atmosphere of fear?

RESOURCES
- *Stranded!* Essential Fiction pages 58–61

SHARED READING

Reread the story *Stranded!*

🔊 **Listening focus** Note how the author describes Tim and Dad's fear.

Collect in and write on the board the words and phrases that describe the characters' fear: 'trembling with fear', 'heart start to race', 'heart beat faster', 'stomach churning so much', 'heart beating fast enough for it to burst right out of his chest' etc. Discuss how authors often describe fear through the physical reactions of characters.

Draw a stick figure of Tim on the board. Draw arrows to various parts of the body and discuss how a physical reaction could convey a sense of fear, e.g. eyes darting wildly around, hands trembling, knees shaking, heart thumping.

Time out Ask the children to choose some other physical reaction to show fear.

WORD WORK

Select some words from the text ('fear', 'race', 'fright', 'beat', 'yell', 'scream') and write these across the board. Ask the class to suggest other words that have a similar letter pattern. Add these in columns. If the word suggested sounds the same but has a different letter pattern write these as a new column, e.g. 'fear', 'near', 'dear' in one column but 'here' and 'steer' in different columns. Talk about how letter patterns produce different long vowel phonemes.

INDEPENDENT WRITING

Ask the children to work in pairs and to imagine the conversation between Tim and his Dad after the whale has chased the shark away. They should write this as dialogue. They should include some reference to the fear they felt and their relief after the shark and whale disappear.

GUIDED WRITING — CORE

Find the following words or phrases in the story: 'trembling with fear' (L4); 'crouching down' (L13); 'without warning' (L19); 'frantically' (L59) 'helplessly' (L62). Talk about their meaning in the context of the story. Ask the children to use the words and phrases to write their own sentences about a fearful situation.

PLENARY

Ask pairs of children to come out and present as a radio play the dialogue they created in the independent work. Ask the other children to comment on the choice of vocabulary. *Have they described the characters' feelings and responses accurately?*

SESSION 5

FOCUS
- How do you write speech accurately?

RESOURCES
- *Quackers* Fiction Skills Big Book page 7
- Resource Sheet 4 'Reporting clauses'

SENTENCE WORK

Select examples of the dialogue the children created during the independent work in Session 4. Demonstrate how to accurately punctuate the dialogue. Draw attention to the importance of setting out the dialogue with each new speaker having a new line.

Time out for thinking Dictate the following sentence to the class and ask them to punctuate it correctly: 'I can see a shark,' said Tim.

Write the sentence correctly on the board. Remind the children about the checklist of features of speech punctuation created in Term 1. Ask them to recall key features, e.g. end of sentence punctuation – comma, exclamation mark and question mark are placed before the closing speech marks. Look again at the Big Book (*Quackers*) and ask the children to identify the features on their checklist in the text itself.

Teacher scribing Write the following sentences on the board and ask the children to suggest examples of reporting clauses:

"The shark is under the boat," (*Tim whispered anxiously or said Dad nervously*)

"What is the whale doing?" (*asked Tim desperately or wondered Tim*)

Talk about how the reporting clause gives the reader an insight into the characters' feelings.

INDEPENDENT WORK

Give each child a copy of RS4. Tell them to add reporting clauses to the speech.

GUIDED WRITING — EXTENSION

Look through a selection of fiction books and collect examples of a range of reporting clauses. The children should write them on the whiteboard for the rest of the class to refer to.

PLENARY

Tell the children to suggest changes to the plot of *Stranded!* by playing 'What if?'. Ask the children to consider how the story would be different ... *if the whale did not rescue Dad; ....if Tim fell in the water; ....if the shark attacked the whale.* Share the reporting clauses collected in the guided writing work.

SESSION 6

FOCUS
- How do paragraphs help when planning a sequence of episodes?

RESOURCES
- *Trapped!* Fiction Skills Big Book pages 32–33
- Screen version of an adventure story (*The Famous Five*)

ORAL LANGUAGE WORK

Look at the picture in the Big Book. Tell the children this is a prompt for them to write an adventure story. Explain that they will need a story plan, to ensure they have a clear sequence of events and a gripping plot. Write the story plan on the board: 'Characters Setting Problem Solution'. Talk about the picture under the headings. Ask questions, e.g. *Who are these children? Where are they? What has happened to them?*

Return to each heading and talk about how to expand each category, e.g. children's names, ages, personalities. Remind the children that it is best to have some tension between characters rather than just making them very similar. So the boy could be cautious and the girl reckless. Brainstorm descriptions for the setting, e.g. an isolated cove, dark clouds building, tide coming in fast, sea rough and dangerous.

Time out for thinking Tell the children to work with a partner and to come up with a means of escaping from the cove before the tide comes in.

Share some of the solutions the children come up with. As they detail the plot ask other children to be thinking: '*How did they feel? What did they say?*' Take suggestions from the class.

WORD WORK

Brainstorm suitable words that children might need when writing their adventure story, e.g. dangerous, frantically, scramble, pounding waves. Talk about spelling patterns for each of these words and remind them of different spelling strategies they can use to help them to remember the spellings.

INDEPENDENT WRITING

Tell the children to complete a story plan for their own story of escaping from the incoming tide. Remind them that the plan should be in note form.

GUIDED WRITING — SUPPORT

Help the children to complete their story plans. Particularly support with spellings that will be useful when the children come to write their story.

PLENARY

Discuss typical features of adventure stories and write these as a checklist for children to refer to.

(Alternatively show a screen extract from an adventure story such as *The Famous Five*.)

SESSION 7

FOCUS
- How does an author build up tension in an adventure story?

RESOURCES
- *Trapped!*; *Caught in the Storm* Fiction Skills Big Book pages 32–33 and 34–35
- Resource Sheet 5 'Adventure story (opening)'

SHARED WRITING

Read the extract from the adventure story *Caught in the Storm*. Ask the children what they think will happen next in the story. Talk about it in terms of the features discussed in the plenary in Session 6. *How successful is it as an opening to an adventure story? How does the author use the setting to create fear and tension?* Underline the words and phrases that contribute to the sense of danger e.g. 'They had been walking for ages.'

Demonstration writing Demonstrate writing the opening paragraph of the story prompted by *Trapped!* in the Big Book. Talk about word choices, punctuation for speech and descriptions to build up fear and tension. (You may wish to use RS5 as a prompt.)

INDEPENDENT WORK

Tell the children to write the opening paragraph for their own adventure story based on the plan they made in Session 6.

GUIDED WRITING — CORE

Challenge the children to use both dialogue and description as they introduce the setting and characters in their opening paragraphs. Ask them to think about how the main characters will behave and how they can use dialogue to show their personalities.

PLENARY

Ask some children to read their opening paragraphs to the class. Ask the rest of the class to look at the class checklist and to note where particular features have been used successfully.

SESSION 8

FOCUS
- What must I remember when writing an adventure story?

RESOURCES
- *Trapped!* Fiction Skills Big Book pages 32–33
- Resource Sheet 5 'Adventure story (opening)'

ORAL LANGUAGE WORK

Revisit the scenario of the picture in the Big Book. Tell the children that the next part of their story needs to describe how they attempt to escape from the tide. Remind them that to hold the reader's attention they must include descriptions not just of what the children did, but of how they felt. Remind them of how the author did this in *Caught in the Storm* and refer to the collection of phrases about the build up of fear collected in Session 4.

Time out for thinking Tell the children to work with a partner and to freeze frame one action as the children realise how hopeless their situation is. You are going to move between the tableaux and touch children on the shoulder. You will ask them to say how they are reacting physically to the fear they are experiencing e.g. *How are you are breathing?* (deeply) *What is your heart doing?* (thumping) *What are your eyes doing?* (darting nervously about) *How do your legs and hands feel?* (trembling, shaking).

EXTENDED WRITING

Tell the children to refer to their story plan, completed in Session 6, their opening paragraph completed in Session 7 and to keep in mind the freeze-frames they have done, and to write the part of the story where the characters try and discuss various ways to escape. They should not, at this stage, write the final solution to their story.

GUIDED WRITING — SUPPORT

Help the group to identify where they have got to in their opening paragraph in the sequence of their plot. Get them to list in sequence two more things the children could do, or consider to do, to escape from the cove. When they write, support their spelling and punctuation.

PLENARY

Choose a child's story so far and relate it to the plan the child completed in Session 6. Will the solution in the plan now fit the story as it has unfolded? Talk to the children about the importance of not sticking to a plan if the story has moved on differently. Tell the children to work with a partner and to check that the stories written so far will still tie in with the original plans. If they do not, they should work together to suggest alternative solutions.

SESSION 9

FOCUS

- What makes a successful solution to a story?

RESOURCES

- *Trapped!* Fiction Skills Big book pages 32–33
- Resource Sheet 6 'Adventure story (ending)'

SHARED WRITING

Demonstration writing Talk to the children about the importance of rounding off an adventure story. *What sort of ending do you like when you get to the end of this type of story?* Remind them that they should all have their own planned solutions to their stories and that you will help them to decide how to finish their stories effectively. Present different options (you may wish to use RS6 as a prompt), e.g. ending based on the characters' personalities; a jokey ending; a repentant ending; a circular ending. Demonstrate how to write the final sentence in each case. Draw attention to the way that you are making links with what we know about the characters and building on elements of the plot.

EXTENDED WRITING

Ask the children to write the solutions for their stories, taking account of the discussion they had with their partners in the plenary of Session 8 and the suggestions for rounding off their stories that you demonstrated earlier. Tell them to think of a good title for their story.

GUIDED WRITING — EXTENSION

Ask the children to read through their stories so far. Are they happy that they have created a sense of tension? Have they described the characters' fear? Support the children in thinking of changes or additions to the plots to make them more exciting.

PLENARY

Share with the class a checklist of items for editing their stories. Ask them to mark in the margin a tick or cross if the following features are included:

Have you written a title that fits your story and which entices the reader?

Have you written an opening which introduces the characters and the setting?

Does the solution link to the problem?

Have you created a sense of fear?

Have you rounded off your story satisfactorily?

Have you used speech marks accurately?

Is the story divided into paragraphs?

Are there any spellings that need attention?

SESSION 10

FOCUS

- How should you present your story?
- What have you learnt from this unit?

RESOURCES

Resource Sheet 6 from Unit 12 'My evaluation sheet'

SHARED WRITING

Give children time to look at their completed, marked, story drafts and to think about anything they will need to change in a final copy. Draw attention to common spelling errors identified through marking and ask the children to think of ways to help them remember the correct spellings.

Discuss with the children different ways to present their stories.

INDEPENDENT WORK

Ask the children to make a final copy of their stories. They should create a fair copy either by rewriting the story or by using the word processor. They should consider how to illustrate their story and discuss how the stories should be displayed.

GUIDED WRITING — SUPPORT

Support the children in identifying areas for changes or improvements in their final story drafts. Advise them on ways to present work effectively.

EXTENDED PLENARY

Give each child a copy of RS6 from Unit 12. Ask them to complete it and to reflect upon what they have learned in this unit.

Bring the class together to discuss the completed review and evaluation forms. Ask the children what they now know about writing stories that they did not know before. Invite some children to share their finished stories.

On the Literacy World Interactive CD for Stage 1 Fiction, you will find the following resources for this unit:

- Copies of all the Fiction Skills Big Book pages for interactive work (*Quackers* page 7 and *Caught in the Storm* pages 34–35)
- Interactive word and sentence work for Sessions 2, 4, 5 and 6
- Extra reading (*The Coral Island*)
- All the Resource Sheets for independent work for you to customise
- Comprehensive Teaching and Planning Guide for the unit are also available on the CD.

SENTENCE WORK: **Cards**

Jack and the Beanstalk game

Jack and his mother were very poor. One day Jack took the cow to market to sell her.

On his way to market Jack met a strange little man who gave him five beans in exchange for the cow.

Jack's mother was furious when she saw the beans and she threw them out of the window. That night a huge beanstalk grew in the garden.

The next morning Jack climbed up the beanstalk. He saw a giant's castle. He heard the giant coming home so he hid in the oven.

The giant counted his pile of gold. Then he fell asleep and Jack stole the gold and hurried back down the beanstalk.

Time went by and Jack decided to climb the beanstalk again.

Once in the castle Jack saw the giant had a hen which laid golden eggs. Jack stole the hen and hurried back down the beanstalk.

But Jack was eager to climb the beanstalk for a third time.

On his third visit Jack stole the giant's magic harp but the harp sang out "Master, Master." The giant chased Jack but Jack grabbed an axe and chopped down the beanstalk.

And that was the end of the giant. Jack and his mother lived happily ever after.

STAGE 1 | TERM 3 | For use with Unit 9 Session 1 as oral language work.
© Harcourt Education Ltd. 2004. Copying permitted for purchasing school only. The material is not copyright free.

Name _____ Date _____

The story of *Jack and the Beanstalk*

Fill in the gaps in the story.

1. Jack and his mother were very poor. One day Jack took the cow to market to sell her.

2. _____

3. Jack's mother was furious when she saw the beans and she threw them out of the window. That night a huge beanstalk grew in the garden.

4. _____

5. The giant counted his pile of gold. Then he fell asleep and Jack stole the gold and hurried back down the beanstalk.

6. _____

7. Once in the castle Jack saw the giant had a hen which laid golden eggs. Jack stole the hen and hurried back down the beanstalk.

8. _____

9. On his third visit Jack stole the giant's magic harp but the harp sang out "Master, Master." The giant chased Jack but Jack grabbed an axe and chopped down the beanstalk.

10. _____

Name Date

Story skeleton

Here is a basic story skeleton. Expand the 'problem' of the story to make it exciting and dramatic.

| Characters
Tom and Ella. | Setting
In the wood. |
|---|---|
| Problem
They go for a walk.
They get lost. | Solution
They find the path and come home. |

Expanded problem

1 They talk about the fact that they are lost.

"Are you sure this is the right way to go?" asked Ella, "I'm sure we passed this tree ages ago."

Tom wasn't sure at all but he didn't want to admit it to Ella.

2 They decide to do something. (*Write what they decide to do.*)

_____

_____

3 That goes wrong. (*Explain what goes wrong.*)

_____

_____

4 They blame each other. (*Write what they say.*)

_____

_____

5 They find the path by accident. (*Write how they find the path.*)

_____

_____

Name Date

Reporting clauses

Add reporting clauses to each of the following sentences. The first one has been done for you.

"Give it to me," demanded the man roughly.
(to show anger)

"I've lost it," _____
(to show misery)

"I've won!" _____
(to show excitement)

"Where is it?" _____
(to show worry)

"I can help you," _____
(to show kindness)

"It's getting closer," _____
(to show fear)

PROMPT: Writing exemplar

Adventure story (opening)

> I know some details about my characters, their names and personalities from the plan I completed earlier … they are brother and sister and they are always quarrelling … I'll start like the author did and go straight into the action with dialogue.

"Tom! Look!" said Amy in alarm. "The tide. It's come right into the cove. How are we going to get back to the bay?"

> I'll introduce the characters, the setting and the problem.

Tom looked up from the rockpool where he was fishing for shrimps.

> Then I'll give a description of the cove and explain what the children have been doing.

His sister was right. The waves, which had been glinting in the distance when they had walked round into the cove, were now rushing up the beach and the sandy path back to the bay had disappeared completely.

> I'll create some drama about the incoming tide …

> … the waves have cut them off from the bay where their parents are.

"Don't worry," he said. He tried to sound confident. "We'll paddle through the water and get back to Mum and Dad." But even as he spoke he knew that the water was too deep and the current too strong. They would have to find another way out.

> Tom is older than his sister and he doesn't want to look as if he doesn't know what to do.

> This is a good dramatic place to end this paragraph. Hopefully I've made the reader curious to know more.

PROMPT: Writing exemplar

Adventure story (ending)

I can choose any number of endings for my story but I must make sure I make links with the rest of my plot and the characters in it:

an ending related to the characters' personalities	"I knew we'd be OK in the end," said Tom cockily. "Oh yeah?" said Amy.
a jokey ending	"Do you know the worst bit of all that?" asked Tom. "Scrambling up the cliff face? Nearly drowning?" asked Amy. "No," said Tom coolly, "losing my shrimping net."
a repentant ending	"Do you think you've learned your lesson?" asked the helicopter rescue man. Tom and Amy nodded.
a circular ending	"It was a bit scary," admitted Tom, "but it won't stop me going back to the cove tomorrow."

STAGE 1 | TERM 3 | For use with Unit 9 Session 9 as a prompt for shared writing.
© Harcourt Education Ltd. 2004. Copying permitted for purchasing school only. The material is not copyright free.

1 3 10 Point of view

KEY INFORMATION

TEACHING OBJECTIVES

TEXT LEVEL

T3 T1	retell main points of story in sequence
T3 T3	distinguish between 1st and 3rd person accounts
T3 T4	consider credibility of events
T3 T5	discuss characters' feelings, behaviour and relationships
T3 T12	write a 1st person account
T3 T13	write more extended stories based on a plan of incidents

SENTENCE LEVEL

T3 S1	use awareness of grammar to decipher new or unfamiliar words
T3 S4	use speech marks and other dialogue punctuation
T3 S5	how sentences can be joined in more complex ways using a widening range of conjunctions

WORD LEVEL

T3 W2	identify phonemes in speech and writing, blend phonemes for reading, segment words into phonemes for spelling
T3 W5	identify misspelled words in own writing
T3 W6	use independent spelling strategies
T3 W12	the collection of new words from reading ... and make use of them in reading and writing

UNIT SUMMARY

RESOURCES

- **Essential Fiction Anthology** *The Toad Tunnel* pages 42–45
- **Fiction Skills Big Book** *The Pied Piper* pages 36–41
- **Resource Sheets** 1–8
- **Literacy World Interactive** Unit 10 (optional)

In this unit children write a first person account from the point of either the Pied Piper or the Mayor of Hamelin.

5–14 GUIDELINES

Reading level B/C
- Reading for enjoyment
- Reflecting on writer's craft
- Knowledge about language

CHILDREN'S TARGETS

READING
I can distinguish between first and third person accounts.

WRITING
I can write a first person account.

SENTENCE
I know how to use speech marks.

WORD
I can collect words I have read and use them in my writing.

GROUP DISCUSSION
I can investigate characters' feelings and behaviour.

GUIDED READING LINKS

Twelfth Floor Kids (Core)
Dinosaur Whodunnit? (Satellites)
Quackers (Comets)

OUTLINE PLAN

STAGE 1 · TERM 3 · UNIT 10

SESSION	WHOLE CLASS WORK		INDEPENDENT WORK	GUIDED GROUPS	WHOLE CLASS WORK plenary
1 Monday	**Shared reading** Read *The Toad Tunnel* in EF and discuss the story. Draw attention to the use of the third person. Introduce first person. Map story onto story planner		**Independent reading** Find words and phrases the author uses to create a sense of fear from a passage in EF	**Guided reading** core Explore the sequence of the story	What will you need to do in this unit? Start class collection of words and phrases describing fear
2 Tuesday	**Word work** Look at words to describe fear. Explore ways to remember how to spell them **W6**	**Oral language work** Explore ways of describing fear. Hot seat child as Tom and prompt questions	**Independent writing** Write a paragraph as first person account of a frightening situation	**Guided writing** core Create new expressions for 'fear'	Create a class poem entitled 'My Worst Fear' using phrases from children's paragraphs
3 Wednesday	**Oral language work** Demonstrate writing from different point of view. Look at *The Toad Tunnel* and scribe the story from Alan's point of view **T4**		**Independent work** Change third person into first person using RS1	**Guided reading** support Adjust from third to first person account	Create first person sentences. Sit in circle and child says next word in sentence
4 Thursday	**Sentence work** How sentences can be joined in more complex ways. Look at conjunctions in *The Toad Tunnel*. Start a class collection of conjunctions **S5**		**Independent work** Use RS2 to add conjunctions to sentences	**Guided writing** extension Extend sentences using conjunctions	Play 'circle sentences' using conjunctions. Aim not to complete the sentence
5 Friday	**Shared writing** Demonstrate how to write an incident from *Jack and the Bean Stalk* as a first person account **S4**		**Independent writing** Write second incident in the first person	**Guided writing** support Orally expand story plan	Say sentences from teacher's point of view. Class to suggest child's point of view
6 Monday	**Shared reading** Show and read retelling of *The Pied Piper* in third person from BB. Discuss story with class. Ask them to identify characteristics of third person narrative **S1 W12**	**Oral language work** Dramatise the story	**Independent writing** Expand the labels with descriptions	**Guided reading** core Perform reading of *The Pied Piper*	Invite guided group to perform their prepared verse
7 Tuesday	**Shared reading** Reread *The Pied Piper* from BB and discuss why the children followed the Pied Piper	**Sentence work** Identify sentences with conjunctions from *The Pied Piper* (links to Unit 17 of GfW) **S5**	**Independent work** In pairs write five sentences from different points of view	**Guided writing** extension Write modern day prose in third person	Teacher hot seats the part of the Pied Piper
8 Wednesday	**Shared writing** Demonstrate retelling the story from the Mayor's point of view		**Independent work** Devise questions they would like the Mayor to answer	**Guided writing** support Consider how to write in first person	Hot seat the character of Mayor and answer questions from independent work
9 Thursday	**Plan for writing** Discuss the character of the Piper. What is his point of view?		**Extended writing** Write the events from where the Piper sees the problem with the rats to where the children leave the town. Writing from Piper's point of view	**Guided writing** support Write first person narrative	Listen to songs from musical *Rats* or ask groups to present tableaux to class
10 Friday	**Shared writing** Use best examples of writing from class. Discuss how well the writer has written from the point of view of the Mayor	**Independent writing** Make fair copies of writing. Discuss ways of presenting work. Use IT if possible		**Guided writing** support Use neat handwriting to present work	*Have you reached your target?* Put the Piper in the dock and ask children to take it in turns to be prosecutor and defence council

Abbreviation key
- **BB** Fiction Skills Big Book
- **EF** Essential Fiction Anthology
- **GfW** Grammar for Writing
- **SPB** Spelling Bank
- **RS** Resource Sheet

143

TEACHING NOTES

SESSION 1

FOCUS
- What is a third person account?

RESOURCES
- *The Toad Tunnel* Essential Fiction pages 42–45

SHARED READING
Read the story *The Toad Tunnel* to the class.
Ask the children the following questions:
- Why is Tom afraid of going down the tunnel?
- Why does Tom change his mind?
- What did the Giant Slime Slug turn out to be?
- How do you think Tom felt when he had cleared the tunnel?

Ask the children: *Who is telling the story? How do you know?* Explain that this is a third person account told by an author. It is as though the author is a cameraman filming all the action. The camera shows what each person does and we know how they feel if they tell us. If it was a first person account then the action is told from the point of view of one of the characters, e.g. Tom. In a first person account we are told how one person feels but we are only told how others feel if the narrator of the story tells us.

Write the sentence on the board: *Alan, Jenny and Tom Sparks lived in London and were spending a weekend with their grandmother in Sussex.* Demonstrate how to change this to a first person account (*Alan, Jenny and I …*). Underline the pronoun changes.

> **Time out for thinking** Read from the top of page 45. Tell the children to work with a partner and to change the first sentence to a first person account.

What difference would it make to the story if it was told in the first person?

EXTENDED INDEPENDENT READING
Tell the children to find words and phrases the author uses to create a sense of fear when Tom goes through the toad tunnel (pages 44–45, lines 80–100).

GUIDED READING — CORE
Tell the children you are going to look at the sequence of events in the story. *Are the events told in chronological order?* Make notes together about the real sequence of events. They should find evidence from the text to support their reasons for the time sequence.

PLENARY
Introduce the targets for the unit and start a class collection of words and phrases about fear from the independent work.

SESSION 2

FOCUS
- How can you describe fear?

RESOURCES
- *The Toad Tunnel* Essential Fiction pages 42–45

WORD WORK
Select some of the words associated with fear from the independent work, e.g. froze, staring, horror, pounding, terror. Ask the children for suggestions of ways to remember how to spell new words, e.g. 'staring'. Ask the children how to spell 'stare' and ask them what has changed. Can they think of a generalisation to cover this spelling feature? (drop the 'e' before adding a suffix which starts with a vowel)

ORAL LANGUAGE WORK
Tell the class about an incident (real or imagined) in which you felt afraid. Describe how you felt. (mouth dry, heart thumping etc)

> **Time out for thinking** Tell the children to turn to a partner and to describe an occasion when they felt afraid.

Allow some children to share their experiences. As they retell the events prompt them to consider how they felt: e.g. *What did your legs feel like? What was your heart doing?*

Hot seating 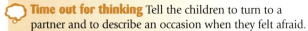 Invite one child to be Tom and to describe his fear. Use questions to prompt the responses: *How did you feel when Jenny and Allan first suggested that you went in the tunnel?*

Remind the children that, in the hot seat, Tom is giving a first person account of events and this can be very dramatic.

INDEPENDENT WRITING
Ask the children to write a paragraph as a first person account about a time when they were afraid. Remind them to describe how they felt.

GUIDED WRITING — CORE
Using some of the expressions from Session 1, and creating new expressions of their own, help the group to write a paragraph including descriptions of how fear is felt in different parts of the body.

PLENARY
Scribe for the children a poem entitled *My Worst Fear* using the phrases generated in the session, e.g. *Knees knocking, heart thumping, I strained to hear, Limbs shaking, hands sweating, I faced my fear.*

SESSION 3

FOCUS
- What must I remember when writing from the point of view of a character?

RESOURCES
The Toad Tunnel Essential Fiction pages 42–45
Resource Sheet 1 'Third to first'

ORAL LANGUAGE WORK

Limbering up Write the following sentences on the board and ask the children to decide from whose point of view they are written.

The toad tunnel will fall on me and I will be trapped. (Tom)

It's lovely to have my grandchildren to stay. (Grandmother)

If I wasn't in this wheelchair I would clear the tunnel. (Mr Burton)

I knew the sign wouldn't stop the cars. (Jenny)

Ask the children if the sentences are in third or first person.

Time out for thinking Ask the children to turn to a partner and to discuss what each character is feeling as they say those words, e.g. Tom is feeling afraid, Grandmother is feeling happy, Mr Burton is feeling frustrated, Jenny is feeling fed up. Talk about how a first person account often allows for the character's feelings to be very obvious.

Demonstration writing Tell the class that you are going to write some of the action of the story from Alan's point of view. Start on the last line (line 26) on page 42 and write *I was furious with Tom. "You've got to go in the tunnel," I shouted.* Do the same with line 62 and line 69. Finally show Alan's change from anger to concern in line 83 when he asks, *"You OK?"*

Discuss how the story is different if we see it through Alan's eyes.

INDEPENDENT WORK

Ask children to complete RS1 and change third person narrative to first person

GUIDED READING — SUPPORT

Work with the children to alter lines 76–82 from a third person account to a first person account. Orally rehearse the changes line by line asking different children to read different lines as Tom.

PLENARY

Arrange the class in a circle. Explain that they are going to create some first person sentences. Start the sentence with 'I'. The next child to the left has to say a word that could follow in a sentence, e.g. 'was'. The next child should say the third word, e.g. 'eating'. Continue in this way. If a child thinks they have come to the end of a sentence they should say 'full stop'.

SESSION 4

FOCUS
- How can sentences be joined in more complex ways?

RESOURCES
- Resource Sheet 2 'Conjunctions'

SENTENCE WORK

Limbering up *What is a sentence?* (a group of words that express a complete thought and make sense; sentences start with a capital letter and end with a full stop or a question mark or an exclamation mark)

Write on the board the following two sentences: *I went to the shop. I bought a cake.* Ask the children how you could join the two sentences.

Explain that these conjunctions (joining words) are very useful but sentences can be joined with a great variety of words, e.g. 'if', 'so', 'that', 'while', 'since', 'although', 'when'. These conjunctions make the links between sentences more precise. Write these conjunctions on the board.

Tell the children to look at the second sentence of *The Toad Tunnel* on page 42. *What conjunction joins the two sentences?* (but) *Look at sentence 3. What conjunction joins the two sentences?* (and) *Look at the conjunctions on the board. Do any of those conjunctions fit in the sentences?*

Start a class list of conjunctions. Display them according to their function, e.g. conjunctions which add two things (and, and then); conjunctions which contrast two things (but, or); conjunctions which explain a reason (because, so, so that, if, since, although); conjunctions which indicate time (when, while).

Time out for thinking Write the following sentence starter on the board: *She smiled …* Tell the children to work with a partner and to think of as many ways as they can to complete the sentence using different conjunctions.

INDEPENDENT WORK

Give each child a copy of RS2. Tell them to add the most suitable conjunction for each sentence.

GUIDED WRITING — EXTENSION

Write the beginning of the story of *Rumpelstiltskin* in short sentences. Write each sentence on a line:

There was once a boastful miller.

He had a beautiful daughter.

Work with the children to extend the sentences using a range of conjunctions.

PLENARY

Arrange the children in a circle. Tell them they are going to play the sentence game again but this time the challenge is to keep the sentence going for as long as possible by using different conjunctions: so, however, but. Can they make one sentence last the whole way round the circle?

145

SESSION 5

FOCUS
- How important is point of view?

RESOURCES
Resource Sheet 3 'The Giant's point of view'

SHARED WRITING
Remind the children of the story of *Jack and the Beanstalk*. Explain that it was a third person narrative and that now you are going to write part of the story as a first person narrative from the point of view of the giant.

Make notes of the key events of the story:

Section 1: Giant returns home, smells Jack. Eats his supper, counts his gold and falls asleep. Jack steals money and giant is furious.

Section 2: Giant returns home, smells Jack. Eats his supper, watches his hen lay golden eggs and falls asleep. Jack steals the hen and the giant is furious.

 Time out for thinking When does the giant come into the story? (after Jack has climbed the beanstalk for the first time) Explain that this is where the first person account will begin.

What pronoun will you be using? (I)

Demonstration writing Explain that you are going to demonstrate how to write the first incident when Jack steals the gold from the giant. (You may wish to use RS3 as a prompt.)

Time out for thinking Tell the children to turn to a partner and to work out how the first sentence of the next section of the first person account might go.

INDEPENDENT WRITING
Ask the children to refer to the plan and write the second section of the story in the first person.

GUIDED WRITING SUPPORT
Orally expand the plan ensuring that the children sustain the first person. Scribe the first few sentences for them up to the point when the giant watches his hen lay the golden eggs. Ask them to complete the section of the story.

PLENARY
Explain that people see the same thing from different points of view. Write the following sentences on the board. Explain that they are from a teacher's point of view. Ask the children to tell you how children might view the same incidents, e.g.

Teacher: Children go to bed far too late.
Children: We're not tired.

Teacher: Pop music is just loud noise.
Children: …

Discuss how this affects the telling of events depending upon whose point of view we are seeing things from.

SESSION 6

FOCUS
- How does the reading of a poem help us to appreciate the story?

RESOURCES
- *The Pied Piper* Fiction Skills Big Book pages 36–41
- Resource Sheets 4 'Hamelin rat' and 'The Pied Piper of Hamelin 1'

SHARED READING
Tell the children the story of the Pied Piper up to the point when the Piper offers to rid the town of Hamelin of rats.

Read the extract from the Big Book. Talk about some of the more challenging vocabulary, e.g. 'ornamental fountain'.

Why might the eyes be described as 'glittering'?

Why would the rats be attracted to the Piper's tune?

What is the 'tide of grey vermin'?

Talk about the simile of the rats' tails.

Why is the word 'ceaseless' repeated?

Is the story told in the first or third person?

Read to the class *The Pied Piper* by Robert Browning (from RS5) up to where the rats are destroyed.

ORAL LANGUAGE WORK
Dramatise the action up to this point. Choose two children to be the Mayor and the Piper and divide the rest of the class into the crowd and the rats. Underline in the Big Book the text that needs to be spoken. Talk about how the rats might whistle and squeal.

INDEPENDENT WRITING
Give each child a copy of RS4. Tell the children to add and expand the labels with descriptions about the rat.

GUIDED READING CORE
Give each child a copy of RS5 with an extract from *The Pied Piper of Hamelin* where the chaos caused by the rats is described.

They should prepare a lively reading of the verse for performance in the plenary. (Remind them of some of the performance marks they learned in Unit 6: Oral and performance poetry.)

PLENARY
Invite the guided group to perform their prepared verse. The rest of the class should share their own ideas about the rats' activities.

Does anyone feel sorry for the rats? From whose point of view are the poem and the story told?

SESSION 7

FOCUS
- How can it help your writing to identify with characters in the story?

RESOURCES
- *The Pied Piper* Fiction Skills Big Book pages 36–41
- Resource Sheet 6 '*The Pied Piper of Hamelin 2*'

SHARED READING
Read pages 39–41 of the Big Book to the class. Talk about some of the more challenging vocabulary and discuss how the meaning can be gleaned from the context e.g. 'recall', (p39) 'taxes' (p40) 'squander', 'caper', 'captivated' (p41)

Discuss the following questions:
- Why does the Mayor lie to the Piper?
- Why are the Piper's clothes changed?
- Why do the people say nothing?
- What does it mean when it says 'children have no sense of business'?
- Why does he play music with two beats?

Share the rest of the story with the class.

Read more from the poem and discuss the following questions:
- Would you have preferred to have gone with the Piper into the mountain, or be the little boy left behind?
- Do you think the Piper was wrong to lure away the children?

SENTENCE WORK
Ask the children to look at page 39 in the Big Book and to identify two conjunctions: 'and', 'when'. Point out that 'but' in line 2 is not a conjunction. Talk about the sentence which starts with 'And'. Turn to page 40. Can the children find a sentence with two conjunctions? ('though' and 'or') (Links with Unit 17 of *Grammar for Writing*.)

INDEPENDENT WORK
Tell the children to write five sentences starting 'If I were … I would …'. They should write from the point of view of the Pied Piper, the Mayor, the stallholder, a rat and a child.

GUIDED WRITING — EXTENSION
Give the group a copy of RS6. Tell them to work together to write a modern-day prose version of the events as a third person narrative, e.g. The Mayor stood with his mouth open … They should write it on a large sheet of paper for the rest of the class to read.

PLENARY
Hot seat the part of the Pied Piper. First ask the children to turn to a partner and to plan two important questions to ask the Piper, e.g. *What have you done with the children? How do you do your magic?*

SESSION 8

FOCUS
- How can understanding a point of view help to make your writing more powerful?

RESOURCES
- *The Pied Piper* Fiction Skills Big Book pages 36–41
- Resource sheets 7 'The Mayor's point of view' and 8 'The Piper's point of view'

SHARED WRITING
Teacher Demonstration Share the writing the children completed in the independent work. Point out that these sentences give us an insight into the point of view of each character.

Tell the children that you are going to write the events from the Mayor's point of view. Remind the children that the Mayor was under a lot of pressure to rid the town of the rats and that he is going to present himself in a good light. Tell the children to imagine that, after the children have been taken away, the townsfolk hold a meeting in the Town Hall and the Mayor has to defend his actions. (Use RS7 as a prompt, if you wish.)

INDEPENDENT WORK
Tell the children to imagine that they are very angry after they have heard what the Mayor has to say. They should work with a partner and come up with six questions that they think the Mayor should answer, e.g. *We heard you promise a hundred pieces of gold. Why are you pretending that you only offered one?* They should then discuss the answers they think the Mayor would have given.

GUIDED WRITING — SUPPORT
Tell the group that they are going to be writing from the Pied Piper's point of view in the next session. Help them to start thinking along the lines of what the Piper might say. Look at the first paragraph of the extract and demonstrate how to use that information to write a first person account (you may wish to use RS8 as a prompt.)

PLENARY
Hot seat the part of the Mayor. Put yourself in the hot seat and let the children fire their questions at you. Then the class should decide upon a punishment for the Mayor.

SESSION 9

FOCUS
- How can you convey a character in a first person account?

RESOURCES
- *The Pied Piper* Fiction Skills Big Book pages 36–41
- Resource Sheet 8 'The Piper's point of view'

SHARED WRITING

Plan for writing Explain to the class that they are going to write the events of the story from the point of view of the Piper from when the Piper promises to get rid of the rats to when the children follow the Piper out of the town.

Share with the class the work from the guided group in Session 8. Talk about seeing things from the Pied Piper's point of view. Remind them of some of the comments made by the Pied Piper in the hot-seat in Session 7.

Make notes about the key incidents:

The Piper promises to get rid of the rats for a fee of 100 gold pieces.

The Mayor agrees.

The Piper plays and the rats follow him and are drowned.

The Piper returns for his money.

The Mayor denies that he promised him any money.

The Piper plays and the children follow him into the mountain.

EXTENDED WRITING

Ask the children to write the story from the Piper's point of view. Give them RS8 which includes an opening sentence, e.g. 'I can get rid of the rats.'

GUIDED WRITING — SUPPORT

Support the children as they complete their independent writing.

PLENARY

Either listen to some of the songs from the musical 'Rats' or divide the children into groups and ask them to select a scene from the story and present it as a freeze-frame. They should present their tableaux to the rest of the class. Move around among the 'statues' and touch them on the shoulder and ask them what they are thinking at that point of the action. Remind the children that these comments would all be first person accounts.

SESSION 10

FOCUS
- How can you improve our writing?

RESOURCES
The Pied Piper Fiction Skills Big Book pages 36–41

SHARED WRITING

Make an enlarged copy of some children's work and edit for the rest of the class to see. Underline where the first person has been used and where the personality of the character comes through.

Talk about how paragraphs help the reader and suggest ways of remembering spellings.

INDEPENDENT WRITING

Return the completed, marked draft copies of the children's writing and ask them to make top copies, correcting any errors. If possible, one group should present their work using IT. They should discuss layout and format and font.

GUIDED WRITING — SUPPORT

Move among the children and support where necessary. Encourage neat handwriting.

PLENARY

Tell the children that the Piper has been called back to explain himself in a court of law. Children should take it in turns to stand in the dock as the Piper and answer questions from the prosecuting counsel (the rest of the class). Children should take their stories with them into the dock and use them in their defence. After giving evidence a judge should decide whether the Piper is guilty of stealing the children or not.

Round off the session by referring to the class targets set out at the start of the unit. They should discuss aspects they particularly enjoyed and areas where they still need more support.

On the Literacy World Interactive CD for Stage 1 Fiction, you will find the following resources for this unit:
- Copies of all the Fiction Skills Big Book pages for interactive work (*The Pied Piper* pages 36-41)
- Audio recordings of *The Pied Piper of Hamelin* and *Rats Musical*
- Interactive word and sentence work for Session 2
- Extra reading (*Karlo's Tale*)
- All the Resource Sheets for independent work for you to customise
- Comprehensive Teaching and Planning Guides for the unit are also available on the CD.

Name   Date

Third to first

Change the text from a third person narrative to a first person.

> Then Tom heard the soft slithering of the Giant Slime Slug and he saw the black monster heading towards him. It had one eye in the middle of its forehead and its mouth was open, showing its huge green fangs. The Giant Slime Slug had looked very hungry and Tom had woken up screaming.

_____

_____

_____

_____

_____

_____

Name _____ Date _____

Conjunctions

Use these conjunctions to fill the gaps in the sentences.

| because | if | so that | although | when |

1 I like swimming _____ it keeps me fit.

2 I like swimming _____ I am not very good at it.

3 I like to swim _____ I have had my breakfast.

4 I will go swimming _____ you will come with me.

5 I practise swimming _____ I can win the race.

Finish these sentences.

1 I was sad because _____

2 I play with my friends when _____

3 I will play with you if _____

4 My dad goes jogging so that _____

5 I like school although _____

PROMPT: Writing exemplar

The Giant's point of view

[The Giant first comes into the story after Jack had climbed the beanstalk for the first time.]

I was on my way home. I was hungry. Fighting other giants always makes me hungry. When I got back to my castle I thought my wife was behaving a little oddly and there was a strange smell. If I wasn't much mistaken it was the smell of fresh boy.

[Direct speech can be used for conversations with Gertrude (his wife).]

"What's that I can smell?" I asked Gertrude.

"That'll be your dinner cooking," she replied. "It's your favourite – cow pie."

I ate all of my supper and then I decided to enjoy my favourite hobby – counting my gold. It takes a long time to count all my gold and my eyelids felt heavy and I must have fallen asleep.

[Activities centre round the Giant.]

[The Giant was asleep so he has to make assumptions about what happened.]

The next thing I knew my money had gone – all of it – all my beautiful gold. Someone had stolen it. They would be sorry. Very sorry.

Name Date

Hamelin rat

Look at the picture of the rat. Describe each feature. Suggest why the people of Hamelin hated the rats so much.

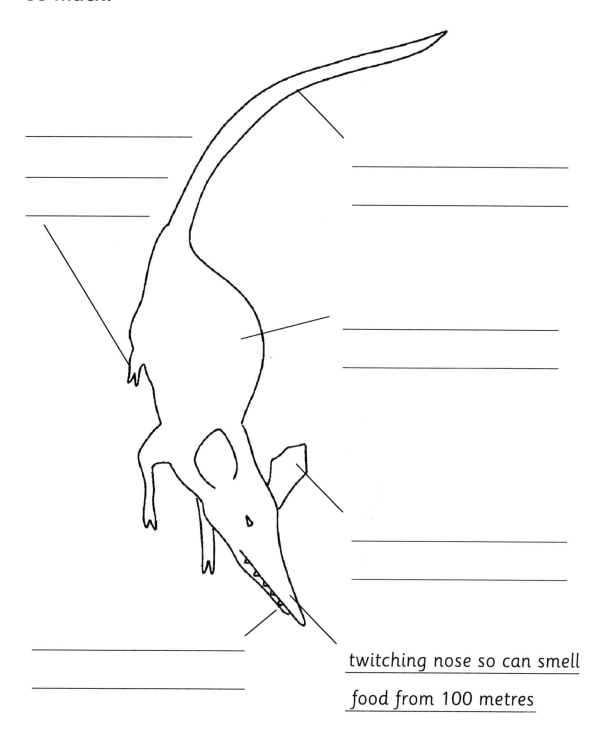

twitching nose so can smell food from 100 metres

The Pied Piper of Hamelin 1
by Robert Browning

Rats!
They fought the dogs, and killed the cats
And bit the babies in the cradles,
And ate the cheeses out the vats
And took the food from the cook's own ladles,
Split open the kegs of salted sprats,
Made nests inside men's Sunday hats,
And even spoiled the women's chats,
By drowning their speaking
With shrieking and squeaking
In fifty different sharps and flats.
Out of the houses the rats came tumbling
Great rats, small rats, lean rats, brawny rats,
Brown rats, black rats, grey rats, tawny rats,
Grave old plodders, gay young friskers,
Fathers, mothers, uncles, cousins,
Cocking tails and pricking whiskers,
Families by tens and dozens,
Brothers, sisters, husbands, wives –
Followed the Piper for their lives.

The Pied Piper of Hamelin 2
by Robert Browning

The Mayor was dumb, and the Council stood
As if they were changed into blocks of wood,
Unable to move a step, or cry
To the children merrily skipping by –
And could only follow with the eye
That joyous crowd at the Piper's back.
When, lo, as they reached the mountain's side,
A wondrous portal opened wide,
As if a cavern was suddenly hollowed;
And the Piper advanced and the children followed,
And when all were in to the very last,
The door in the mountain-side shut fast.
Did I say, all? No! One was lame,
And could not dance the whole of the way.

PROMPT: Writing exemplar

The Mayor's point of view

This is a first person account so I must remember to use the personal pronoun 'I'.

"Quiet please, ladies and gentlemen, I can explain everything. As you know we were recently visited by a very peculiar character who played a pipe.

I was keen to send him on his way but many of you seemed to think he would be helpful in getting rid of the plague of rats which tormented the town.

I must pretend that I wasn't interested in the Piper getting rid of the rats so I'll tell a lie.

I'll pretend that it was the townspeople's fault.

I was prepared to go along with your ideas but, of course, I wanted to be careful with your taxes so I suggested that he did the job first and then we would pay him one gold piece.

I mustn't admit that I ever even mentioned 100 gold pieces so I'll just say that it was one gold piece.

You will also remember that this coincided with the rats choosing to leave our town and although it might have looked as if it was something to do with the Piper, I am sure they really wanted to have a swim in the river but they had forgotten they could not swim.

I think I'll tell my biggest lie. I'll pretend that the rats leaving had nothing to do with the Piper, but that the the rats left of their own accord.

I'll try to make the people think that the Piper was a liar.

Then the ridiculous character made up a story that I had promised him one hundred gold pieces. What a lie!

I really cannot say anything about your children. Children often wander off to play and I'm sure they'll be back by supper-time.

I must pretend to know nothing about the children.

I am going on holiday immediately so if you've any more questions please send a letter to the Mayor's office."

The crowd are getting angry so I had better find some way of getting out of here.

STAGE 1 | TERM 3 | For use with Unit 10 Session 8 as a prompt for shared writing.
© Harcourt Education Ltd. 2004. Copying permitted for purchasing school only. The material is not copyright free.

The Piper's point of view

Continue to write the story from the Piper's point of view.

I can rid the town of rats. But you will have to pay me.

My fee is 100 gold pieces.

1 3 11 Humorous poetry

KEY INFORMATION

TEACHING OBJECTIVES

TEXT LEVEL

T3 T6	compare forms or types of humour
T3 T7	select, prepare, read aloud and recite by heart poetry that plays with language or entertains; to recognise rhyme, alliteration and other patterns of sound that create effects
T3 T15	write poetry that uses sound to create effects, e.g. onomatopoeia, alliteration, distinctive rhythms
T3 T21	use IT to bring to a published form – discuss relevance of layout, font, etc. to audience

SENTENCE LEVEL

T3 S1	use awareness of grammar to decipher new or unfamiliar words
T3 S7	become aware of the use of commas in marking grammatical boundaries within sentences

WORD LEVEL

T3 W4	discriminate syllables in reading and spelling
T3 W8	identify short words within longer words as an aid to spelling
T3 W11	use the apostrophe to spell further contracted forms e.g. couldn't
T3 W13	collect synonyms which will be useful when writing dialogue
T3 W14	explore homonyms which have the same spellings but different meanings and explain how the meanings can be distinguished in context

UNIT SUMMARY

RESOURCES

- **Essential Fiction Anthology** *How Can I?; My Dad's Amazing; Recipe for a Disastrous Family Picnic; Through the Staffroom Door; At the End of School Assembly* pages 34–37, 46–47, 49, 62
- **Fiction Skills Big Book** *Sunday in the Yarm Fard; The Grumpy Princess; Baira and the Vultures; Teacher Said…; All The Things You Can Say* pages 3, 42–45
- **Resource Sheets** 1–6
- **Literacy World Interactive** Unit 11 (optional)

In this 2-week unit, children read and respond to humorous poems, learning to recognise devices such as alliteration and onomatopoeia and consider their effect. They write their own poems and perform them to the rest of the class.

5–14 GUIDELINES

Reading level B
- Reflecting on writer's craft
- Reading for enjoyment
- Reading aloud

CHILDREN'S TARGETS

READING
I can choose a funny poem that I like and learn it off by heart.

WRITING
I can write a poem using sound to create effects, present it using IT and perform it to the rest of the class.

SENTENCE
I can work out unfamiliar words using the meaning of the sentence and check that the word looks and sounds right.

WORD
I can work out the meaning of homonyms by reading the whole sentence.

SPEAKING AND LISTENING
I can perform poems with expression.

OUTLINE PLAN

SESSION	WHOLE CLASS WORK		INDEPENDENT WORK	GUIDED GROUPS	WHOLE CLASS WORK plenary
1 Monday	**Shared reading** Introduce focus Read *Sunday in the Yarm Fard* from BB Discuss poem with the class What made them laugh? **T6**		**Independent work** Make a list of animals and their noises and create spoonerisms	**Guided writing** extension Create own spoonerism poem	Introduce targets *What do you need to learn in this unit?* Extension group to read own poem
2 Tuesday	**Shared reading** Read *How Can I?* and *My Dad's Amazing* from EF Discuss the expressions in the poems **S1**	**Word work** Look at homonyms **T7**	**Independent work** Complete RS1 on common expressions	**Guided reading** support Learn own poems by heart	Discuss the suggestions from the independent work
3 Wednesday	**Shared reading and writing** Read *Recipe for a Disastrous Family Picnic* from EF Scribe ideas for *A Disastrous School Outing*		**Independent writing** Complete RS2 and write own poem for *Disastrous Shopping Trip*	**Guided reading** support Discuss ideas for 'what to do' section of poem	Act out the poem *Recipe for a Disastrous Family Picnic*
4 Thursday	**Shared reading** Read *Through the Staffroom Door* from EF and talk to the class about the alliteration Look at the punctuation	**Word work** Look at syllables in the poem **W4**	**Independent reading** Count the syllables in the poems	**Guided reading** support Identify syllables in words	Act out *Through the Staffroom Door*
5 Friday	**Shared writing** Demonstrate how to write a poem about *Ten Cheeky Children*		**Independent writing** Complete the poem, writing the lines from numbers six to one	**Guided writing** support Rehearse oral performance of own poems	Share work from independent task
6 Monday	**Sentence work** Look at the place of commas in texts Commas for embedded clauses **S7**		**Independent writing** Use RS4 for building sentences	**Guided reading** core Practise reading and obeying punctuation	Play 'Silly Sentences' game
7 Tuesday	**Shared reading** Read *At the End of School Assembly* Look at effect of onomatopoeia **T15**	**Word work** Learn spellings - words within words **W8**	**Independent work** Complete the sentences on RS5	**Guided writing** support Complete poem on RS5	Play 'Word Challenge' game *How many little words can you find in these longer words?*
8 Wednesday	**Shared reading** Read *Teacher Said* in BB to the class Discuss alliteration and rhyme	**Word work** Look at apostrophe for contractions **W11**	**Independent work** Speech verbs RS6	**Guided writing** core Use thesaurus to find synonyms for 'say' RS6	Prepare a performance of the poem
9 Thursday	**Shared reading and writing** Read *All the things you can say to places in the UK* from BB to the class. Create rhymes for place names. Model writing new lines		**Extended writing** Select place names and link with rhyming words	**Guided writing** support Orally rehearse lines for place names	Discuss onomatopoeia and alliteration
10 Friday	**Shared writing** Select ten best place name rhymes. Look at ways of presenting poems		**Independent work** Make fair copies of poems Encourage use of IT Present as class poetry book **T21**	**Guided writing** support Discuss ways to present own poems	Look at the targets for the unit Perform favourite poem **T7**

Abbreviation key
- **BB** Fiction Skills Big Book
- **EF** Essential Fiction Anthology
- **GfW** Grammar for Writing
- **SPB** Spelling Bank
- **RS** Resource Sheet

TEACHING NOTES

SESSION 1

FOCUS
- What are spoonerisms?

RESOURCES
- *Sunday in the Yarm Fard* Fiction Skills Big Book page 42

EXTENDED SHARED READING

Introduce this unit by talking about things that make the children laugh. Link this with poems to be read in this unit.

Time out for discussion Tell the children to turn to a partner and to think of two things that make them laugh.

Share the children's ideas and introduce the idea of spoonerisms (where the first letter of two words are transposed), e.g. par cark.

Share with the children the poem *Sunday in the Yarm Fard*. Talk about the spoonerisms and sort out what the words should have been, e.g. the cat meowed. Discuss with the children suitable sound effects for each animal. Reread the poem and ask the class to make the relevant noise. In the last verse they should make the noise after each verb, e.g. dacking (quack, quack), changing (ding dong).

Introduce the word 'onomatopoeia' (words which echo sounds associated with their meaning). Talk about how to say the word 'meowed' as if a cat were making the sound. Do the same with the other sounds in the poem.

Encourage the children to learn by heart the first two verses of the poem.

INDEPENDENT WORK

Ask the children to make a list of animals and to transpose the first letter to make spoonerisms, e.g. rion loared.

GUIDED WRITING — EXTENSION

Tell the children they are going to create a poem based on *Sunday in the Yarm Fard* but it will be *Sunday in the Pafari Sark*. First they should think of animals in the park and their animals' noises. They should be thinking which possible noises could rhyme for lines 2 and 4, e.g. the giger trowled and the hunkey mowled, the snoth slored and the carrot pawed.

PLENARY

Ask the extension group to share their poem *Sunday in the Pafari Sark*. Invite the rest of the class to identify which animals are making the sounds. Then see if the animal spoonerisms created by the rest of the class could be combined to make a rhyming verse.

Read through the unit targets and talk about the work that you will be doing in this unit to help the children meet the targets.

SESSION 2

FOCUS
- What are other kinds of word play?

RESOURCES
- *How Can I?*; *My Dad's Amazing* Essential Fiction page 46 and 49
- Resource Sheet 1 'Homonyms'

SHARED READING

Read the poem *How Can I?* which uses word play but not spoonerisms. Talk about the phrases the poem is based on. Discuss the difference between the way the phrases are normally used and their literal meanings. Ask the children to think of how the following phrases could be taken literally, e.g. people who pull faces, hot cross buns, changing your mind.

Read the poem *My Dad's Amazing* to the class. *Have you heard any of these expressions before?* Talk to the children about the meaning of the different expressions. *How does the poet make them funny?* (he presents them as literal)

WORD WORK

Write the word 'wind' on the board. Ask the children what word you have written. Talk about the fact that the word can be pronounced in two different ways. Introduce the word 'homonym'. Emphasise the importance of reading the whole sentence to work out the meaning. Write the word 'bulb' on the board. Write a sentence with each meaning, e.g. 'The bulbs she planted flowered in the spring.' or 'The bulbs in the classroom are very bright.'

Time out for thinking Ask the children for the two meanings of the following words: bank, bat, note and letter. They should suggest a sentence which brings out the meaning of the word.

INDEPENDENT WORK

Using RS1 ask the children to explore the difference between the literal and figurative meaning of expressions.

GUIDED READING — SUPPORT

Reread one of the poems from shared reading. Talk through each line, checking that children understand the expressions used. Help the children begin to learn the poem off by heart.

PLENARY

Ask the guided group to act out the expressions they discussed. Can the rest of the class guess the expression and then talk about the meaning? Start a class collection of common expressions.

SESSION 3

FOCUS
- Can a recipe be a poem?

RESOURCES
- *Recipe for a Disastrous Family Picnic* Essential Fiction page 63
- Resource Sheet 2 'Recipe for a disastrous shopping trip'

SHARED READING AND WRITING

Ask the children what they know about the instruction genre, e.g. recipes (heading describes what is to be made; ingredients listed separately; what to do = a set of sequenced steps each starting with an imperative verb; does not include personal opinions). Jot these down for the class to refer to.

Read the poem *Recipe for a Disastrous Family Picnic* to the class. Talk about the poem and ask the following questions:

Why do you think the recipe would work best near a herd of cows?

How has the poet made links between the Ingredients and the Method?

Refer to the list of text characteristics for instructions. Can they identify in the poem?

Time out for thinking Ask the children to turn to a partner and to come with three items for the list of ingredients for writing a recipe poem for 'A Disastrous School Outing'. Remind them of how the poet linked the Ingredients and the Method. They should think about quantities, e.g. 1 harassed teacher, 4 exhausted helpers.

Collect in the suggestions and agree on a final list.

Teacher scribing Model for the children how to use the ingredients to describe funny incidents on the outing, e.g. *Place 1 harassed teacher, 4 exhausted helpers, 1 grumpy bus driver and 30 excited children in a hot coach.*

Time out for writing Ask the children to work with a partner and to come up with a postscript to the poem, e.g. *Please note that this recipe works best if served …*

INDEPENDENT WRITING

Ask the children to make up their own poem, using RS2 and the same model as above.

GUIDED READING — SUPPORT

Discuss RS2 with the group. Ask them to think what might happen in the 'What to do' section. Scribe their ideas drawing attention to spelling choices and familiar letter patterns.

PLENARY

Divide the class into groups of five. Tell them they are going to act out the disastrous family picnic. Each child should take a role, e.g. an adult, or the baby. They should do or say things that fit in with the poem, e.g. *What are the children arguing about? What do the parents do to show they are fed up?*

SESSION 4

FOCUS
- What are rhyming couplets?

RESOURCES
- *Through the Staffroom Door* Essential Fiction page 62

SHARED READING

Read the poem to the class.

Time out for thinking Ask the children to pick out the rhyming words in the poem. What do they notice about the pattern of rhyming words?

Point out the alliteration in the line 'Ten tired teachers'. Talk about the effect of this repetition. Note that the first line of each couplet starts with a number and the second line ends 'then there were …'. Explain that the comma in the middle of the second line of each couplet helps us to read the poem. Demonstrate this by writing the line 'one gave an enormous sneeze, then there were five'. Remove the comma from its correct place and put it after 'gave'. Discuss how this spoils the meaning of the sentence.

Brainstorm rhyming words for the numbers 'nine' to 'none': 'seven' is very difficult, e.g. Devon, heaven, eleven. Display these for use in Session 5.

Talk about how the number of beats in the first line of each couplet should be the same as in the second line.

WORD WORK

Explain that a syllable is a beat in a word. So 'child' has only one syllable or beat and 'children' has two. Say each word of line 1 and demonstrate how to clap for each syllable (12 claps). Ask the children to clap the syllables in line 2 (13 claps).

Time out for thinking Tell the children to work with a partner and to count the syllables in the second couplet.

Look at the two syllable compound words: staffroom, playtime. Ask the children what two words make up the compound word. Can you find four more compound words in the poem? (playground, cupboard, getaway, afternoon)

INDEPENDENT READING

Tell the children to draw four columns headed 1 to 4. They should look through the poem *Recipe for a Disastrous Family Picnic* and find five examples of words with 1 to 3 syllables and one example each of a word with 4 syllables (ingredients) and 5 syllables (unreliable).

GUIDED READING — SUPPORT

Give each pair a number fan 1–3. Select words from the poem and ask the children to identify the number of syllables in each word. They should show the number with their fan, e.g. 'ten' (1), 'teachers' (2), 'enormous' (3).

PLENARY

Act out *Through the Staffroom Door*. Divide the class into three groups of ten. All the children should say the lines and demonstrate what happens to each teacher reducing the group size down to none.

SESSION 5

FOCUS
- How can you use what you have learned about rhyming couplets to write your own poem?

RESOURCES
- *Through the Staffroom Door* Essential Fiction page 62

SHARED WRITING

Explain to the children that you are going to write four rhyming couplets based on the model of *Through the Staffroom Door* and they are going to complete the poem. Tell them that your poem is going to be about ten cheeky children and you are going to make it as funny as you can.

Ask the children how you should start your poem (*Ten cheeky children*). Explain that you have chosen the adjective 'cheeky' because it is alliterative with 'children'. Display the list of rhyming words for each number (made in Session 4). Remind them that the end of your first line must rhyme with nine, e.g. line, fine, pine, dine, mine. So you are going to choose 'line'. So your first line goes:

Ten cheeky children wouldn't stand in line.

The teacher put one in the bin, then there were nine.

Do the same with nine cheeky children. Remind them that seven is difficult to find a rhyme so you will choose 'Devon', e.g.

Eight cheeky children went off to Devon.

One fell off a cliff, then there were seven.

INDEPENDENT WRITING

Tell the children to complete the poem with numbers 6–1. Remind them of the rhyming words they have already brainstormed and the rhythm of the lines. If possible allow some children to work directly onto a word processor.

Extension Encourage these children to create a poem of their own with different characters, e.g. Ten massive monsters.

GUIDED WRITING — SUPPORT

Read through the class poem and help children to rehearse each verse before they write. Support them in referring to the list of words that rhyme with each number. Encourage them to keep reading and rereading their lines to make sure they are happy with them.

PLENARY

Ask individual children to share their poems. Invite the rest of the class to comment on the success of the rhyme and rhythm and if necessary suggest alternatives.

SESSION 6

FOCUS
- How are commas used to mark boundaries within sentences?

RESOURCES
- *The Grumpy Princess* Fiction Skills Big Book page 3
- *Baíra and the Vultures* Essential Fiction pages 34–37
- Resource Sheets 3 'Commas' and 4 'Making sentences'

EXTENDED SENTENCE WORK

Reread the opening paragraph from *The Grumpy Princess*. Cover the commas with Post-it notes. Then read it a second time omitting all pauses for commas. Ask the children to explain the differences between the first and second readings. Discuss where the commas are needed and why. Draw a comma on each of the Post-it notes and place them randomly in the text. Read the text obeying the new commas. Does the text make sense? Talk about how commas help the reader to work their way through a longer sentence, keeping bits of the same information together.

Give out the cards from RS3. Invite the children to come out and make sentences, e.g. Rover likes to do tricks. Demonstrate how to add in the phrase 'my dog' and mark this with commas. Do this with other sentences, e.g. Amy, my sister, is eleven.

Time out for writing Write the following sentence: *Miss Tick marks our books.* Ask children to write on their whiteboards the sentence with 'our teacher' added in and marked with commas.

INDEPENDENT WRITING

Give each child a copy of RS4 and ask them to build sentences with commas and a full stop.

GUIDED READING — CORE

Turn to the story of *Baíra and the Vultures*. Explain to the group that they are going to practise reading aloud with fluency and obeying all the punctuation. Remind them to look carefully at the commas.

PLENARY

Using the sentences from RS4, invite children to make 'silly' sentences, e.g. 'My friend, Mr Cross, hid under the table' or 'The headteacher, Tinkerbelle, has a new bike'. Recap the conventions for using commas investigated in the session.

SESSION 7

FOCUS
- **What is a metaphor?**

RESOURCES
- *At the End of School Assembly* Essential Fiction page 47
- Resource Sheet 5 'How did the children leave the classroom?'

SHARED READING
Read the poem *At the End of School Assembly* to the class. Ask the children how the author has made the poem funny. (linked the teacher's name to the verb) Talk about the effectiveness of this link. Ask them why the final line of the poem is written differently. *Which line do you think is the funniest? Can you think of a teacher's name in the school which could easily be linked to a verb of movement, e.g. Mrs Potter's class ambled out.* Talk about the difference between the first two verses and the second two verses. (the first two use action verbs and the second two use common expressions) Explain that the poet has used metaphors to make comparisons between the teachers' names and the way the children leave the class.

Time out for thinking Ask the children to work in pairs and to think of how to present some of the lines of the poem, e.g. *How would you say 'Mrs Steed's lot galloped out.'?* (trying to make the word sound like the action).

Explain that this is onomatopoeia (when words sound like their meaning). Talk about the effect of this in the poem.

WORD WORK
Tell the children that one way to spell longer words is to see smaller words inside them. Demonstrate this with the word 'bothered' – both, other, the, he, her, here, red. Tell them to work with a partner and to find 20 words in the poem which have smaller words inside them.

INDEPENDENT WORK
Give each child a copy of RS5. Ask them to think of verbs to complete each of the sentences.

GUIDED WRITING — SUPPORT
Look at RS5. Ensure the group understand that they are selecting verbs which will describe how someone with one of those names might leave the classroom. Scribe answers for the group, talking about spelling options as you write.

PLENARY
Find out who has the longest list of words from the shared activity.

Write the following words on the board and challenge the children to find as many smaller words inside them as possible: friend (1), because (3), important (5), together (6), something (7).

SESSION 8

FOCUS
- **How can you make dialogue interesting?**

RESOURCES
- *Teacher Said …* Fiction Skills Big Book page 43
- Resource Sheet 6 'What did they say in the following ways?'

SHARED READING
Limbering up Ask the children to think of three things that teachers often fuss about when children are writing stories.

Take in the children's ideas and talk about using different speech verbs after a character has spoken.

Time out for thinking Tell the children to think of three alternatives to 'said'.

Before reading the poem to the class, cover the last line. ('…SAID my teacher.') Read the poem to the class and ask them to guess the final line. Ask the children why they think the poet has ordered the speech verbs in the way she has. (alliteration and rhyme)

Write a speech sentence on the board, e.g. 'Come over here.' Ask the children to choose a speech verb and say the sentence in accordance with that speech verb, e.g. very quietly for 'muttered'.

WORD WORK
Look at the contraction 'don't' in the poem. Ask the children why the apostrophe is needed. Demonstrate how 'could not' can be contracted to 'couldn't'.

Time out for discussion Write 'should not' on the board and ask the children to write it as a contraction.

Explain that sometimes the contraction loses more than just one letter, e.g. 'won't' is the contraction for 'will not'.

Write 'they are' on the board and 'they're'. Ask the children what letter is missing. Ask them to do the same with 'we are' and 'you are'. (Draw attention to the difference between 'you're' and 'your'.)

INDEPENDENT WORK
Give each child a copy of RS6. Tell the children to think of sentences appropriate for each speech verb.

GUIDED WRITING — CORE
Use a range of thesauruses to find as many different words for 'say' (talk, speak) excluding the ones used in the poem. Write the words on an A3 sheet for the class to refer to.

PLENARY
Prepare a performance of the poem. Give each child in the class one of the speech verbs and tell them to be prepared to say it appropriately to go with its meaning. You act as narrator and link together the speech verbs. All the class together should read the repeated line, 'but don't use SAID!'
The last line should be read by one child very quietly.

SESSION 9

FOCUS
- How can you write a poem following a model?

RESOURCES
- *All the things you can say to places in the UK* Fiction Skills Big Book pages 44–45
- Road atlases

SHARED READING AND WRITING

Limbering up Tell the children to think of five different names of places in the UK.

Collect in the place names. Explain that you are going to write a poem with words that rhyme with place names. Have a look at the class list and decide which place names will be easy to find a rhyme for and which are impossible!

Time out for thinking In pairs ask the children to generate rhymes for the place names that are easy to rhyme with.

Show children the map of the UK in the Big Book. Point out where the school is.

Read the poem pointing at each place on the map as you read the relevant line. Explain that they are going to write a poem about things to do in places all over the UK.

Talk about the rhyme in the poem. Demonstrate how to clap the metre. (4 beats in each line)

Demonstrate how to link the place names suggested by the children to make a line with internal rhyme like the poem, e.g. Drink some tea in Swansea. Buy a new dress in Inverness.

EXTENDED WRITING

Give each group of children a road atlas. Tell the children to select place names and make up a line with internal rhyme of something to do in that place.

GUIDED WRITING — SUPPORT

Help the children to identify suitable place names. Talk about creating a line with internal rhyme, rehearse it together orally and then act as scribe for the group.

PLENARY

Remind the children of poetic devices explored in the unit (alliteration, onomatopoeia). Ask the children to look at the lines they prepared in the independent work. Work together to build in alliteration or onomatopoeia in the lines, e.g. Slurp some tea in Swansea.

SESSION 10

FOCUS
- Can you write a poem using internal rhyme?

RESOURCES
- *All the things you can say to places in the UK* Fiction Skills Big Book pages 44–45

SHARED WRITING

Ask the children to read through their independent work from Session 9. Tell them to choose their ten best place names and rhymes they created in Session 9.

Time out for thinking Tell the children to try out their lines on partners. *Does the internal rhyme work? Have you included something to do in the chosen place? Does the rhythm of each line match all the other lines? Could you improve any of the lines by adding alliteration or onomatopoeia?*

Talk to the children about various ways of presenting their poems. They may like to sketch an outline of the UK (or draw round a template).

INDEPENDENT WORK

Ask the children to prepare a top copy of their poem. One group could present their poem using IT.

GUIDED WRITING — SUPPORT

Support the children as they read through the poem they created in the previous session. Ask them to write out their own copy, in their best handwriting.

EVALUATION AND REVIEW

Invite the children to share what they consider to be their most successful lines. Discuss how the finished poems could be displayed.

Refer to the targets shared at the beginning of the unit. Remind the children of all the things they have learned.

Round off the unit with a performance of their favourite poem.

On the Literacy World Interactive CD for Stage 1 Fiction, you will find the following resources for this unit:

- Copies of all the Fiction Skills Big Book pages for interactive work (*Sunday in the Yarm Fard* page 42, *Teacher Said …* page 43 and *All the things you can say to places in the UK*, pages 44–45)
- An audio recording of *Recipe for a Disastrous Family Picnic*
- Interactive word and sentence work for Sessions 5, 6 and 8
- All the Resource Sheets for independent work for you to customise
- Comprehensive Teaching and Planning Guides for the unit are also available on the CD.

Homonyms

These pictures show literal meanings of phrases. Write a sentence to show the real meaning of the phrase.

Answer: to wind somebody up means _to annoy them_

Answer: traffic jam means
_____

Answer: fish fingers means
_____

Answer: crossroads means
_____

Answer: catching a bus means
_____

Name _____ Date _____

Recipe for a disastrous shopping trip

Make up your own poem using these ingredients.

1 tired Mum   1 crying baby
2 arguing children 1 wonky buggy
1 late bus   1 broken shopping bag

What to do

Place _____

Mix in _____

Then _____

Next _____

_____

_____

_____

_____

Please note that this recipe works best if _____

_____

SENTENCE WORK: Cards

Commas

Cut out the cards and use them to demonstrate how to add commas to sentences.

Rover	likes	to	do	tricks
Luke	is	very	tall	my friend
Amy	is	eleven		my sister
my dog	,	,	.	.

STAGE 1 | TERM 3 | For use with Unit 11 Session 6 as sentence work.

Name _____ Date _____

Making sentences

Choose one item from each box to make a sentence. (Don't forget the commas and full stops!)

My friend	The old lady next door
Our kitten	The headteacher

Rani	Mrs Jones
Tinkerbelle	Mr Cross

has a new bike	likes reading
hid under the table	is good at football

_____
_____
_____
_____
_____

 STAGE 1 | TERM 3 | For use with Unit 11 Session 6 as independent work.
© Harcourt Education Ltd. 2004. Copying permitted for purchasing school only. The material is not copyright free.

Name _____ Date _____

How did the children leave the classroom?

Look at the children's names. Complete the sentences using words which describe how each child might have left the classroom.

The first one has been done for you.

Amir Rann	_____raced_____	out of the classroom.
Megan Dance	_____	out of the classroom.
Tom Ball	_____	out of the classroom.
Helen Skip	_____	out of the classroom.
Tony Carr	_____	out of the classroom.
Jasmine Joy	_____	out of the classroom.
Ryan Rivers	_____	out of the classroom.
Chloe Tapp	_____	out of the classroom.
Ken Walker	_____	out of the classroom.
Mary Fisher	_____	out of the classroom.

STAGE 1 | TERM 3 | For use with Unit 11 Session 7 as independent work.
© Harcourt Education Ltd. 2004. Copying permitted for purchasing school only. The material is not copyright free.

Name _____   Date _____

What did they say in the following ways?

Write in some speech that each character might have spoken in the style suggested by the speech verb.

The first one has been done for you.

1 " <u>I've lost my homework</u>," muttered the boy.

2 " _____," groaned the footballer.

3 " _____," grumbled the dinner lady.

4 " _____," bellowed the farmer.

5 " _____," squealed the excited children.

6 " _____," howled the toddler.

7 " _____," screeched the terrified girl.

8 " _____," shrieked the girls.

STAGE 1 | TERM 3 | For use with Unit 11 Session 8 as independent work.
© Harcourt Education Ltd. 2004. Copying permitted for purchasing school only. The material is not copyright free.

1 3 12 Stories by the same author

KEY INFORMATION

TEACHING OBJECTIVES

TEXT LEVEL		SENTENCE LEVEL		WORD LEVEL	
T3 T8	compare and contrast works by the same author	T3 S2	identify pronouns and understand their function in sentences	T3 W4	discriminate syllables in reading and spelling
T3 T9	be aware of authors and discuss preferences and reasons for these	T3 S3	ensure grammatical agreement in speech and writing of pronouns and verbs	T3 W12	continue the collection of new words from reading and other subjects
T3 T14	write book reviews for a specified audience based on evaluations of plot, character and language	T3 S4	use speech marks and other dialogue punctuation appropriately in writing	T3 W16	collect, investigate, classify common expressions from reading…

UNIT SUMMARY

RESOURCES

- **Essential Fiction Anthology** *The Hodgeheg; King Max the Last* pages 50–53, 54–57
- **Fiction Skills Big Book** *Dinosaur School* pages 46–48
- **Resource Sheets** 1–6
- **Literacy World Interactive** Unit 12 (optional)
- Screen version of *Babe*

In this optional 1 or 2-week unit children read a selection of extracts from books by Dick King-Smith. They look for similarities in author style and write a book review.

Week 1 stands alone and covers all the objectives. Week 2 is optional. It builds on the work in Week 1, reinforcing all the objectives and widening children's experience of the work of one author.

- If possible, coordinate this unit with a class reading of a Dick King-Smith title, e.g. *The Hodgeheg* in Week 1 and *Dinosaur School* in Week 2.

5–14 GUIDELINES

Reading level B/C
- Reflecting on writer's craft
- Reading for enjoyment
- Knowledge about language

CHILDREN'S TARGETS

READING
I can say why I like an author's stories.

WRITING
I can write a book review saying what I liked and disliked in a story.

SENTENCE
I know how to use speech marks.

WORD
I understand some common expressions.

GUIDED READING LINKS

- *Mrs Dippy* (Core)
- *Pet Rescue* (Satellites)
- *Goat-skin Lad and other Tales* (Comets)

OUTLINE PLAN

STAGE 1 • TERM 3 • UNIT 12

SESSION	WHOLE CLASS WORK		INDEPENDENT WORK	GUIDED GROUPS	WHOLE CLASS WORK plenary
1 Monday	**Shared reading** Introduce unit Look at the writing of Dick King-Smith Read extract from *The Hodgeheg* from EF Draw story plan on board and discuss		**Independent writing** Look at dialogue and present as speech bubbles using RS1 **S4**	**Guided writing** extension discuss dialogue that would have taken place between characters	What have you learned about hedgehogs from the story?
2 Tuesday	**Shared reading** Discuss presentation of speech/speech marks	**Word work** Look at common expressions **W16**	**Independent writing** Add punctuation to speech using RS2	**Guided writing** support Insert correct punctuation into sentences	Act out the dialogue for three characters in story
3 Wednesday	**Shared reading** Read *King Max the Last* from EF Look at links with previous story Reread extract as a play		**Independent writing** What did Max mean to say? Use RS3 to explain	**Guided reading** core Devise muddled sentences	Share muddled sentences with class
4 Thursday	**Sentence work** Play 'Pronoun game' (links to Unit 16 in GfW) **S2**	**Shared writing** Look at book reviews Model writing a review **T14**	**Independent writing** Prepare for writing a book review on Dick King-Smith	**Guided writing** support Talk through book reviews	Play 'Guess my book'
5 Friday	**Sentence work** Change the pronoun cards **S3**	**Shared reading** Look at features of writing in Dick King-Smith. Look at humour and information included	**Independent writing** Write a book review on story by Dick King-Smith on RS4 **T14**	**Guided writing** core/extension Review other books	Share the book reviews from independent work
6 Monday (optional)	**Shared reading** Read *Dinosaur School* from BB Discuss the story	**Word work** Break words into syllables **W4**	**Independent work** Map opening of *Dinosaur School* onto story plan	**Guided writing** support Learn high frequency words	Share story charts from independent work
7 Tuesday (optional)	**Shared reading and writing** Demonstrate how to write introductory sentence		**Independent writing** Write opening sentence in style of Dick King-Smith	**Guided writing** support Scan internet for information on brontosaurus	Research group to present findings
8 Wednesday (optional)	**Shared reading** Discuss presentation of speech	**Sentence work** Speech punctuation	**Independent work** Text marking on RS5	**Guided writing** extension Add dialogue to opening sentence	Use dialogue from extension group – what extra information has been included?
9 Thursday (optional)	**Shared writing** Demonstrate selecting and writing quotations		**Extended writing** Select book and quotation for class mobile – make first draft	**Guided writing** support Work on class mobile	Children to argue for best Dick King-Smith title Make class mobile
10 Friday (optional)	**Shared writing** Write a letter to Dick King-Smith about books **T9**	**Shared viewing** Show class opening of *Babe* and ask class to identify characteristics of the author			Review and evaluate unit Complete RS6

Abbreviation key
- **BB** Fiction Skills Big Book
- **EF** Essential Fiction Anthology
- **GfW** Grammar for Writing
- **SPB** Spelling Bank
- **RS** Resource Sheet

TEACHING NOTES

SESSION 1

FOCUS
- What Dick King-Smith stories do we know?

RESOURCES
- *The Hodgeheg* Essential Fiction pages 50–53
- Resource Sheet 1 'What are Max and Pa saying?'

SHARED READING

Limbering up Ask the children to name any Dick King-Smith books they have read. Write these on the board.

Introduce the unit by explaining that they are going to look at stories by Dick King-Smith and write a book review.

Read the extract from 'The Hodgeheg' to the class. Ask the following questions:
- Has anyone read this story? What happens to Max at the end?
- What has happened to Auntie Betty?
- Why do Max's family want to cross the road?
- How should humans cross a busy road safely?

Draw a story plan on the board: Characters/Setting/Problem/Solution. Ask the children to help you to fill in the first three sections. Then they should speculate on a possible solution.

Time out for thinking Ask the children to work with a partner and to look again at lines 1–11. They should work out what they have learned about Pa hedgehog and Ma Hedgehog from this dialogue. Talk about how dialogue can convey character.

Remind the children of the difference between direct speech and using speech bubbles. Demonstrate with line 3: "Oh, no!" cried Ma. "Where?"

INDEPENDENT WRITING

Give each child a copy of RS1. Ask them to put into speech bubbles the dialogue between Pa Hedgehog and Max.

GUIDED WRITING — EXTENSION

Tell the group to look again at page 52 (lines 36–43). Ask the group to discuss the actual dialogue that would have taken place between Ma and Pa Hedgehog.

PLENARY

Ask the children what facts they have learned about hedgehogs from this extract. Write the headings: Appearance, Habitat and Diet on the board and enter the information under the headings.

Introduce the targets for this unit.

SESSION 2

FOCUS
- How does the author make common expressions amusing?

RESOURCES
- The Hodgeheg Essential texts pp50–53
- Resource Sheet 2 'Dialogue'
- Completed RS1 from Session 1

SHARED READING

Limbering up Tell the children to work with a partner and read the speech bubble dialogue on RS1 that they completed in Session 1.

Reread the extract from the story.

Listening focus Ask the children to listen for the differences between spoken dialogue and prose.

Stop after line 44 and ask the children in the guided writing group to read the dialogue they created for lines 36–43 on RS1.

Write an example of dialogue on the board, e.g. line 49: "What are you talking about, Ma?" he said. Explain all the speech punctuation.

WORD WORK

Write the following story on the board: *On Saturday I got out of bed on the wrong side and that made me very out of sorts. I met my friend and she was in the same boat.*

Time out for thinking Ask the children to work with a partner and to identify the common expressions.

Can they work out what the expressions mean?

Tell the children that Dick King-Smith frequently uses common expressions in his stories. Can they find examples in this extract? (l1 'copped it', l26 'night's sport', l28/ l29 'hard life and that's flat', l46 'bright boy', l53 'mind your own business')

Start a class collection of common expressions.

INDEPENDENT WRITING

Give each child a copy of RS2 and ask them to add the correct punctuation.

GUIDED WRITING — SUPPORT

Write the following sentence without punctuation and ask the children to write it on their whiteboards with the correct punctuation: *I'm going to find out a safe way to cross the road said Max*

PLENARY

Tell the children to work in groups of three and to take the parts of Max, Pa or Ma. They should scan the extract for the dialogue and prepare a radio performance of dialogue. Invite groups to perform their reading for the rest of the class.

SESSION 3

FOCUS
- How do we know that this story is a sequel?

RESOURCES
- *King Max the Last* Essential Fiction pages 54–57
- Resource Sheet 3 'Max's muddles'

SHARED READING

Read pages 54–55 from *King Max the Last* to the class.

🔊 **Listening focus** Tell the children to listen out for evidence that this story is a sequel to *The Hodgeheg*.

After reading, ask the class what they noticed that linked this story to the previous one. Ask which two paragraphs sum up the main action of the story of *The Hodgeheg*. (lines 8–19)

Look closely at lines 12–13 where Max gets his words muddled after the blow to his head. *What did Max mean to say? Why was he known as a Hodgeheg?*

Discuss the following questions:
- *Why did the men capture Max?*
- *Why couldn't they fit a radio collar on Max?*
- *How did they solve the problem?*
- *Why did they add a light to the transmitter?*

Ask the children to look for any common expressions in this extract. (line 35 'turn up', line 67 'no neck to speak of')

Tell the children that Dick King-Smith is famous for using puns and playing on words. Talk about this in connection with lines 90–91 ("I'm absolutely stuck".)

Reread the extract as a play. Tell the 'scientists' that Dr Dandy-Green is the one with the torch and Professor Duck is the man with the net at the top of page 55. You should read the part of the narrator.

INDEPENDENT WRITING

Give each child a copy of RS3. Ask the children to write what Max meant to say.

➤ **Extension** Ask the group to write a book review of something they have read recently. (A Dick King-Smith book would be ideal.) They should include in the book review what they thought of the book, who would enjoy the book and whether they would recommend it to other children.

GUIDED WRITING — CORE

Tell the group to imagine that it is the time when Max had the bump on his head. Help the group to devise further muddled sentences that Max might speak.

PLENARY

Share the muddled sentences created by the guided group. Invite children from the independent work to share their book reviews. Have they read any other Dick King-Smith books? Were they worth reading? Would they recommend them? What did they like best?

SESSION 4

FOCUS
- How do pronouns make reading easier?

RESOURCES
- *King Max the Last* Essential Fiction pages 54–57
- Resource Sheet 4 'Book Review'

SENTENCE WORK

Write the following text on the board:
"The hedgehog's not all that old, by the size of the hedgehog. The hedgehog will do nicely."

Ask the children if they notice anything odd about the sentences. (The pronouns have been replaced by nouns.) Do they think the word 'hedgehog' has been used too many times. *What could you do to change the sentence?*

Now write: *"He hasn't come home," he said.*

"He probably decided to stay there and have a good day's sleep," he said.

Ask the children what's the matter with these sentences. Explain that pronouns are helpful to hold a text together but the trick is not to use too many or too few.

Play the 'Pronoun game' where children say, *I like eating ice cream*, then point to someone to substitute 'you' for 'I', 'they' for 'I' etc. (Links with Unit 16 of *Grammar for Writing*.)

SHARED WRITING

Look again at the book reviews from the independent work in Session 3. Talk about the purpose and audience of a book review. Look at published book reviews (e.g. Junior Education, Books for Keeps, or use a website.) Explain that a book review summarises the plot and gives information to help readers decide whether or not they want to read it.

Tell the children you are going to write a review of a book you have shared with the class recently. Remind them of the purpose and audience so the tone should be lively and the writing should tempt the reader to read or put them off.

Write a brief review. (You may wish to use RS4 as a prompt.)

INDEPENDENT WRITING

Tell the children to prepare for completing their book review in Session 5. Explain that their review is going to be about either *The Hodgeheg* or *King Max The Last*. They should make notes under the headings you used in the shared writing.

GUIDED WRITING — SUPPORT

Talk through the headings with the group and help them to identify the 'problem' and the 'best line'. Make notes, based on their suggestions, for them to use in the next session.

PLENARY

Play 'Guess my book'. Give children clues to books and see if they can identify them, e.g. I live in a Children's Home and I'm waiting for my mother to come and get me. (*Tracey Beaker*)

SESSION 5

FOCUS
- What are the features of Dick King-Smith's books?

RESOURCES
- *The Hodgeheg* or *King Max the Last* Essential Fiction pages either 50–53 or 54–57
- Resource Sheet 4 'Book Review'
- Pronoun cards: he she it they him her them

SENTENCE WORK
Give the pronoun cards to seven children.

Write the following sentences on the board: *Mr Jones gave the book to Lucy.*

Ask the children to come out and place their pronoun card (He, it, her) in the correct place in the sentence.

Tell the children to pass on their pronoun cards and then write the following sentences on the board:

The children gave their homework to the teacher. (They gave it her/him.) Talk about choosing the correct pronoun depending on whether the teacher is male or female.

The man took the dogs for a walk. (He, them). Discuss how using 'it' for 'the walk' wouldn't be right.

Talk about how an overuse of pronouns can lead to ambiguity.

SHARED READING
Tell the children you are going to make a list of features of Dick King-Smith's writing. Read some of the titles from the list started in Session 1. Draw attention to how many titles refer to animals, e.g. *The Great Sloth Race, The Invisible Dog.* Explain that Dick King-Smith nearly always writes with animals as the main characters who speak and think like humans. Write on the list: *usually animal stories but the animals have human thoughts and feelings.* Ask the children to find examples of this in *The Hodgeheg*.

Talk about the different kinds of humour (play on words – muddled words – spoonerisms – deadpan humour).

Remind the children that Dick King-Smith books always include specific information about the animal characters, e.g. page 51 (Plenary in Session 1).

INDEPENDENT WRITING
Give each child a copy of RS4 and ask them to write their book review based on the notes they made in Session 4.

GUIDED WRITING CORE/EXTENSION
Work with those children who have decided to write their review on a Dick King-Smith book other than *The Hodgeheg* or *King Max the Last*.

PLENARY
Share some of the book reviews.

Discuss with the class how well they have met their targets.

SESSION 6 OPTIONAL

FOCUS
- What features of Dick King-Smith stories can you see in *Dinosaur School*?

RESOURCES
- *Dinosaur School* Fiction Skills Big Book pages 46–48

SHARED READING
Refer to the list created in Session 5 about the features of Dick King-Smith's stories.

Listening focus Tell the children to listen out for those features in the opening of *Dinosaur School*.

Read pages 46–48 from the Big Book to the class.

Take in responses from the listening focus. Which features were evident?

Discuss the story by asking the following questions:
- Why were the other dinosaurs teasing Basil?
- What have we learned about brontosaurus in this excerpt?
- What is the secret Araminta tells Basil?
- What do you think Basil will do when he goes back to playschool the next day?

WORD WORK
Write *brontosaurus* on the board. Explain that the 'saurus' part of the word means 'lizard' and it is in 'dinosaur', 'stegosaurus' and 'ankylosaurus'. Show the children how to break down the word 'brontosaurus' into syllables: bront/o/saur/us.

Explain that each syllable division has a vowel in it. Ask the children to count the syllables in the following words: 'morning', 'variety'. Can they identify the vowels in each syllable? Explain that 'y' functions as a vowel in these circumstances.

 Time out for thinking Dictate the following words to the class and ask them to count the syllables and then spell them on their whiteboards: stupid, shallows, carefully.

INDEPENDENT WORK
Tell the children to map the opening of *Dinosaur School* on to a story plan: 'Characters/Setting/Problem/Solution'. Tell them to complete the sections as far as they can and to suggest a solution for Basil.

GUIDED WRITING SUPPORT
Select ten high frequency words from the story *Dinosaur School* and share with the group different ways to remember how to spell the words.

PLENARY
Share the story plan the children completed in the independent work. What different endings did they come up with?

SESSION 7 OPTIONAL

FOCUS
- How can you write a good opening sentence?

RESOURCES
- *Dinosaur School* Fiction Skills Big Book pages 46–48

SHARED READING AND WRITING

Reread the opening paragraph of the story.

Time out for thinking Tell the children to list all the information the author gives the reader in the first paragraph. Using the acetate overlay, underline the words and phrases in the text that provide this information.

Demonstration writing Explain that it is possible to introduce all the important information to open a story in just a single sentence, e.g. *Little Norah Rat scurried down the rubbish tip in great excitement.*

Time out for discussion Ask the children what information they have learned in this opening sentence. Draw out the following: name is a play on words, rats live in rubbish tips and the character is very excited. Explain that the reader now knows who the main character is, where they live and how they are feeling. The feelings give a clue about the main problem of the story.

Demonstration writing Explain that you can use exactly the same model to introduce a different story, with another main character and a different setting:

Little Claudius Tiger sprang angrily down from the Acacia branch and stormed up to his mother.

Time out for discussion Ask the children what information they have learned from this opening sentence. (character, setting and a clue to the problem)

INDEPENDENT WRITING

Tell the children to write an opening sentence for a Dick King-Smith story. Remind them they are trying to include information about the character, the setting and a hint of the problem in the one sentence.

GUIDED WRITING — SUPPORT

Work with the group to research on the Internet to find more information about brontosaurus, especially about appearance, habitat, diet and having two brains. Help them to make brief notes based on their research.

PLENARY

Invite the group who had done the research to present their findings. Set it up as a TV panel programme with the 'researchers' as 'experts'. The rest of the class should ask of the 'experts' questions.

SESSION 8 OPTIONAL

FOCUS
- How can dialogue move a story forward?

RESOURCES
- Resource Sheet 5: Features of Dick King-Smith's writing
- *Dinosaur School* Fiction Skills Big Book pages 46–48

SHARED READING

Divide the class into groups of three. Give them a copy of RS5. Tell them they are going to read the opening of *Dinosaur School* as a play. They should each choose a part and mark on the resource sheet the actual words they will be speaking. They should check their marked resource sheets to ensure there is no overlap. (Narrator, Araminta, Basil)

Invite groups of three to perform their play to the rest of the class.

SENTENCE WORK

Look again at the speech in the story. Draw attention to commas, question marks and exclamation marks within speech marks. Ask the children how the punctuation helped them when they were reading the story in the style of a play. *Did it give clues as to how to say the words?* (e.g. question marks, exclamation marks). Ask the children what Basil might have said when he returned to playschool the next morning. Write their sentences on the board and talk through the punctuation.

INDEPENDENT WORK

Tell the children to use RS5 that they marked for their play reading and to use coloured pencils to indicate examples of characteristics of Dick King-Smith's writing i.e. humour, play on words, animal facts.

GUIDED WRITING — EXTENSION

Tell the children that they are going to write some dialogue to add to the opening sentence they wrote in Session 7. Look again at the Big Book to see how Dick King-Smith uses dialogue to move the story on. Ask the children to write an exchange between two main characters. Make an OHT of two examples of work to share in the Plenary.

PLENARY

Look at the dialogue created in the guided writing work. Ask the class what extra information about the Characters, Setting or Problem through the dialogue has been added then ask them to note if the dialogue has been punctuated correctly. Did this dialogue move the story on?

SESSION 9 OPTIONAL

FOCUS
- Can you explain why you enjoy reading a particular book?

RESOURCES
- A collection of books by Dick King-Smith

SHARED WRITING

Limbering up Ask the children about book reviews: *Why are they written?* (Purpose) *What do they look like?* (Form) *Who is a book review for?* (Audience)

Talk about quotations being memorable lines from a book. Choose a quotation from *Dinosaur School* to demonstrate and explain why you chose it as a favourite quotation.

Tell the children they are going to make a Dick King-Smith mobile to display in class. It will have their recommendations of their favourite books by the author.

Time out for thinking Ask children to work in pairs. Talk about the Dick King-Smith books they have read (or heard). Each child should choose a favourite Dick King-Smith title (using *The Hodgeheg* or *King Max The Last* if they have not read any others).

Write up the following headings on the board and explain that this is the information that they need to display on the mobile about their chosen book.
Title:
Funniest part of the story:
Quotation:

Give children time to discuss their chosen book with a partner, using these headings.

EXTENDED WRITING

Ask the children to complete a first draft of their mobile book review and check it through with a partner for correct spelling and punctuation. Read through, and mark the work. Then ask the children to draw an outline of the main animal character onto the card, cut it out and write the information on one side.

GUIDED WRITING SUPPORT

Support the group where necessary in making their mobiles.

PLENARY

Invite the children to come to the front of the class and to select the Dick King-Smith title which is their favourite. They should present their arguments as to why they think it is the best.

After the session, display the finished reviews. Make a class mobile using two pieces of dowling. Write a banner for the mobile: *Dick King-Smith* and suspend the cut-out animal reviews from the dowling. Display in the book corner.

SESSION 10 OPTIONAL

FOCUS
- Where can you learn more about an author apart from in her/his books?

RESOURCES
- Screen version of *Babe*
- Resource Sheet 6 'My evaluation sheet'

SHARED WRITING

Tell the children that they are going to help you to write a letter to Dick King-Smith in which you tell him how much you have enjoyed reading and talking about his books. Explain that authors are very busy and it may be a long time before there is a reply and the reply might be from the publisher not the author himself.

Time out for thinking Tell the children to work with a partner and to think of two important things they would like to say about Dick King-Smith's books.

Teacher scribing Take in the children's suggestions and demonstrate on the board how to arrange a letter and how to set out the school address.

Keep the letter brief but to the point. Explain that such a letter should be signed off 'Yours sincerely' because it was addressed to Dick King-Smith by name.

Tell the children that the letter will be sent to the author's publisher who will forward it to the author.

SHARED VIEWING

Show the children the opening of the film *Babe* which is a film version of Dick King-Smith's book *The Sheep-Pig*.

Ask the children if the characteristics noted in the class checklist of features are evident in the film version.

EXTENDED PLENARY REVIEW AND EVALUATION

Discuss the targets for the unit. What have the children learned about writing book reviews? Ask the children to complete RS6.

On the Literacy World Interactive CD for Stage 1 Fiction, you will find the following resources for this unit:
- Copies of all the Fiction Skills Big Book pages for interactive work (*Dinosaur School* pages 46–48)
- An audio recording of *Dinosaur School*
- Interactive word and sentence work for Sessions 2 and 8
- All the Resource Sheets for independent work for you to customise
- Comprehensive Teaching and Planning Guides for the unit are also available on the CD.

Name _____ Date _____

What are Pa and Max saying?

Fill in the speech bubbles.

Name _____ Date _____

Dialogue

Add the correct punctuation to this conversation between Max and Pa.

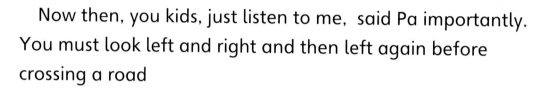

Now then, you kids, just listen to me, said Pa importantly. You must look left and right and then left again before crossing a road

Why do we have to do that asked Max

Because you need to look out for the traffic said Pa.

What should we do if we see a car in the distance asked Max.

Wait on the pavement said Pa firmly. Cars can move much faster than we can so don't ever try to outrun them.

Is it safer to cross at night asked Max.

Not really said Pa There is less traffic but those lights can dazzle little hedgehogs and many have come to a sticky end crossing in the dark

What's a sticky end asked Max

STAGE 1 | TERM 3 | For use with Unit 12 Session 2 as independent work.
© Harcourt Education Ltd. 2004. Copying permitted for purchasing school only. The material is not copyright free.

Name _____ Date _____

Max's muddles

When Max was knocked over by the lorry he bumped his head and he started to talk in a funny way. Read the funny things he said. Write what he meant to say.

"Ma," said Max, "I'm walking for a go."

_____

"Yes, of course," said Max, "I'll be quite KO."

_____

"Am I where?" said Max looking around him.

_____

"Oh!" said Max, "I peg your bardon."

_____

"Yes, thanks," said Max. "Trouble is, I go to want home, but I won't know the day."

_____

_____

STAGE 1 | TERM 3 | For use with Unit 12 Session 3 as independent work.
© Harcourt Education Ltd. 2004. Copying permitted for purchasing school only. The material is not copyright free.

Name   Date

Book review

Choose a book you have read. Use the chart to write your review.

Title	Author	Genre
Main character(s):		
Problem for the main character(s):		
Funniest part:		
Part I liked best:		
Best line:		
Comment:		
Star rating:		

 | STAGE 1 | TERM 3 | For use with Unit 12 Sessions 4 and 5 as independent work.
© Harcourt Education Ltd. 2004. Copying permitted for purchasing school only. The material is not copyright free.

Name _____ Date _____

Features of Dick King-Smith's writing

Read the story as a play.

Mark these features using three colours:

☐ animals like humans ☐ play on words ☐ animal facts

Little Basil Brontosaurus came home from his first morning at playschool in floods of tears.

"Whatever's the matter, darling?" said his mother, whose name was Araminta. "Why are you crying?"

"They've been teasing me," sobbed Basil.

"Who have? The other children?"

A variety of little dinosaurs went to the playschool. There were diplodocuses, iguanodons, ankylosauruses and many others. Basil was the only young brontosaurus.

"Yes," sniffed Basil. "They said I was stupid. They said I hadn't got a brain in my head."

At this point Basil's father, a forty-tonne brontosaurus who measured twenty-seven metres from nose to tail-tip, came lumbering up through the shallows of the lake in which the family lived.

"Hello!" called Araminta. "Did you hear that? The kids at playschool said our Basil hasn't a brain in his head." Herb considered this while pulling up and swallowing large amounts of waterweed.

Name _____   Date _____

My evaluation sheet

The focus for this unit was _____

_____

My Reading target was _____

_____

My Writing target was _____

_____

The best piece of writing I did was _____

_____

The things I still need to work on are _____

_____

My Sentence level target was _____

_____

I have learned to _____

_____

My Word level target was _____

_____

I now know how to _____

_____

The part of the unit I enjoyed most was _____

_____

STAGE 1 | TERM 3 | For use with Units 9 and 12 Session 10 as review and evaluation.
© Harcourt Education Ltd. 2004. Copying permitted for purchasing school only. The material is not copyright free.